D0935583

THE OTHER THEATRE

[*Angus McBean*

THE GATE THEATRE: John Mills and Niall MacGinnis in Norman Marshall's production of Steinbeck's *Of Mice and Men*.

THE

OTHER THEATRE

NORMAN MARSHALL

JOHN LEHMANN

LONDON MCMXLVIII

Second Impression

FIRST PUBLISHED IN 1947 BY
JOHN LEHMANN LTD.
MADE AND PRINTED IN GREAT BRITAIN BY
PURNELL AND SONS, LTD.
PAULTON (SOMERSET) AND LONDON

SECOND IMPRESSION JUNE 1948

FOREWORD

As most of my work and much of my playgoing has been done in what for want of a better description is usually called "the non-commercial theatre", I thought it might be worth while to attempt to make some record of the pioneer theatres in England during the past twenty-five years. But the book I have written is not quite the book I intended to write. I had planned to divide my space impartially among the various theatres and managements according to what seemed to be the importance of their work; but what I have done is to give most space to those theatres of which I have first-hand knowledge, and less room than they deserve to those of which my knowledge is less personal. For instance, I have devoted two chapters to the Gate Theatre because I happen to know a great deal about that theatre, while other theatres perhaps more important have been given only a few pages. So this book can make no claims to being a comprehensive and impartial history. It is no more than a personal record of what I have seen in the kind of theatres which have provided me with most of my happiest experiences, either as a playgoer or a producer.

A book of this sort cannot be written without pestering a great many people for information. The list of all these to whom I am indebted is too long to print here, but I am particularly indebted to Miss Enid Collett and Mr. Michael Russell-Smith for undertaking much of the duller work connected with the making of this book, to the keepers of the Enthoven Collection at the Victoria and Albert Museum, and to Miss Coates, the Librarian of the British Drama League.

NORMAN MARSHALL

TO

JENNIE AND ELSIE CAMPBELL
WHO HAD FAITH IN
THE OTHER THEATRE
WHEN FAITH WAS RARE

CONTENTS

CHAPTER		PAGE
I.	The 'Twenties	11
II.	J. B. Fagan and the Oxford Playhouse	17
III.	Nigel Playfair and the Lyric, Hammersmith	30
IV.	Peter Godfrey and the Gate	42
V.	The Festival Theatre, Cambridge	53
VI.	The Sunday Theatre	72
VII.	The Amateur Theatre	85
VIII.	Back to the Gate	105
IX.	Lilian Baylis and the Old Vic	125
X.	Ninette de Valois and the English Ballet	139
XI.	Barry Jackson	162
XII.	The Shakespeare Memorial Theatre	175
XIII.	The Repertory Theatres	190
XIV.	Many Others	208
XV.	Twenty-five Years Later	224

LIST OF ILLUSTRATIONS

THE GATE THEATRE: *Of Mice and Men.* Frontispiece

Between pp. 64–65

LYRIC THEATRE, HAMMERSMITH: *The Way of the World*

LYRIC THEATRE, HAMMERSMITH: *La Vie Parisienne*

LYRIC THEATRE, HAMMERSMITH: *The Would-be Gentleman*

LYRIC THEATRE, HAMMERSMITH: *When Crummles Played*

THE GATE THEATRE: *The Eater of Dreams*

THE GATE THEATRE: *Uncle Tom's Cabin*

THE GATE THEATRE: *All God's Chillun*

THE GATE THEATRE: *Peer Gynt*

FESTIVAL THEATRE, CAMBRIDGE: *Alcestis*

FESTIVAL THEATRE, CAMBRIDGE: *Antigone*

FESTIVAL THEATRE, CAMBRIDGE: *The Eunuch*

FESTIVAL THEATRE, CAMBRIDGE: *Twelve Thousand*

THE AMATEUR THEATRE: *God Bless the Guv'nor* at Unity Theatre

THE AMATEUR THEATRE: *The Arbitration* at the Questor's Theatre, Ealing

THE AMATEUR THEATRE: *My Heart's in the Highlands* at the Unnamed Society's Theatre in Manchester

THE AMATEUR THEATRE: *The First Legion* at the Crescent Theatre, Birmingham

THE GATE THEATRE: Robert Morley as Oscar Wilde

THE GATE THEATRE: Hermione Gingold in *The Gate Review*

THE OLD VIC: *Hamlet* in modern dress

THE OLD VIC: *The Taming of the Shrew*

THE OLD VIC: *The Country Wife*

THE OLD VIC: *Richard III*

Between pp. 128–129

SADLER'S WELLS BALLET: *Douanes*

SADLER'S WELLS BALLET: *Job*

SADLER'S WELLS BALLET: *The Rake's Progress*

SADLER'S WELLS BALLET: *Dante Sonata*

COURT THEATRE: *Macbeth* in modern dress

THE MALVERN FESTIVAL: *Gammer Gurton's Needle*

BIRMINGHAM REPERTORY THEATRE: *The Winter's Tale*

BIRMINGHAM REPERTORY THEATRE: *Czarina*

STRATFORD ON AVON: *Two Gentlemen of Verona*

STRATFORD ON AVON: *Doctor Faustus*

STRATFORD ON AVON: *Cymbeline*

STRATFORD ON AVON: *Love's Labour's Lost*

THE PLAYHOUSE, LIVERPOOL: *Street Scene*

GLASGOW CITIZEN'S THEATRE: *A Babble of Green Fields*

NORTHAMPTON REPERTORY THEATRE: *Androcles and the Lion*

PASSION PLAY at MADDERMARKET THEATRE, NORWICH

WESTMINSTER THEATRE: *Mourning becomes Electra*

GROUP THEATRE: *The Ascent of F6*

ARTS THEATRE CLUB: *The Constant Couple*

HAYMARKET THEATRE REPERTORY SEASON: *The Duchess of Malfi*

THE COMPANY OF FOUR: *The Trojan Women*

THEATRE ROYAL, BRISTOL: *Twelfth Night*

THE MERCURY THEATRE: *This Way to the Tomb*

CHAPTER I

THE 'TWENTIES

I HAD forgotten how exciting it was, that season of 1925–26. Hunting up facts for this book, I was rummaging in a cupboard stuffed with old programmes and press cuttings when I came across a bundle labelled in careful, rather schoolboyish writing, "Shows seen, September 15, 1925–June 1, 1926". That was the year I came down from Oxford. Living for the first time in London I was at last able to go to the theatre as often as I liked instead of cramming two shows a day into brief end-of-term visits to town on my way home to Scotland. Judging from the size of that bundle of programmes, I must have made the most of my opportunity.

It was a wonderful season for a young man gluttonously eager to see fine plays. I doubt if there can ever have been a season when so many of the classics were to be seen in London. According to these programmes I saw thirteen plays of Shakespeare, half-a-dozen Elizabethan and Restoration classics, all five of Chekov's full-length plays, and one apiece by Molière, Ibsen, Gogol, Calderon, Andreyev Dostoievsky, Turgenev, Hauptmann and Benavente. The contemporary dramatists were equally well represented that season. Among the names on these programmes are Granville Barker, Flecker, Pirandello, Cocteau, Lenormand, O'Neill, Kaiser, James Joyce, Capek, Jean-Jacques Bernard, O'Casey and Shaw, whose *Man and Superman* was given in its entirety that season.

Surely there can have been little wrong with the London theatre of the middle 'twenties if it could offer such richness and variety within the space of a single season.

Unfortunately the answer is that there was a very great deal wrong. Hardly any of these plays were given within that ramshackle edifice known as "The West End Theatre". The theatre which staged most of them was struggling for existence in strange out-of-the-way places such as a drill hall in Hampstead rechristened The Everyman Theatre, a forgotten playhouse in Hammersmith which for years had been a furniture store, a cramped little cinema out at Barnes where Komisarjevsky was performing miracles of production on a tiny stage, and a back street attic in Covent Garden in which the Gate Theatre had just been started. In the Waterloo

Road the Old Vic, housing its own opera company as well as a Shakespeare company, managed to put on ten plays during the course of the season, while at King's Cross the Euston Palace of Varieties, rechristened The Regent, had become another refuge for plays denied entrance to the West End. The rest were hurried into ordinary theatres on a Sunday night and hustled out again after sometimes being allowed to give a second performance on Monday afternoon. To legalise these performances there were upwards of a dozen "private" Sunday play-producing societies whose nominal privacy, besides allowing them to give Sunday performances, also enabled them to produce some of the many distinguished European and American plays which the Lord Chamberlain ruled to be unfit for public performance in England. Among the most active of these societies were The Stage Society, The Three Hundred Club, The Repertory Players, The Phoenix, The Play-Actors, The Renaissance, The Fellowship of Players, The Venturers, The Playmates and The Pioneer Players.

What had the West End to offer to compare with the work of these exiled groups of players? There was Lewis Casson's spectacular production of *Henry VIII* at the Empire, and a lifeless, old-fashioned production of *Much Ado* at the New. There was also the modern dress *Hamlet* at the Kingsway, though the West End could hardly claim as its own this production acted by the company which Barry Jackson had brought to town from his repertory theatre in Birmingham. The serious continental theatre was represented by one solitary production, *A Doll's House* at the Playhouse. The only new plays of any distinction were *They Knew What They Wanted*, imported from America, and Benn Levy's *This Woman Business*, bought from one of the Sunday night societies. Most of the wit and intelligence and style which the West End season had to offer was contained in Cochran's revue at the London Pavilion, with a little left over for Archie de Bear's *R.S.V.P.* at the Vaudeville—and there were the Astaires at the Palace in *Lady, Be Good.*

Occasionally a fine play managed to edge its way into some small and unfashionable theatre which had escaped the clutches of the theatrical combines because its seating capacity was not large enough to yield big profits. J. B. Fagan presented The Irish Players in *Juno and the Paycock* at the Fortune, and in *The Plough and the Stars* at the Royalty. It was also at the Royalty that Anmer Hall gave *A Month in the Country*. At the Little, Philip Ridgeway, who was responsible for the Chekov season at Barnes, put on *The Seagull.* At the Ambassadors there was a brief revival of Granville Barker's *The Madras House* and at the same theatre Paul Robeson appeared for a few performances of O'Neill's *The Emperor Jones*. But in spite of these occasional flickers of light on the fringes of the West End, it would have been a dreary season for that eager young man from Oxford had it not been for that other theatre struggling against the timidity of the theatrical manager and the tyranny of the Censor, who between them were reducing the English theatre to a dead level of mediocrity.

This book is a history of that struggle, a struggle which was waged unceasingly throughout the twenty years between the two wars, but which was at its height during that season of 1925–26. In the years that followed many of the leaders of the revolt gave up through weariness and disillusionment. The Lyric, Hammersmith became empty once more; the Everyman and the Regent were surrendered to the films; Komisarjevsky was finally defeated by the limitations of the tiny stage at Barnes; Barry Jackson withdrew from London, disillusioned and embittered; The Stage Society, oldest and greatest of the Sunday societies, became pitifully enfeebled, and its offshoot, The Phoenix, expired together with many of the other Sunday societies. In the provinces two theatres of exceptional courage and enterprise, The Leeds Civic Playhouse and the Cambridge Festival Theatre, came to an end in the early 'thirties, while Fagan at Oxford abandoned his theatre to the humdrum routine of ordinary repertory.

The chapters that follow are so full of mortality that at first sight this book might seem to be largely a record of failure—gallant and exciting failure, perhaps, but nevertheless failure. On the contrary, it is a Success Story. Nearly everything that was most worthwhile in the English theatre in the period between the two wars was due to the influence of these rebel organisations. If this book were merely the record of various out-of-the-way, hole-in-the-corner theatre and play producing societies for the entertainment of coterie audiences it would hardly be worth writing. Actually it is a record of how the English theatre was saved from stagnation and sterility by the small group of producers, players and playgoers who, supported by many of the dramatic critics, refused to accept the drab monotony imposed upon the theatre by the managers and by the Censor, seemingly united in a determination to keep the theatre in a state of arrested development.

It is astonishing how few even of the West End theatre's biggest box office successes, apart from musicals, farces and thrillers, were originally created by the West End managers. For instance, Noel Coward owed his first real success both as an actor and a playwright to the Everyman, where *The Vortex* was produced after it had gone the rounds of the West End managers in vain. Emlyn Williams' first London production was given him by a Sunday society which afterwards persuaded a West End management to put on the play for a run. John Gielgud established himself as a West End star through the success of *Richard of Bordeaux*, originally produced on a Sunday night at the Arts. Everybody knows the story of *Journey's End*, produced by the Stage Society after it had been rejected by every management in London, but perhaps by now most people have forgotten that long runs such as *The Barretts of Wimpole Street*, *Young Woodley*, *Outward Bound*, *The Man with a Load of Mischief*, *The Lady with the Lamp*, *Strange Orchestra*, *Musical Chairs*, *George and Margaret*, *The Applecart*, *Love on the Dole*, *Victoria Regina*, and *Jeannie*, to name but a few, were all first produced by so-called "non-commercial" managements. In fact I can only think of three playwrights of any note which the West End managements discovered for themselves during these twenty years. They are A. A. Milne, Dodie Smith and Clemence Dane. Although J. B. Priestley's early plays were given their first performances in West End theatres, he could only achieve this by backing them himself.

The extent to which the West End had become dependent on the private theatres and Sunday societies for their plays during these twenty years was fully revealed when the war put an end to the activities of this other theatre. Helplessly the West End managers fell back upon revivals and importations from America. There were times when these outnumbered new plays by three to one, and most of the few new plays were of the lightest and most trivial sort. Even in their choice of revivals of more serious plays the managers were guided mainly by the work of the "non-commercial" managements in the past. Take for example two of the outstanding successes among the revivals of 1943. *A Month in the Country* had already been twice produced in London by Anmer Hall, who had also given it in the provinces, while *Love for Love* had been produced three times in London (twice by Sunday night societies and once by the Old Vic), twice at the Cambridge Festival Theatre and once by J. B. Fagan at the Oxford Playhouse where John Gielgud first played Valentine.

Jeering at the West End managers for their lack of enterprise and their consistent under-rating of the public taste is an old game and an easy one. It is more interesting to examine the reasons for a state of affairs in which a timid and reactionary commercial theatre existed side by side with an immensely vital and progressive group of rebel theatres and play-producing societies. It was a state of affairs which existed in no other country. In Paris, in pre-Nazi Berlin, in New York, in Prague, in Vienna, they had no need for theatre clubs and play-producing societies. There the ordinary commercial theatre was adventurous and contemporary in the best sense of the word. The reasonably intelligent playgoer and the more enterprising actors and producers found no need to form their own organisations in self-defence against the standards of commercialism.

Incidentally, at this point it occurs to me that officially I am myself one of that row of battered Aunt Sallies labelled "West End Managers". At least, I am a member of the Society of West End Managers, and on occasions I have made considerable sums of money in Shaftesbury Avenue and on Broadway. But I am one of the little men. It is only when theatre business is bad that we are allowed to disport ourselves unmolested in the West End playground. As soon as there is any sign of a boom we are jostled off by the big combines shoving and scrummaging for the bricks and mortar. I was luckier than most of the little men. I owned a converted skittle alley called The Gate Theatre with a subscription audience that was large, steadfast and intelligent. There I was able to put on plays which appealed to my own taste, unmolested by the Censor and untroubled by an avaricious landlord waiting to evict me as soon as a play showed any falling off in receipts.

It was, of course, the boom of 1914–18 which first brought the combines into the theatre. Theatres were sold and resold, let and sublet over and over again, each time at a bigger price. For anyone who had the bricks and mortar, knowledge of the theatre was unneccessary. It was only too easy to make money out of the completely uncritical war-time audience. Old established managements were squeezed out of business. Control of the theatre passed from the hands of men of the theatre into the hands of men of money. Before 1914 the playgoer was served by managers running their own theatres according to their own taste and policy. Often the manager was also a distinguished actor, playing and producing in a theatre which he owned. During the war of 1914–18 theatres became just another asset on the list of properties held by business magnates, regarded as impersonally as the factories, the hotels, the chains of shops, the blocks of flats which also figured on the list. With the individual managers no longer in control, a frightful sameness descended upon the English theatre. The public was given what they wanted. At least, it seemed to be what they wanted, as theatres were packed, but they were given no chance of proving whether they wanted anything else.

By 1920 the boom had passed and with it had gone many of the war-time managements. The harm they had done remained. The theatre was crippled and disabled, staggering under the burden of gigantic rents, and further weighed down by the entertainments duty and increased rates and taxes. To take a single instance, a West End theatre which I rented in the 'thirties cost me exactly three times as much as the figure at which it used to be rented in 1914. Yet on its post-war rental none of the extraordinary collection of landlords, sub-landlords, lessees and sub-lessees who had got themselves tangled up in this theatre were receiving more than a comparatively small return on their money.

One of the most serious results of the crazy economics of the post-war theatre was that it prevented the return of the independent manager prepared to rely on his own taste and judgment. The expenses and consequently the risks of theatre management had now become so great that no new management could reasonably hope to last long without very considerable capital behind it. The few older managements that had survived were bewildered by the problems bequeathed to them from the war years. Those of the war-time managements that still remained were finding normal peace-time audiences very different from the days when a floating war-time population thronged London with plenty of time and money and in no mood to be selective or critical. Timid and uneasy, managements played for safety—or at least what they hoped would be safety. They confined themselves to the most conventional and stereotyped sort of play. Authors' agents found that the best way to sell a play was to recommend it as "another so-and-so"—naming some past success. Freshness and originality were unsaleable qualities.

Such was the state of affairs that in the early 'twenties led to the revolt against the standards of commercialism which is the subject of this book.

CHAPTER II

J. B. FAGAN AND THE OXFORD PLAYHOUSE

If I were ever to write my autobiography that chapter entitled "Early Years" would be dull reading. My boyhood recollections of the theatre are sadly tame compared with those colourful experiences I read about so enviously in other peoples' books. I was never nearly trampled underfoot in the mad race up the gallery stairs for front seats to see Irving's Shylock. I never went without lunch every day for a week in order to have enough money to book a seat when Forbes Robertson visited the town. I never played truant from school to see Duse when she appeared for a flying matinée. I never walked on as a local super in *Julius Caesar* and stood breathless with awe and excitement only a yard or two away from Osmund Tearle as he declaimed "Friends, Romans, countrymen". I never woke sweating with fear in the night after seeing Tree as Svengali. I never fell hopelessly in love with Ellen Terry, saving up my pocket-money for weeks to send her, anonymously, a bouquet of flowers. I never saw Sarah Bernhardt.

My early experiences of the theatre consisted of sitting primly with my mother in the front row of the dress circle of the Lyceum Theatre, Edinburgh, first in an Eton suit, later in a dinner jacket, watching a succession of touring versions of musical comedies beginning with *Oh, Oh Delphine!* and continuing with *The Pearl Girl, Tina, The Dancing Mistress, The Marriage Market, Gipsy Love, The Sunshine Girl, The Girl from Utah, Betty, High Jinks, To-night's the Night, The Maid of the Mountains, Theodore and Co.*,—and lots of others that I have forgotten. The straight plays that I saw were mainly the stock successes of the touring theatre of those days, *When Knights Were Bold, Are you a Mason?, The Private Secretary, Charley's Aunt, Brewster's Millions.* Of course I saw the D'Oyley Carte; and "The Terrys" in *The Scarlet Pimpernel* and *Sweet Nell of Old Drury*; and Martin Harvey in *The Only Way, The Cigarette Maker's Romance* and *The Breed of the Treshams.* I can remember seeing Matheson Lang in a rip-roaring drama about the Flying Dutchman, and Owen Nares in a play about a girls' school. Otherwise I can't remember seeing anyone of any particular fame apart from Cicely Courtneidge who used in those days to play the ingénue parts in the tours of her father's musical comedies.

To-day a boy brought up in a big provincial city is able to see most of the important London productions on tour with the original cast, while the local repertory theatre gives him the chance of seeing other plays besides current successes, including a few of the classics. But I was in my 'teens during the war and its aftermath when the provincial theatre was at it lowest ebb. Although I immensely enjoyed my theatre-going, nothing I saw gave me any inkling of the fact that the theatre could provide me with experiences every bit as vivid and thought-provoking as those I was at that time excitedly discovering for myself in books. In those days published plays were not easy to get, and the school play-reading society, now as normal an institution in most schools as the debating society and the literary society, did not exist. Only a very daring headmaster would have given his approval to his boys meeting together to read plays by modern dramatists such as Shaw, Ibsen and Granville Barker, all of whom were considered immoral writers on the strength of each having had a play banned by the Lord Chamberlain. Even Galsworthy was suspect. There were "dangerous ideas" in plays such as *Strife*, *The Skin Game* and *The Mob*. Synge was ruled out because of "the language", and most parents would have sat down and written a sharp letter to the headmaster had they heard that their sons had been reading *The Importance of being Earnest* or any other "tainted stuff" by Oscar Wilde. In case I seem to exaggerate, it is worth recalling that the Vice-Chancellor of Oxford University forbade a touring company to bring Stanley Houghton's *Hindle Wakes* to Oxford, and as late as 1923 the authorities of my own college at Oxford refused to allow the college dramatic society to produce *Androcles and the Lion* on the grounds that it was blasphemous.

When I went up to Oxford I was so little interested in the theatre that I made no effort to join the O.U.D.S. I did not even bother to become a member of the college play-reading society.

The local theatre provided much the same sort of fare as I had been accustomed to in Edinburgh. During my first two years all I can remember seeing were some more musical comedies, Seymour Hicks in a farce, Irene Vanbrugh in *Mr. Pim Passes By*, a thriller called *The Cat and the Canary*, and again the D'Oyley Carte. Perhaps I would have gone to the theatre more often had I not become an earnest rowing man. I was constantly in training with the crew, which entailed going to bed at ten o'clock every night, and ruled out the theatre unless one was prepared to leave long before the end. It was probably for this reason that I did not see the Stratford

Company, the Macdona Players, and the Birmingham Repertory Company which all visited Oxford during my first two years as an undergraduate.

It was in 1923, at the beginning of my third year at Oxford, that J. B. Fagan opened the Oxford Playhouse. An undergraduate friend, more enthusiastic than myself, persuaded me to become one of the several hundred season ticket holders for which Fagan was appealing. Fortunately a torn muscle had put an end to my unnatural existence as a rowing man, so I could not plead early-to-bed as an excuse for refusing.

Fagan started his Oxford venture handicapped by a dismal, gimcrack building which had once been a big game museum. The flimsy walls were anything but sound-proof against the noise of traffic in the Woodstock Road. On wet nights the rain drumming on the tin roof added to the din. The auditorium was gaunt and cheerless. There was no foyer, no bar, and smoking was not allowed. Most of the seats were wickedly uncomfortable wooden chairs which contributed their quota of noise by creaking complainingly throughout the evening.

The stage was somewhat on the same lines as Copeau's at Le Vieux Colombier. There was a wide, deep apron stage; behind it a smaller inner stage with curtains drawing across in front of it. In fact it was not unlike an Elizabethan stage, but without the Elizabethan gallery at the back. Settings were suggested simply and economically by using scenery only on the inner stage. Scenes could be played on the apron while another scene was being got ready behind the curtains of the inner stage. It was difficult to see any other advantages. At the end of an act the cast had to be manœuvred upstage off the apron so that the curtains could draw in front of them. When it was necessary to have props or furniture set downstage they had to be placed on the apron stage during the interval in full view of the audience. I remember the incident John Gielgud mentions in his book, when during *Monna Vanna* the spectacle of two white-coated stage hands carefully placing a large and voluptuous-looking couch on the forestage was received with ribald cheers by the delighted undergraduate audience.

Fagan had assembled a very young but extremely talented company, including Tyrone Guthrie, Alan Napier, James Whale, Peter Creswell and Richard Goolden. His leading lady was his wife, Mary Grey. John Gielgud, who had only recently left the R.A.D.A., joined the company a little later, and other additions included Flora Robson, Raymond Massey, Fred O'Donovan, Veronica Turleigh, Glen Byam Shaw, Robert Morley and Reginald Denham, who became assistant producer. With the exception of Mary

Grey and Fred O'Donovan all these were new and unknown names. Obviously Fagan had an exceptional gift for recognising young talent.

The Playhouse was opened in the Michaelmas Term of 1923 with *Heartbreak House*. The rest of the programme consisted of *The Importance of being Earnest*, Goldoni's *Mirandolina*, St. John Hankin's *The Return of the Prodigal*, *The Master Builder*, De Musset's *No Trifling with Love*, and *The Rivals*.

This was a programme which showed a sound understanding of the undergraduate audience. The undergraduate is not an easy audience. He is in an uncomfortable state of semi-sophistication which makes him intellectually self-conscious and warily on the defensive against emotion in the theatre. He is so afraid of being thought sentimental that he is apt to mistake sentiment for sentimentality. Many of the more mature passions are still so far beyond his experience and understanding that they merely seem to him faintly comic. Because he is so unsure of himself, so frightened of being swayed by emotion, he protects himself behind an over-developed sense of the ridiculous. On the other hand he is the best possible comedy audience. He appreciates style, understands verse, delights in wit, and is intensely interested in argument. His reactions to everything that he enjoys are quick, lively and generous.

Six out of the seven plays which Fagan chose for his first programme are acknowledged masterpieces, but with the exception of *The Master Builder* they are plays which rely less on emotion than upon wit, style, gaiety and disputatiousness. The undergraduate audience accepted *The Master Builder* quite happily because they were so busy puzzling over its symbolism that they were not unduly disturbed by its emotions. One of the biggest successes of the season was St. John Hankin's now almost forgotten play, *The Return of the Prodigal*. It is a witty, audacious play which turns a conventional belief upside down, mocks at pomposity and snobbery, and has an impudent, amoral hero. All this was very much to the undergraduate taste.

For me the season was, quite literally, a revelation. I had no idea that the theatre could be so varied, so amusing, so provocative. The acting surprised and excited me as much as the plays. The Oxford Players, as the company called themselves, were so young and inexperienced that much of their acting must have been raw and fumbling, but it had freshness and eagerness and imagination. I had never seen those qualities on the stage before. I had been accustomed to performances which were copied from the original London cast, or to conscientious repetition by touring stars of parts that had been in their repertoires for years, or to an occasional

West End actor repeating on tour a performance with which he had probably already become bored long before the end of the London run. At the Playhouse I was seeing for the first time performances that were newly created and had, whatever their faults, the freshness and zest and nervous tension which inevitably vanish from a performance through repetition.

It must be remembered, however, that the Oxford Players were not an ordinary repertory company. The qualities they possessed are rare among repertory actors churning out a play a week all through the year, often basing their performance on a rough guess at how So-and-So must have played the part in the original production, using a slick, superficial technique to cover up the deficiences in their acting, and relying again and again on a stock collection of tricks and mannerisms which they know to be "safe". At the Playhouse there were only twenty-one productions during the year, divided into three seasons of seven weeks each. The shortness of the seasons made it possible for the actors to rehearse much more intensively than is usual in repertory companies. The ordinary repertory actor has got to conserve his energy. Rehearsals have to be cut down to the barest minimum in order to give him time for a certain amount of leisure and relaxation. Otherwise he cannot last the pace week after week, month after month. But in a seven weeks season the actor can work himself to the last ounce, knowing that at the end of the seventh week he will have a rest to recover from his exhaustion. I saw some bad performances at the Playhouse, but I never saw one that was stale or perfunctory or merely slick.

The quality of the acting at the Playhouse was not, of course, merely due to the brevity of the seasons. The company was an exceptionally talented one. Many of them are now famous names in the theatre. In 1923 nearly all of them were little more than beginners; but although they lacked many of the qualities which they were later to develop through experience, they offset these deficiencies by other qualities which since then they have had to surrender in exchange for maturity and experience and technique.

Watching John Gielgud as Valentine in *Love for Love* at the Haymarket in 1943 I found myself remembering his original performance of the part at the Oxford Playhouse twenty years earlier, and comparing the two performances as far as I was able. I am not going to pretend that I could remember the earlier performance in detail, but I did not need to rely on my memory to know that the young Mr. Gielgud never spoke that lovely speech to Angelica beginning "You are a woman" as exquisitely as it was spoken at the Haymarket twenty years later. This was the sort of acting which is the reward of experience and technique allied to sensitiveness and imagination. Nor can the young Mr. Gielgud's timing possibly have been so exact, the phrasing of his lines so beautifully balanced, his touches of business so illuminating, his sense of period so unfailing. But there were qualities in that earlier performance which I can still remember vividly and which I missed at the Haymarket. Gaiety and impudence and high spirits, fresh, ringing tones, a youthful, self-confident dash and swagger. The two performances were very different, similar only in their imaginativeness, sensitiveness and feeling for language. Both were enchanting. That is the point. Like all young actors of more than ordinary talent, Gielgud at the beginning of his career was able to use the qualities of youth to compensate for the lack of experience and technique. Perhaps the point may seem so obvious that it is hardly worth making, but the tendency in the theatre since the end of the 'twenties has been to place too exclusive a trust in experience and technique, making too little use of the fresh and vivid qualities of youthful talent. It is regrettable that the Old Vic, which once created its own stars from among its youthful companies, has for many years now relied mainly on older, well-established players and ready-made stars. That original company at the Oxford Playhouse, like the Vic companies in the 'twenties and the Birmingham Repertory Company of the same period, proved how exciting the acting of a young company can be if it is chosen with skill and properly produced.

Fagan was not, by ordinary standards, a good repertory producer. He was unused to working against time and taking short cuts. Often on a Monday night his productions were obviously unfinished and the company far from word-perfect. The competent repertory producer rapidly arranges his groupings and moves, indicates the characterisation in bare outline, and bothers his cast as little as possible so that they can concentrate on learning their lines. The result usually has sufficient slickness to deceive the audience into thinking that they are seeing a complete performance of the play. Fagan, who had learned his producing from Granville Barker, was too scrupulous a producer to be capable of smearing a veener of polish over unfinished work. In the limited time at his disposal he strove to develop the style and mood of the play, and to reproduce the author's characterisation as exactly and vividly as possible. The result might often be rough and unpolished through lack of time, but the qualities of the play were always clearly and plainly revealed.

Fagan's greatest gift as a producer was his ability to fire the imagination of his cast. As a result, the acting invariably had vitality and gusto. The Playhouse was an exciting theatre because of the atmosphere of enthusiasm both on the stage and in the auditorium. Nobody ever "dropped in" at the Playhouse to pass away an evening. The theatre was too out-of-the-way, too horribly uncomfortable. One had to be a real enthusiast to endure the rigours of an evening in that barbarous building. Often the audience was small, but it was always eager and responsive.

By the time I went down from Oxford I had seen six seasons at the Playhouse. The plays, besides those already mentioned, included *Captain Brassbound's Conversion*, *Candida*, *Getting Married*, *The Lady from the Sea*, *John Gabriel Borkman*, *The School for Scandal*, *She Stoops to Conquer*, *Twelfth Night*, *Oedipus*, Sierra's *Madame Pepita*, Maugham's *Smith*, Pinero's *Dandy Dick*, and a dozen or so of one-act plays. Each season three or four one-act plays were generally given as a complete evening's entertainment. The one-act bill is not a particularly satisfying entertainment, rather like a dinner consisting of hors-d'oeuvres, soup, sweet and a savoury, but I am grateful that I was able to see at the Playhouse miniatures such as Pirandello's *The Man with a Flower in his Mouth*, Strindberg's *The Stranger*, Yeats' *Land of Heart's Desire*, Turgenev's *Country Cousin*, Lady Gregory's *The Workhouse Ward*, Shaw's *Dark Lady of the Sonnets*, Galsworthy's *The First and the Last*, Lennox Robinson's *Crabbed Youth*, and Benavente's *His Widow's Husband*.

There were three productions I remember particularly vividly. Synge's *Deirdre of the Sorrows* with Veronica Turleigh giving a performance of rare and exquisite quality as Deirdre; Richard Hughes' *A Comedy of Good and Evil*; and *The Cherry Orchard*, never before publicly performed in England. A week or two previous to this production William Archer had been staying with me in Oxford. He had come up to speak to a University club of which I was the president. I remember him advising me not to waste my time and money on going to *The Cherry Orchard*, which he had seen when it was produced by the Stage Society. I have often wondered what went wrong with the Stage Society's production of this play that it so bewildered not only William Archer but also most of the critics and audience. Perhaps it was not the production but the audience which was at fault. Ibsen and Shaw were the dramatists-in-chief of the Stage Society in those days. The members were primarily interested in the theatre as a discussion ground for social and moral problems. No doubt they were puzzled and irritated by Chekov's refusal to pass judgment on his characters or draw any moral from his story. But even if the sociologically minded Stage Society audience were exasperated to find that Chekov had "nothing to say" it is hard to understand how they were unmoved by the pity and tenderness of the play, or unamused by its humour.

I went to the Playhouse rather doubtfully that Monday evening, expecting to be bored and bewildered. It was one of the most exciting evenings of my life. This play had a reality such as I had never imagined to be possible in the theatre. For the first time I was seeing ordinary men and women on the stage. Always before they had been drawn larger than life, or reduced to types, or allowed only such characteristics as were convenient to the dramatist's purpose. They had seldom been allowed to talk and behave and think completely naturally. Generally their behaviour had been governed by the necessity for pointing a moral, expressing an idea, developing the plot, raising a laugh, squeezing a tear. Here was a play in which the author seemed content to be no more than an impartial witness, telling the truth about his characters but passing no judgment on them, recording their doings and sayings but making no obvious attempt to control their behaviour so as to fit them into some prearranged plan of his own. William Archer had been grumbling about the play's shapelessness and untidiness. To me it was all the more real because the author had refused to over-simplify life in order to make a neatly finished picture. Gerhardi says that the thrill which one gets from making the acquaintance of Chekov for the first time is the discovery that our vaguely apprehended half-suspected thoughts concerning the fluidness, complexity and elusiveness of life have been confirmed articulately. That evening at the Playhouse I was not able to analyse my emotions. I only knew that I had seen a play full of the beauty and strangeness of life, its humour and its sadness and its absurdity, a play full of understanding and tenderness unblurred by sentimentality, by a man without illusions but without bitterness. For the first time I realised that the theatre can achieve a reality deeper and more poignant than is possible in any other art.

Since then I have seen many productions of *The Cherry Orchard* in many countries. I still think Fagan's production the best of them all. I never saw the Stanislavsky production, but I am told by someone whose judgment I respect, and who has also seen the play many times, that Fagan's production was closest in spirit to Stanislavsky's. Fagan had never seen this production; he had never been to Russia; but he had the advantage of being an Irishman. The Ireland that Fagan knew had much in common with the Russia that Chekov wrote about. Those isolated, feckless country families, their great houses falling into decay, their estates gradually dwindling away, their retinues of servants reduced to two or three old retainers, were as familiar to Fagan as they were to Chekov. The people living in these houses had the same belief in the past, the same feeling that for them there was no present, the same vague hope that something would happen in the future to change the course of their lives.

But Fagan had more than this in common with Chekov. The Slav and the Celt share a natural melancholy, a quality which the Englishman finds difficult to understand. He usually confuses it with mere gloominess and depression. English producers of Chekov, misunderstanding the true quality of melancholy, and fearing that the play may seem gloomy to the audience, usually overstress the humour at the expense of the other and deeper emotions of the play. They justify themselves by pointing out that Chekov described *The Cherry Orchard* as a farce. This he never did. In a letter to his sister while he was writing the play he merely remarked that some of the scenes were nearer to farce than to comedy.

This intrusion of farce at the most unexpected moments is apt to bewilder English audiences. They lack the mental and emotional agility to move swiftly from one mood to another without warning. This agility—call it emotional instability if you prefer—is a quality as Celtic as it is (or was) Slav. Compare a play by Chekov with an Irish play—by O'Casey, for example—and in both plays one finds the same sudden transitions from comedy to tragedy, from tragedy to farce, from farce to pathos. The success of Fagan's production was largely due to the certainty with which he handled the ever-changing moods of the play, never leaving the audience wondering whether the author expected them to laugh or to cry.

I have seen no other production of a Chekov play which was at the same time so full of laughter and so full of emotion. The Oxford audience that night, unlike the members of the Stage Society, found this play neither bewildering nor pointless. After the long diminuendo which brings the play so movingly to its end the audience sat for a few moments in complete silence. When the applause came it started quietly, but soon it had swelled into a roar of cheering which, in the words of the critic of one of the undergraduate papers, "would not have disgraced a football match".

At the end of the season Fagan took *The Cherry Orchard* to London, first to the Lyric, Hammersmith, then to the Royalty.

To-day, when *The Cherry Orchard* is acknowledged as one of the great masterpieces of the world, it would be a brave critic who would dare to dismiss it as "pretentious twaddle", "aimless maunderings", "dreary rubbish", "theatrically incompetent"—yet these are some of the phrases from criticisms of the play when Fagan produced it in London. One critic of some eminence stated that he could see no reason at all why this "silly, tiresome, boring play" had ever been translated. But the better critics rose to the occasion, and Fagan summed up the attitude of the Press by quoting two typical opinions on the bills advertising the play. One was "fatuous drivel", the verdict of the critic of a popular daily; the other was James Agate's "an imperishable masterpiece".

After I went down from Oxford in 1924 I still occasionally saw a show at the Playhouse. There was often a play which made the journey to Oxford well worth while. For instance, Strindberg's *The Spook Sonata.* Fagan had a particular enthusiasm for this dramatist, who is still insufficiently known and appreciated in England. He produced three more of Strindberg's plays at Oxford—*Intoxication, Easter*, and *The Thunderstorm*, making his own translations in collaboration with Erik Palmstierna. Other plays I remember journeying to Oxford to see were Marcel Achard's *Marlborough Goes to War*, De Musset's *Fantasio*, Vanbrugh's *The Confederacy*, and Coleman's *The Jealous Wife*. I have often wished I had taken the trouble to go up to see a new play called *Full Moon*. It was by an undergraduate at Christ Church whose name was Emlyn Williams.

Meanwhile Fagan was finding it increasingly difficult to keep an intelligent theatre open in Oxford. An arrangement made with the Cambridge Festival Theatre to exchange companies one week in each term proved a lopsided bargain. The Oxford Players did well in Cambridge, but the Festival company played to wretched business at the Playhouse with productions which at Cambridge had packed the theatre. In 1927 and 1928 the Playhouse was closed during the summer terms. In 1929 it did not re-open after the Christmas vacation, but it was rumoured that this was because the Playhouse was to be rebuilt. Terence Gray, of the Cambridge Festival Theatre, had acquired a site for a theatre in London, and he proposed also to build a new theatre on the site of the Playhouse, the three theatres exchanging companies, with Gray and Fagan jointly in control of the scheme. But the local authorities insisted that if a new building was to be put up on the Playhouse site the frontage must be set back a number of feet sufficient to make the already cramped and awkward site too small for the building of an adequate theatre. This was a bitter disappointment for Fagan, but he gallantly refused to allow himself to be disheartened by it and re-opened the Playhouse in the Michaelmas Term of 1929. His programme was as courageous as ever. It consisted of *The Mask and the Face*, Gogol's *Marriage*, Andreyev's *He Who Gets Slapped*, Yeats' *Deirdre*, Gilbert Murray's version of *Iphigenia in Tauris*, Strindberg's *The Thunderstorm*, and a new play, *The Beaten Track* by J. O. Francis.

The Oxford Magazine, referring to a "short and courtly speech" by Fagan on the first night of the season, remarked that "as he stood upon the stage we could not help but feel the heaviness of the debt we owe to one who has done so much for us, and the irony of the fact that he should pay so heavily for the privilege of doing so. Surely it is an amazing fact that Oxford cannot support a theatre where fine plays are finely produced."

At the end of the season Fagan at last admitted defeat. The Oxford Playhouse was converted into a midget golf course.

It is a shameful fact that Fagan received no help or recognition from the University authorities. Oxford, which so magnificently houses its books, its pictures and its museum collections, seemed quite unembarrassed by the fact that its drama was so wretchedly accommodated in that miserable building in the Woodstock Road. As far back as 1926 the Government report on "The Drama in Adult Education" considered it "a matter of great regret" that the works of the dramatists were studied in the universities "from an antiquarian, philological or purely literary standpoint, and not in relation to the art of the theatre for which they were written". It was not until twenty-two years later that Oxford showed any signs of interest in the theatre as part of the normal education of its undergraduates, and then only because Sir Alexander Korda prodded them into action by presenting the University with a cheque for five thousand pounds to send a party of dons to the United States to see for themselves the importance which the American universities attach to the theatre. On their return the Oxford Drama Commission announced that "we think a great benefit would be conferred on the studies of Oxford if it owned a theatre in which plays could be performed freely and experimentally, so as to explore their full significance". The report went on to express the hope that with the acquisition of a theatre "it might be possible in co-operation with other universities, to work out a system in which productions such as we have in mind could be undertaken by companies of professional players". It is ironical that Oxford could not realise this twenty years earlier when Fagan was providing Oxford at his own expense with the sort of drama which the authorities now realise should be seen in a great university town. When Fagan and Terence Gray attempted to bring about a co-operation between the theatres in two university towns on the lines recommended by the Drama Commission report, neither university showed the slightest interest.

As a midget golf course the Playhouse was no more successful than it had been as a theatre. For a time the building stood empty. Then, in 1930, posters appeared bearing the somewhat surprising announcement that Sir Philip Ben Greet was about to present *Rookery Nook*. This was the beginning of a new management (Edward Wilkinson, Arthur Brough and Stanford Holme were the other directors) whose policy, announced Ben Greet in his first night speech, was "to entertain and not to educate". It must have surprised Fagan to hear that during his years at the Playhouse he had been attempting to educate anybody. He was simply a man of admirable taste to whom the plays of the great writers were considerably more entertaining than *Rookery Nook* and the succession of rather faded light comedies and farces with which the new management sought to entertain the apathetic Oxford public. After several years of losing money they threw up the sponge. A group of Oxford residents came to the rescue and raised a guarantee fund. Ben Greet and Brough retired from the management and Stanford Holme, who had produced all the plays, took charge. His programmes were unadventurous, but that was the fault of Oxford rather than of Stanford Holme. A fine play almost invariably lost money—and he had very little money to lose. The only sure-fire winner he could depend upon among the giants was Shaw. Apart from him, Novello, Travers, Ellis and Coward appeared to be Oxford's favourite dramatists. But perhaps the Playhouse audience in those days was not altogether representative of Oxford. Fagan drew his audience mainly from the University. His successors appealed more to the residential population of North Oxford, though Stanford Holme maintained some connection with the University through the O.U.D.S. His actresses took part in the O.U.D.S. productions, and many undergraduate actors joined the Playhouse company after they had gone down or during their vacations. One of these young men was Eric Dance, who conceived the idea of building a new theatre for repertory in Oxford. He persevered in the face of every sort of discouragement, and the present Playhouse in Beaumont Street, a pleasant and comfortable theatre seating 592, was opened in the autumn of 1938.

The first production at the new theatre was Fagan's *And So To Bed*, a graceful gesture. The rest of the season's programme consisted of *Death Takes a Holiday*, *Hail Nero*, *Fanny's First Play*, *The Silver King*, *Dandy Dick*, *The Great Adventure*, *The Passing of the Third Floor Back*, and *Mr. Pim Passes By*.

The excuses that had always been given for the poor attendances at the old Playhouse were discomfort and its distance from the centre of the town. The new theatre was comfortable and it was central, but audiences were no larger. It was depressingly obvious that Oxford was not theatre-minded. Only when Oxford and the surrounding districts became crammed with service men, evacuees and the staffs of government departments did the Playhouse at last begin to play to full houses. By then Stanford Holme was in the Fire Service and Dance a prisoner of war.

The new prosperity encouraged the interim management to vary their succession of old West End successes with an occasional classic. Here is a term-time programme for 1945: *Tony Draws a Horse, Murder Without Crime, School for Scandal, The Sacred Flame, A Doll's House, Three Men on a Horse, Pride and Prejudice*, and *Caesar and Cleopatra*. In a small provincial town with no other theatre except the repertory, this jumble might pass as a reasonably well assorted programme; but surely Oxford, which has another theatre to house the tours of London successes, should be able to support a more definite and progressive policy at its repertory theatre. One can hardly blame the management of the Playhouse for having its doubts. Oxford has yet to prove that it has anything like the real interest in the theatre which Cambridge has displayed in recent years.

CHAPTER III

NIGEL PLAYFAIR AND THE LYRIC, HAMMERSMITH

I WENT down from Oxford in 1925 knowing exactly what I wanted to do but with little hope of doing it. I wanted to become a producer. I had no desire to act or to write plays or design scenery. I only wanted to produce.

I have often wondered how other producers came to adopt their odd profession. Some are disappointed actors or authors *manqués*. Such producers are a nuisance to the actor and a menace to the author. Others are really stage directors, more interested in lighting and scenery and effects than in the play and the actor. These producers do less harm, but little good. Good producers are, I think, rather humble-minded people with no urge to create, but possessed of a great admiration for the work of the creators. My own ambition to produce developed from an intense interest and delight in plays. Whenever possible I read the plays which Fagan produced at the Playhouse, both before and after seeing them. Often it seemed to me that justice had not been done to the merits of the play. I used to reproduce the plays in my imagination. Knowing nothing of the difficulties of producing, or of the limitations imposed by repertory, I was ingenuously surprised to discover how often a play was underdeveloped in the Playhouse productions, how frequently a character was misinterpreted. With the lunatic self-confidence of youth I thought that given the experience I could sometimes have done better than Fagan. I decided to become a producer.

I knew nobody connected with the theatre. I had just enough sense to realise that I would have to begin by learning about the stage as a small part actor or as an assistant stage manager, but I had no idea of how to set about getting a job. Eventually I managed to get a letter of introduction to Nigel Playfair.

Playfair listened amiably to my ambitions, hinted cautiously that he might be able to find me a job as an assistant stage manager, but suggested that before finally deciding to make the stage my profession I should have a talk with his stage director, Stephen Thomas. It is a peculiarity of the members of the theatrical profession that however successful and contented they may be, they invariably consider it their duty to do their best to dissuade anybody wishing to join their profession. Stephen Thomas was no exception. With gloomy relish he predicted my future. After a long apprenticeship as an assistant stage manager, I might rise to being stage manager of a touring company. Years in the provinces would perhaps eventually lead to a job as stage manager in a London theatre. Then if I were lucky—but only if I were very, very lucky—I might get an occasional production for an obscure Sunday night society, which in turn might lead—though it was most unlikely—to an engagement to produce in the West End. By that time I calculated I would be at least forty. It seemed a long time to wait to discover whether I had any talent for producing. Stephen Thomas was, as now, a man of impressive manner. He spoke gravely and with authority. I took him very seriously—probably much more seriously than he intended or expected. Sadly but, as I thought, sensibly I laid aside my ambitions and spent the next year in advertising and journalism.

I have always regretted that I did not take the chance of working at the Lyric. I would, I think, be a better producer to-day had I worked under Nigel Playfair. As it was, I did learn much from him, though only as one of his audience. I saw all his productions at the Lyric with the exception of the first two. Later I got to know him personally and to learn about him through hearing his actors discuss him and from reading his books.

The story of how Playfair started at the Lyric is well known. In *Hammersmith Hoy* he has described how in 1918, when he was a small-part actor, he was searching for some scenery for a charity matinée and came upon a derelict theatre in an old-clothes market in Hammersmith, surrounded by whelk stalls and fish-and-chip shops. Its official name was The Lyric Opera House; locally it was known as The-Blood-and-Flea-Pit. Because he had grown tired of acting small parts in other people's shows, and because he had some ideas which he thought it would be amusing to express, he bought the theatre. One of the first plays which he presented ran for a year, and he followed it almost immediately with another which ran for nearly fifteen hundred performances. For fourteen years he continued to direct the Lyric, producing plays by Sheridan, Gay, Dryden, Congreve, Bickerstaff, Molière, Shakespeare, Goldsmith, Wilde, Pinero and Pirandello. When in 1932 he gave up the management of the theatre, it relapsed once again into complete obscurity. That briefly, is the history of Nigel Playfair at the Lyric, Hammersmith.

In the profession, when a popular manager is successful he is described as having a flair. If he is not so popular he is dismissed as being merely lucky. Playfair was always described as lucky, not because he was personally unpopular, but because he was always suspected of being an amateur. He did not embark upon his Hammersmith venture from any of the recognised professional motives such as ambition to make a great deal of money, or to give himself good parts, or to educate the public by producing the plays which they ought to see but didn't want to see. Instead, he frankly regarded his theatre simply as a place in which he could amuse himself by producing the plays he liked in the way he liked. This, to the profession, seemed a thoroughly frivolous and selfish way of setting up in management. The fact that it proved an extremely successful method made it all the more exasperating. If he had been a little more serious-minded about his work, if he had considered himself a man with a mission, his colleagues would have accepted him as one of themselves. To make matters worse, outside the theatre he mixed very little with the members of his own profession. Talking shop frankly bored him. "If there is anything which I really hate talking about when I go out", he wrote in his autobiography, "it's the theatre and anything to do with it. I spend on an average twelve hours a day within its walls and when I do escape I like to talk about things of which my knowledge is scanty, like Baroque Architecture and Einstein and Prisoner's Base."

Playfair was perfectly well aware of his reputation, and it often amused him, when talking to one of the more solemn members of his profession, to exaggerate his air of taking the whole thing as a great joke. Yet there *was* something essentially amateurish in his whole attitude to the theatre. Whether one liked or disliked his work depended on whether one liked the atmosphere of charade which he gave to all his productions. He was an extremely poor producer of a realistic play. The hard, detailed, technical work required for this sort of production bored him. He was only happy when working on a play which gave him opportunities to invent, to fantasticate and to caricature. He had none of that deep sense of responsibility toward the theatre which is the mark of the true professional. When he grew tired of the Lyric he abandoned it as casually as a child grown tired of a toy. He made no real effort to ensure that the tradition which he had built up there should be continued. It was nothing more to him than a place where he had happily amused himself.

Although he was an amateur in spirit, he managed his theatre and produced his plays with an ability that was thoroughly professional, though it was concealed by an air of casualness. An ideal host, he managed his theatre with the same expansive geniality with which he ran his parties. He welcomed each newly assembled company to the Lyric with the cordiality of a charming host looking forward to a delightful evening's entertainment. His zest, his enthusiasm for the play in rehearsal, his certainty that it was going to be the most enchanting entertainment ever produced at the Lyric, infected everybody. Just as a party which is a success "goes" with very little apparent assistance from the host, so some of his most successful productions seemed to produce themselves. Because of this, many actors who worked for him under-rated him as a producer. It seemed to them that he "did practically nothing". It is true that he usually embarked upon rehearsals with apparently only a very vague plan of production in his mind, and he left a great deal of the duller work, which bored him, to his extremely able stage director, Stephen Thomas. But Playfair had a gift for communicating his own enjoyment of the play to the cast. Many of the actors who worked at the Lyric were exasperated by the way he conducted rehearsals as if he were getting up an after dinner rag, but he was so amiable about it that most of the cast were willing to join in and to think and invent on their own, perhaps seldom realising to what extent they were being controlled and inspired by the producer, or how much their performances owed to an occasional casual remark or to those touches of business with which Playfair could transform an ordinary performance into a first-rate one.

It was a method of production which very largely depended on having the right sort of actors. Playfair had a real genius for casting and a gift for discerning talent in even the most inexperienced player. For instance, his opening production, Milne's *Make Believe*, included in the cast Herbert Marshall, Angela Baddeley, Hermione Baddeley and Leslie Banks, all of whom at that time were practically unknown.

He showed the same flair for finding the right people in his choice of collaborators. It was essential for his extremely individual style of production that he should have designers whose ideas were in harmony with his own. It is difficult to judge how much his productions owed to his designers or how much his designers owed to his productions—which is a proof of good collaboration. In his choice of composers he was as successful as he was in his choice of actors and designers. His production of *The Beggar's Opera* was as perfect an example of collaboration as has been seen in the English theatre. Those who wished to belittle Playfair used to say that the real credit for the show belonged to Frederick Austin and Lovat Fraser, but as Giles Playfair points out in *My Father's Son*, "if by some trick of circumstances Frederick Austin and Lovat Fraser had come together under any other auspices the result would have been very different. Whether it would have been successful or not it is impossible to say. But I do say it would have been very different".

To say that Playfair's productions had a style and effectiveness of their own is not sufficient to explain why the West End was willing to journey to Hammersmith to see the eighteenth century classics. In London in those days a theatre could not be successful solely on its artistic merits. It had to be fashionable as well. The fact that the Lyric achieved this was largely due to Arnold Bennett who for seven years was Playfair's co-director at the Lyric. According to Giles Playfair, as a theatre director Arnold Bennett certainly had made faults. "His predictions were almost invariably wrong and he had little knowledge of what kind of play was likely to succeed or fail. He was conceited and obstinate. Experience never taught him or made him admit the error of his ways. And he was often relentlessly determined that his own works should be produced. But his virtues outweighed, in my opinion, his faults. He had a tremendous business sense and an acute grasp of figures. While he was in command he saw to it that no member of the staff was paid too much or too little and that every penny spent was a necessary disbursement. What was still more important, he lent the theatre a cachet of his own. An aura of success surrounded him and he was a born publicist. His presence in a box on the first nights seemed to personify stability and prosperity. While he remained chairman of the board of directors, the Lyric was never long out of the news."

Playfair's own personality also did much to make the Lyric fashionable. Unlike most stage people he had an enormous number of friends outside the theatre. He was a man with a lively, superficial interest in a large number of subjects and a dry, rather caustic sense of humour which made him a capital conversationalist. His parties were the most entertaining in London. The personal, friendly atmosphere at the Lyric was to some extent due to the fact that an astonishingly large number of the audience knew Playfair personally. But he made no conscious effort to be hail-fellow-well-met with his audience. In fact, he was seldom seen about the theatre in the evenings. Watching his own productions bored him.

It took some little time for Playfair to develop his policy at the Lyric. The opening production of Milne's *Make Believe* was little more than a hurried attempt to get something on in time for the Christmas holidays. The next three plays, Stanley Houghton's *The Younger Generation*, John Drinkwater's *Abraham Lincoln* and St. John Ervine's *John Ferguson*, had little in common with what afterwards came to be known as "the Lyric tradition". The first two were both produced by Stanley Drewitt. *The Younger Generation* was already well known as one of the best products of the Gaiety Theatre, Manchester, under Mrs. Horniman's direction, and *Abraham Lincoln*, which ran for over a year, was imported from the Birmingham Repertory. But with *The Younger Generation* was presented a one-act operetta by Pergolesi, *La Serva Padrona*, which was the advance guard of the series of eighteenth century plays and operettas which was to make the Lyric famous. It aroused very little interest and few people took much notice of the settings and costumes which were Lovat Fraser's first work for the theatre.

It was *As You Like It*, the production following *John Ferguson*, which gave Lovat Fraser his first real opportunity. This was the production which Playfair always said he would most like to be remembered by. Yet when it was played at Stratford before being brought to Hammersmith it aroused such indignation that when Playfair entered the lounge of the hotel where he was staying people got up and left the room in protest. Compared with most present-day Shakespearian productions it was very straightforward. The audience seemed to have been upset because the verse instead of being spoken in "the Shakespearian manner" was taken lightly and rapidly, and because the gay, colourful costumes seemed to them "cubist" and "futuristic", although actually the colours and designs were taken from fourteenth century French missals. But what annoyed Stratford even more was that Playfair would not use a very ancient stuffed stag which at Stratford was invariably carried on in the forest scene and was specially kept in the Museum for that purpose. In London the production caused much less sensation and only ran at the Lyric for six weeks. On the whole the critics were unfavourable. Some of them considered that it was played as if it were a modern drawing-room comedy, and most of them disliked the dresses on the grounds that they were far too extravagant in colour and "out of key with Shakespeare".

The next production, *The Beggar's Opera*, was the last which Lovat Fraser designed at Hammersmith. He died during its run. His influence on the English theatre has been so great that it is not generally realised how extremely small was the total amount of his work for the stage. In addition to the three productions already mentioned, all that he designed were two ballets for Karsavina at the Coliseum, a special production of Holst's *Savitri*, and Dunsany's *If*. At the time when Lovat Fraser began to work for the stage the standard of design in the English theatre was extremely low. Scenery attempted to be elaborately and extravagantly realistic but usually only succeeded in looking flimsy. Costumes were dull in colour, seldom properly related to one another. Like all good stage designers, Lovat Fraser had a fine mechanical sense, and he was the first designer in England to give serious attention to the problem of designing for a small stage. To-day every repertory theatre in England still uses from time to time some version of his permanent architectural setting which he designed for *The Beggar's Opera*, an arrangement of arches and steps planned so that changes from exterior to interior scenes could be made with the minimum of scene-shifting. Perhaps it is because Lovat Fraser's style has been so constantly copied and debased that he is now very much underrated as an artist of the theatre. Unfortunately most of his imitators have merely reproduced the simplicity of his work, failing completely to reproduce its essential elegance. The simplicity of his settings was based on an extraordinarily detailed understanding and appreciation of eighteenth century architecture. His colour schemes, although superficially bold and brilliant, were actually so subtle and exact that often he was only able to achieve his effects by dyeing the materials himself. In the work of his imitators the freshness of his colour has been copied as if it were a mere obvious juxtaposition of primary colours.

The Beggar's Opera, which ran at Hammersmith for three years and was constantly revived to tide the theatre over periods of financial stress, was the first of a series of eighteenth century productions which made the theatre famous and included *The Way of the World*, *The Duenna*, *The Rivals*, *The Beaux' Stratagem*, *Marriage à la Mode*, *Lionel and Clarissa*, *Love in a Village*, *She Stoops to Conquer* and *The Critic*.

The lack of interest displayed by the audience in *La Serva Padrona* had shown Playfair that the eighteenth century was very much out of fashion. In *The Story of the Lyric, Hammersmith*, he remarked that at that time purity of harmony "could set on edge the teeth of the musical critic in a way no cartwheel could. In literature we were all romantics, in the seventeenth and early nineteenth century manner, or else realists (which generally, in Drama, means romanticists turned sentimental or sadists); and it was the thing to regard the eighteenth century as a temporary chrysaliding of civilisation—an attack of frostbite from which mankind did not recover till the genial rays of 1800 Romanticism."

It was, I think, this realisation of the difficulty of making the eighteenth century interesting to his audience which first led Playfair to put so much emphasis on the decorative trimmings of the period, on its airs and graces and fopperies. Some of the means which he used to give his audience a sense of period were irritatingly obvious, such as the bewigged and dressed-up theatre orchestra in *The Way of the World*, and he had a maddening fondness for footmen promenading around the stage lighting or extinguishing candles. But his manner with these plays was not one which he assumed cynically for mere managerial reasons. The eighteenth century classics gave him a legitimate opportunity for indulging in a style of production which was the most natural expression of his own mind and personality.

It is arguable that he either failed to appreciate or deliberately ignored the real spirit of some of these plays. He changed *The Beggar's Opera* from a ferocious, scurrilous satire into a gay, neat, dainty entertainment. He sponged away much of the cynicism and acidity from *The Way of the World* and substituted a kind of jaunty playfulness. He treated both Sheridan and Goldsmith with the same decorative formality, as if he saw little difference between the two. But it is unfair to judge Playfair as if he had been attempting serious and faithful productions of the classics. His aim was, quite frankly, to make new entertainments out of old plays. At a time when the English theatre was sadly lacking in style of any sort, the audiences gratefully accepted these decorative productions for their lively invention, their elegant, highly coloured settings and costumes, their formalised groupings and gestures, their use of music and dancing, their attractive airs and affectations. But style alone can never bring audiences to a theatre month after month. They went also to see the brilliance of the acting and the genuine, honest humour which underlay the sophisticated glitter of the trappings. In recent years Playfair's reputation has suffered because people are apt to remember only the externals of his productions.

He is often blamed for having started the present-day fashion for fantasticating the classics, but there is a great difference between Playfair's work and that of the exhibitionist school of producers who are so afraid of being dull that they laboriously think out new stunts, far-fetched business, freak casting and unlikely settings to ginger up the plays. Playfair's productions were neither affected nor self-conscious. He produced the plays the way he did because he saw them that way. Even when his own style was theoretically in opposition to the style of his author, he usually succeeded in overcoming the seeming incongruity and blending the two together because his production was the honest and complete expression of his own individual point of view.

Playfair's most original entertainment was his revue, *Riverside Nights*. It has often been said that it was the model for many subsequent intimate revues, but there has never been a revue since which was quite like *Riverside Nights*. It was the most completely individual of all Playfair's productions, the one which was the best illustration of his own taste. In his autobiography Playfair explains that his idea of revue was "frankly to furnish the sort of turns and items which I myself, being precious or highbrow or just vaguely discontented, as you choose to think, would rather see in any entertainment of the kind than what I generally do see". This is the only way in which revue ought to be produced. No revue can be a success unless it is the expression of the taste of one man, and of one man only. He can be either a producer-manager like Playfair or Cochran, or an author-manager like Herbert Farjeon. The essential thing is that he must be in absolute and complete control, responsible to nobody but himself. A revue can have no style or personality if it is a mere hotchpotch of the tastes of the backer, the manager, the producer and the leading lady. In producing the Gate revues, which were usually written by a round dozen of authors and composers, I simply followed the principle of choosing the items which *I* liked, ruthlessly excluding anything which did not appeal to my own personal taste, however good I thought it, however certain everybody else in the cast may have been that it was just what the audience would like.

Producing a revue according to this method came naturally enough to Playfair whose success as a manager was very largely due to the fact that he was an enthusiast who instead of trying to find out what the public wanted always believed that there were plenty of people who would like what *he* liked. "The public may not like a play", wrote A. A. Milne in his epilogue to *The Story of the Lyric Theatre, Hammersmith*, "but it certainly won't if the manager doesn't like it. If he but hold a pipe through which a dozen windy acquaintances, partners, rivals, backers and other experts make music as they pass, nobody will care to listen; but if he blow happily and enthusiastically for himself, the crowd will soon be round him. Mr. Playfair is often accused of knowing, in some occult way, the tunes which the public really likes. He has much more valuable knowledge than this: he knows the tunes which he himself really likes—and is not afraid of them".

To some extent *Riverside Nights* was inspired by *La Chauve Souris*. Playfair had the idea that there was plenty of picturesque material for a revue to be found among our own literature and music. The revue contained some surprising items, such as Walter Savage Landor's *Imaginary Conversation*, and *An Illustration of a Poem by Wordsworth*, and *A Dramatic Pastoral* by Bickerstaff and Thomas Arne. But there were other ways in which *Riverside Nights* was quite unlike other revues. There was no chorus, no black-out sketches, no production numbers, and no star. In fact, it did not contain a single name known to the ordinary West End revue-goer. Playfair was the only revue producer I have ever known who was not obsessed by the necessity for scurrying his show along and cutting his items down to a maximum of three or four minutes. There were at least four items in *Riverside Nights* which played for over fifteen minutes each. To look at, it was quite the most satisfactory small-scale revue I have ever seen, which is not unnatural in view of the fact that it was designed by John Armstrong, George Sheringham, Laurence Irving and Michel Sevier. *Riverside Nights* ran for eight months, and lost £4,000.

To make matters worse the successor to *Riverside Nights*, a very lovely production of Anstey Guthrie's version of Molière's *The Would-Be Gentleman*, was a complete failure. Happily the fortunes of the Lyric were saved by *The Beaux' Stratagem*, which finally established the reputation of Edith Evans whose Mrs. Sullen was an even greater performance than her Millamant. There was so little money left that the theatre could not afford to build new scenery or buy new costumes, so a make-shift set was constructed out of *The Duenna* scenery, and the play was dressed from costumes already in the wardrobe. There were no costumes of the right period, so in a programme note Playfair apologised for placing the play "for reasons of urgent personal convenience" in a later period than that in which it was written.

The Beaux' Stratagem was followed by *When Crummles Played*, an elaborate joke of Playfair's own invention which fell extremely flat. "My idea," he wrote, "and surely it was a good one, was to assemble in a prologue, taken with a minimum amount of adaptation from *Nicholas Nickleby*, the Crummles family and troupe, and to set them to act one of the plays which they did act, or at least, might very well have done." The play he chose was Lillo's *George Barnwell: or The London Merchant*. It was the first time that Playfair had made the mistake of relying more on his gift for invention and burlesque than upon the play, and the failure of the attempt was a severe blow to his self esteem. He was hurt and puzzled that his audience did not like what he considered to be one of his best productions at the Lyric.

A little bewildered, his confidence badly shaken, he decided to play for safety. In the theatre success almost invariably seems to be the reward of courage, and playing for safety usually in the end proves to be an unwise policy. Nothing could have seemed safer than a return to the combination of music and the eighteenth century which had always packed the Lyric. Nevertheless, Bickerstaff's *Love in a Village* proved to be the first eighteenth century production at the Lyric that failed to draw the town. Playfair had always regarded the eighteenth century plays and operettas as the only form of subsidy which the Lyric possessed and the failure of *Love in a Village* following on the failure of *When Crummles Played* shook his confidence in himself and his audience. From now onwards his work lacked its former spontaneity. His style lost much of its freshness and became dangerously like a mere formula. He began to find the Lyric a worry and a burden. The immediate difficulties were solved by letting the theatre for six months to the Old Vic company, who were temporarily without a home owing to the reconstruction of the Vic. *She Stoops to Conquer* and *The Critic* which followed were both reasonably successful. It was during the next production, *A Hundred Years Old* by the brothers Quintero, that the tenth anniversary of Playfair's management of the Lyric was celebrated. "I felt upon this evening", he wrote, "that I should have liked to have announced my retirement from active management, that ten years of the constant strain and anxiety is enough for any man, as indeed it is, and I would willingly hand the theatre with its goodwill to a younger man."

By now the theatre seemed to have regained some of its old prosperity and Playfair was encouraged to break fresh ground with a production of Offenbach's *La Vie Parisienne* adapted by A. P. Herbert. Although it achieved a reasonable run, it failed to make money. The public was beginning to weary of Playfair's style of production, which itself was beginning to look a little tired. From now onwards he continued to repeat himself. Frequently he fell back on revivals of his previous successes, which invariably proved to be disastrous. He made a brief return to his old form with a production of *The Importance of Being Earnest* with John Gielgud in the lead, but all the money made on this production was lost on Dryden's *Marriage à la Mode*, and his other return to the eighteenth century, a production of Congreve's *The Old Bachelor*, was even more unfortunate. Compared with *The Way of the World* it is a poor play and to make matters worse Edith Evans' part was a very feeble one compared with those in which she had previously appeared at Hammersmith. Even the production was flat and dull. An attempt was then made to establish a tradition of light opera by modern authors and composers with *Tantivy Towers* and *Derby Day*, but as a producer Playfair had lost his gaiety and inventiveness, his casting was careless and the scenery far below the Lyric standard. *Derby Day* was Playfair's last production at Hammersmith. It was the only time he produced anything at Hammersmith which he did not care for personally and his production showed it.

The end of Playfair's régime at the Lyric was a severe loss to the London theatre. For fourteen years he had run the Lyric as a place where people could unfailingly rely on finding intelligent entertainment extremely well acted and produced with distinction and style. He had brought the eighteenth century classics back into the English theatre, and had done much to raise the standard of stage designing through the opportunities he gave to Lovat Fraser, George Sheringham, Doris Zinkeison and Norman Wilkinson. It is not generally realised that as a producer he re-introduced a style that had vanished from the English theatre. When he began his work at the Lyric the whole technique of acting and production in England was based on a pretence of ignoring the audience and isolating the actors in their own world behind the footlights. Playfair's method was to accept the presence of the audience, to make them a partner in the play, and to establish a feeling of intimacy between the stage and auditorium. It was a method of production ideally suited to the Lyric with its small, friendly auditorium and whenever a production was transferred from Hammersmith to another theatre it invariably failed.

Both the success and the eventual decline of the Lyric were due to the fact that it was essentially a producer's theatre. Although the standard of the plays was extremely high, the policy of the theatre was based less on the plays themselves than on the manner in which they were produced. Because it was a very personal and individual manner, it was impossible for Playfair, when he grew old and tired, to employ other producers and confine his own energies simply to the direction of the theatre. It is all to the good of the theatre as a whole that there should occasionally be producers' theatres, but such theatres can have no permanence. They can exist only so long as their directors can maintain their freshness and powers of invention. No theatre can have real stamina and staying power if it neglects the importance of the living author as the only person who can continually supply it with fresh ideas and renewed energy. During all these fourteen years Playfair did not produce a single straight play for the first time. His policy of new English light operas came too late, when he was tired and dispirited. Even his taste for the classics was limited to the plays of a comparatively brief period of theatrical history. Though it would be unfair to say that he lacked appreciation for the plays of other periods, as a producer his style was too definite and too limited to allow him much variety in his choice of plays. But within these admittedly narrow limits he had more effect on the art of production in the English theatre than any other producer of his time.

CHAPTER IV

PETER GODFREY AND THE GATE

I WAS not impressed on my first visit to the Gate. I thought it a squalid looking place. Worse, I suspected it of being arty. In those early days it was on the top floor of a ramshackle warehouse in a Covent Garden alley called Floral Street. The more enterprising small boys of the district used to charge twopence to pilot would-be members of the audience who had lost their way among the maze of dark narrow alley-ways surrounding the theatre. When one had found the entrance there was a gruelling climb up many flights of rickety stairs to the theatre itself. The "theatre" was little more than a large garret holding an audience of eighty crammed together on cruelly narrow and uncomfortable seats. There was the minimum of ventilation and no foyer to escape to in the interval. But at the back of the room there was a coffee bar presided over by the amiable Mrs. St. Lo who from the first day the Gate was opened until its last performance in 1940 continued to provide the best coffee in London and to be the kindliest but shrewdest critic of the shows.

The stage of those Floral Street premises could hardly have been smaller, and the dressing-room accommodation was so limited that several of the cast used to have to make their changes on the stage itself during the intervals. The front curtain was of sacking. On it someone had started to paint something that looked as if it would eventually develop into an antelope but had given up after finishing only the hindquarters. I think it was this writhing, prancing half-an-antelope which more than anything else made me suspect that the Gate smelt of artiness. But I was wrong. It smelt of dirt and size and coffee and greasepaint and sweating humanity, but it was not arty. Peter Godfrey, its founder, was thoroughly professional in the best sense of the word. Although he was still in his early twenties he was widely experienced in the theatre. He had begun as a boy conjurer "on the halls"; he had toured Ireland with a fit-up; he had been a member of Ben Greet's Shakespearian company, travelled with a circus as one of the clowns, worked as a film extra, and acted and produced with repertory companies at Southend, Wakefield and Plymouth. It was while he was at Plymouth that he began reading the new "expressionistic drama" that was being produced in

Germany and America. These plays, which at that time seemed so excitingly unorthodox in their technique and choice of subject, made Godfrey more than ever discontented with the succession of stale West End successes which were all that the repertory theatres would allow him to produce or act in. So he and his wife, Molly Veness, conceived the fantastic idea of founding in London a theatre of their own. It was a fantastic idea because they had no money. Week by week they saved on their tiny salaries, and at last they had enough to rent that top floor in Covent Garden.

It was not originally Godfrey's intention to run the Gate as a private theatre. Later it became labelled as a theatre to which people went to see banned plays, so it is interesting to note that in the first season of eighteen plays only one of these could possibly have been refused a licence by the Lord Chamberlain. The Gate was opened as a private theatre not to escape from the jurisdiction of the Lord Chamberlain, but because the London County Council not unnaturally refused to license as a public theatre a loft in Floral Street to which the only entrance and exit was a rickety wooden staircase.

The decision to run the theatre as a private club was a bold one and entirely new. At that time there of course existed several Sunday night play producing societies performing for members only, but this was the first time that anyone had conceived the idea of using the privileges of a theatrical club not merely for one or two performances but for a nightly run of two or three weeks.

The Gate opened on October 30, 1925, with Susan Glaspell's *Bernice*. The opening production ran for a fortnight and was followed by a double bill consisting of *The End of the Trail* by Ernest Howard Culbertson and Copeau's *The House Into Which We Are Born*. Then came Strindberg's *The Dance of Death* and another double bill consisting of Schnitzler's *The Wedding Morning* and de Musset's *A Door Must Be Either Open Or Shut*. The Christmas production was Molière's *George Dandin*.

Up to now the theatre had been struggling along without attracting any particular notice. The tiny capital had long ago been eaten up. There were some weeks when the salaries of the cast amounted to only a few shillings each. Even a charwoman was a luxury which the theatre could not afford. The two directors used to come down each morning an hour or so before rehearsals and clean the theatre themselves.

Had it not been for James Agate, it is very unlikely that the Gate would have been able to exist long enough even to finish its first season. It was Agate's notice of the next production, *From Morn to Midnight*, which was the turning point in the early history of the

Gate. Up to then Agate, in common with most of the dramatic critics, had paid very little attention to the Gate, but in his notice of *From Morn to Midnight* he more than made amends. He did more than just write an enthusiastic notice of the play and production and urge his readers to go to the Gate. He gave full details of how to join, and even included the theatre's telephone number in his notice. "Breathes there a serious playgoer", he wrote, "with soul so dead that he will neglect to support a theatre of such aim and achievement as I have outlined? I refuse to think so. If I may add a further recommendation", he continued, "it is that people who intend to be interested should be interested now; it is no use bringing the tube of oxygen after the patient is dead. What is wanted is practical sympathy now and not the *beau geste* when it is too late."

On the Sunday evening of the day this article appeared the Gate was packed. By Monday morning applications for membership were pouring in by telephone and by post. By Monday evening every performance for the rest of the run of the play was sold out.

The run could easily have been extended for several weeks, but Godfrey had promised his members a long programme for the season and he very wisely refused to break faith with them for the sake of making as much money as possible out of a single production. At the end of its three weeks run at the Gate the production was transferred to the Regent where Claude Rains took over the part played by Peter Godfrey, who refused to leave the Gate.

Expressionism is now a dead formula, both in writing and production, although J. B. Priestley and Basil Dean between them made a belated attempt to revive it years later in *Johnson Over Jordan.* But in 1925 it had only just been heard of in England. *From Morn to Midnight* was the first completely expressionistic production to be seen in London. The tremendous vitality and excitement of this production was due to the fact that Peter Godfrey was not painstakingly following the continental formula, but was quite independently working out his own style of production. In all his previous productions at the Gate there had been some touch of expressionism. Lack of money made any form of solid realistic scenery out of the question. Even if the money had been available, the tiny stage made it impracticable. From the beginning, his method had been to use a permanent black background, indicating the locale of the scene by the minimum of properties and furniture, relying for atmosphere and effect entirely on purely unrealistic lighting. Even his favourite method of opening a play by drawing the curtains on a pitch dark stage and then gradually bringing up the lights had a practical origin. The theatre could not afford curtains of a material heavy enough to be impenetrable by light.

From Morn to Midnight was, of course, deliberately written for an extreme form of expressionistic production. But Godfrey brought to it the methods he had already worked out for himself. He succeeded in inspiring his cast to achieve a completely stylised form of acting which avoided any suggestion of lifelessness. Each scene was dominated by its own rhythm—the steady chinking of money in the opening scene at the bank, the rhythmic sobbing of the children in the cashier's home, the nagging syncopation of the jazz band in the night club, the hectic, jigging movement of the spectators at the bicycle race, the thumping of the big drum in the Salvation Army scene. I still count this production among the best I have ever seen.

During that first season at the Gate there were eighteen changes of programme, comprising twenty-three plays (sixteen full-length and seven one-acters), making altogether a total of two hundred and fifty-two performances. In addition to the plays already mentioned, the season's programme included Ibsen's *Hedda Gabler*, Hauptmann's *Rosa Bernd*, Toller's *Hinkemann*, Masefield's *The Tragedy of Nan*, Capek's *The Land of Many Names*, Evreinoff's *The Theatre of the Soul*, Dostoievsky's *The Brothers Karamazov*, and *The Race with the Shadow* by Wilhelm von Scholz. It was one of the most remarkable programmes ever given in a single season by any one theatre, especially when one considers the incredible difficulties under which the actors and the producer were labouring. Their achievement is made all the more remarkable by the fact that the theatre was seldom closed for more than two days between each production.

The next season was a little less hectic, as this time there were only fourteen changes of programme (comprising thirteen full-length plays and five one-act plays). These included Gorki's *The Lower Depths*, Maeterlinck's *Monna Vanna*, Jules Romains' *Dr. Knock*, Elmer Rice's *The Adding Machine*, Wedekind's *Erdgeist*, and Chatrian's *The Polish Jew*. The programme was shorter than the previous one because in March the Floral Street premises were closed. New premises had been obtained in Villiers Street.

There were the usual difficulties and delays over the reconstruction. The first two productions of the third season had to be given at the Rudolf Steiner Hall. The new theatre was not opened until November 22, 1927. The play was Simon Gantillon's *Maya*.

The building was being used as a skittle alley when it was acquired by the Gate. At one time it had been part of the old Gatti's Restaurant and Music Hall. In the process of being converted from a restaurant to a skittle alley, with an interim period when it was practically derelict, the building had lost every pretension to any kind of architectural style. Huge, fly-blown gilt mirrors along the walls were the only remnants of its one-time glory. It had been altered, added to and propped up without any attempt at anything but achieving the necessary ends by the cheapest possible means.

The adaptation of this ramshackle building, measuring only fifty-five feet by thirty feet, was done with extraordinary skill and ingenuity at the minimum of cost. Godfrey's wisest step was to plan the stage first and the auditorium afterwards. As a result the Gate possessed a well-proportioned stage, which in size was out of all normal proportion to the auditorium. It occupied, in fact, over one-third of the floor space of the entire building. It must have required considerable determination to resist the temptation to sacrifice a few feet of stage-space for the sake of that extra row of stalls which would have made all the difference to the finances of the theatre.

Godfrey showed further originality and courage in completely ignoring all the usual principles of theatre design. As the roof of the building was, for the purposes of a theatre, comparatively low, he built the stage only eighteen inches high so as to obtain the greatest possible height for his settings. He compensated for this by steeply raking the auditorium. The stage was so close to the audience that those sitting in the front row could—and sometimes did—sit with their feet resting on the edge of the stage. At first it was terrifying for an actor to have to play a long emotional scene with the spectators sitting at little more than arm's length, but actually the advantages of this outweighed the disadvantages. From the point of view of the actor the Gate combined most of the advantages of the theatre with those of the radio and the cinema. With his voice he could get over to the audience subtle variations of tone usually only possible in a broadcasting studio. Facial expressions which are ordinarily only effective to an audience if magnified by a close-up were perfectly visible from the back row of the Gate. The actor could play far more rapidly and intimately at the Gate than is possible in a normal sized theatre. He did not have to magnify and project his performance to reach the back rows of a gallery or an upper circle. Without the no-man's-land of the orchestra pit or the barrier of a row of footlights his contact with the audience was instant and direct. On the other hand, because of this extreme intimacy between stage and auditorium, insincerity was at once detected by the audience. The Gate mercilessly revealed any sort of trickery or stageyness. Yet although over-acting was so relentlessly magnified, it was possible for the actor to let himself go as full out at the Gate as at any other theatre, providing that he was acting with absolute sincerity and never overstraining. Proof of this is that actresses such as Flora

Robson, Beatrix Lehmann, Gwen Ffrangcon-Davies and Margaret Rawlings, all of them emotional actresses in the grand manner, gave some of their finest performances at the Gate.

There is another feature of the way the Gate was constructed which, although at first sight it appeared to be a disadvantage, was actually a help to the actor. Owing to lack of space the dressing-rooms were built on either side of the stage, only a few feet from the wings, so that all through the performance both the play and the reaction of the audience could be heard in the dressing-rooms. In the ordinary theatre, where the dressing-rooms are separated from the stage by a long passage and perhaps two or three flights of stairs, the actor is completely isolated from the play until he is standing in the wings a moment or two before he makes his entrance. As soon as he makes his exit and leaves the wings his contact with the stage is broken again, and each new entrance means a renewed effort to attune himself to the key of the performance. At the Gate, without any conscious effort, almost subconsciously, the actor was "in" the show even when he was in his dressing-room. It is interesting that the importance of this was realised by Tairov when he designed his new theatre, the building of which was in the end abandoned owing to his fall from favour with the Soviet. The theatre was so planned that the dressing-rooms bordered the sides of the stage in exactly the same way as at the Gate.

New theatres are seldom successful when they first open. The new Gate proved to be an exception. *Maya*, with Gwen Ffrangcon-Davies in the lead, was easily the Gate's greatest success up to date. It ran for fifty-three performances, and was followed by another success, O'Neill's *The Hairy Ape*, which ran for thirty-three performances. Other successes of this season were a revival of *From Morn to Midnight*, Cocteau's *Orphée*, and *20 Below* by Robert Nichols and Jim Tully. In all, two hundred and forty performances were given this season, with nine changes of programme.

The fourth season was less successful. The longest run achieved by any of the plays was twenty-seven performances of a revival of *The Race with the Shadow* by Wilhelm von Scholz. Toller's *Hoppla!* would probably have achieved a considerably longer run had it not been for the fact that after nineteen performances the entire cast was stricken with mumps. As a long run had been anticipated, no production was in rehearsal and the theatre would have closed had not the Cambridge Festival company come to the rescue at the end of their own season and performed W. J. Turner's *The Man Who Ate the Popomack* for a fortnight.

The most notable feature of this season was that at Christmas Peter Godfrey inaugurated the series of musical burlesques which he produced so brilliantly. The first was Mrs. Mowatt's *Fashion: or High Life in New York*, which was afterwards transferred to the Kingsway. Subsequent Christmas shows included *Ten Nights in a Bar Room: or Ruined by Drink*, *The Red Rover's Revenge*, *Uncle Tom's Cabin*, *Little Lord Fauntleroy* (with Elsa Lanchester in the title role), and two revues under the title of *Peter's Parade*, in which Hermione Gingold, who was afterwards to be the star of many Gate revues, made her first appearance at the theatre.

The outstanding success of the fifth season was Alfred Savoir's *The Lion Tamer: or English as She is Eaten.* With Ernest Thesiger and Jeanne de Casalis in the leading parts it ran for forty-one performances. But perhaps the two most distinguished plays on the programme were Lenormand's *The Eater of Dreams* and Jean-Jacques Bernard's *Martine*, which was afterwards seen at the Ambassadors.

It is interesting to note that *Martine* was the least successful production of the whole season, running for only nineteen performances. Evidently Bernard was very little to the taste of the Gate audience in those days, but later he was to become one of the most popular dramatists in the Gate repertoire. More plays by Bernard were produced at the Gate than by any other author.

The sixth season, 1930–31, was remarkable for a series of magnificent performances by actors and actresses then almost entirely unknown, opening with a firework display by Veronica Turleigh and Eric Portman in Vaijda's *The Professional Lover*. Eric Portman gave another fine performance later in the season in O'Neill's banned play *Desire Under the Elms*. Playing opposite him was an unknown actress called Flora Robson. It is a performance which I still think the finest Flora Robson has ever given. Another then unknown actress who made her reputation that year at the Gate was Margaret Rawlings, who acted in Wilde's *Salomé* with a cast which also included Flora Robson, Robert Speaight, John Clements, Hedley Briggs and Esmond Knight. The dances were arranged by Ninette de Valois, settings and costumes were by John Armstrong, and the music was composed by Constant Lambert. At Christmas Elsa Lanchester brilliantly burlesqued *Little Lord Fauntleroy*; and Wilfrid Walter, partnered by Miriam Adams, brought off a *tour de force* in his own play *Happy and Glorious*, which has a cast of only two. It was during this season that Esme Percy appeared twice at the Gate, giving brilliant and completely contrasting performances in Moeller's *Douaumont* and Antoine Bibesco's *The Heir*.

This season was easily the most successful in the history of the Gate up to date, several of the plays running for over forty performances each. From now onwards began the steady decline ending in Peter Godfrey finally relinquishing the theatre.

When he opened the next season he was no longer in partnership with Charles Spencer, who for the last four years had been in joint control. Spencer's absence was at once noticeable in a deterioration in the quality of the programmes from 1931–32. Two or three of the plays were far below the standard which the Gate had set itself, and towards the end of the season it was necessary to fall back on past successes, including *From Morn to Midnight* and *Maya.* There was also a noticeable deterioration in the casting, and often the productions were unexpectedly limp and uninspired. After six years' incessant work under exceptionally difficult conditions, Peter Godfrey was a tired man. Forced to reassume much of the work and responsibility which Spencer had taken off his shoulders, his productions inevitably suffered.

Fully realising this himself, he sought a remedy for the season of 1932–33 by amalgamating with the Cambridge Festival Theatre. In theory the plan was an excellent one. Both theatres had similar aims, and both directors had very similar tastes in plays. An interchange of companies would obviously give far more time for rehearsals, and each director had to find only half as many plays as before. In practice the scheme was a failure. As the Festival Theatre was a public one under the jurisdiction of the Lord Chamberlain, this at once limited the Gate's choice of plays. Although the methods of production of both theatres were broadly similar insofar as both were anti-realistic, the two stages were far too dissimilar in size and design for productions rehearsed for one theatre to fit comfortably into the other. The establishment of two permanent companies automatically reduced the standard of casting at the Gate. It had always been possible to get together a distinguished cast at the Gate who were prepared to play for a nominal salary for four or five weeks, but successful actors and actresses could hardly be expected to play for a whole season at the very small salaries which could be paid. All these handicaps might have been overcome had the amalgamation been made at a time when the Festival Theatre was at its best. Unfortunately, Terence Gray's passion for experiment had by that time declined into sheer eccentricity. The production of Ashley Dukes' *One More River*, which was the first Festival production to be seen at the Gate did not even shock or infuriate Gate audiences as Terence Gray had, I think, rather hoped. It merely bored and irritated them.

By December the steady decline in the size of the audiences at the Gate led to the abandonment of the scheme. I saw all the productions of this period and can only remember one with any pleasure—*Peer Gynt* with Peter Godfrey in the title role.

The failure of this scheme left Peter Godfrey without a programme for the Gate. A new version of his revue, *Peter's Parade*, saw him over Christmas and he then fell back on revivals of *The Race with the Shadow* and *Hinkemann*. The next production, a play of his own, called *I Hate Men*, was little more than a hotch-potch of characters and scenes out of some of the more sensational Gate productions in the past.

Wilfrid Walter's *Let Sleeping Dogs Lie* which followed proved to be much less successful than the same author's *Happy and Glorious*, which had been presented two seasons before. To end the season, Godfrey had to resuscitate *Peter's Parade* yet again.

At the beginning of the season 1933–34 the situation was desperate. The membership was now only one-third of what it had been two years before. Nevertheless, the season opened promisingly with Pirandello's *As You Desire Me*, in which Jean Forbes Robertson gave an exquisite performance. Two very feeble plays followed, and then Jean Forbes Robertson made another appearance at the Gate in *The Lady of the Camélias*. Even this, however, only ran for three weeks.

At Christmas, Godfrey suddenly returned to his old form with a superbly entertaining version of *Uncle Tom's Cabin*. But this recovery came too late. Many of his audience has lost faith in him, and the membership showed no signs of increase. He fell back on yet another revival, Langer's *The Outskirts*. The production and acting were lamentably inferior to those of the original performance and it failed completely.

Then, for the one and only time in the history of the Gate, the theatre was let. The tenants were a company of marionettes. At one performance the total takings at the box office were only seven shillings and sixpence. This disastrous experiment was followed by what proved to be the last of Peter Godfrey's productions. It was an interesting play, Jean Serment's *The Marriage of Hamlet*, but by now the Gate no longer had an audience and the play only survived for eight performances.

During its run, the members received the following announcement:

"I started the theatre in Floral Street with the object of giving London a chance of seeing the amazing experiments that were being made in the theatre all over central Europe and in America just after the war. I achieved my object and now I feel that the vast experience I have had in the work of the theatre (in nine years I have produced over 350 plays) should have a larger field and so I am reluctantly handing over the Gate to a new company, which I am sure will carry on the high standard of acting and production that the Gate audience has come to expect. Further details will be posted to you in due course.

"I want to thank you all sincerely for the way you have supported my enterprise in the past.

"Good-bye,

"PETER GODFREY."

It would be unfair to blame Godfrey for the decline of the Gate. For nine years he had directed the theatre under the most difficult circumstances. The constant change of programme never allowed him to let up for an instant. As soon as one production was launched, the next had to be cast. As the Gate was not able to offer a definite contract or a reasonable salary to any actor, this meant that often during rehearsals members of the cast had to relinquish their parts for the sake of a more profitable engagement. Even during the run of the play itself there was always the danger that someone might be spirited away, so that the casting alone was a continual source of strain and anxiety. The stage and its lack of facility for stacking or flying scenery demanded the greatest possible ingenuity and invention on the part of the producer, whose task was further complicated by the fact that the smallness of the theatre made it imperative that every possible economy should be practised. It was so essentially a one-man theatre that the business side, the stream of correspondence and the vast pile of plays waiting to be read, meant that such time as Godfrey had to spare from his actual production work had to be devoted to what was really a full-time job for at least two people. Not even his evenings were his own, as often he was acting in his productions.

To complicate matters still further, it was only in the most prosperous years of the Gate that its director was able to draw a salary sufficient to make him financially independent, so he was seldom in a position to refuse the offer of other work, such as a production in an ordinary West End theatre or the direction of a film. During the last year of Godfrey's régime at the Gate the income from the theatre was so small that he was forced to accept an offer to compère non-stop variety at the London Pavilion, with the result that he could give only his mornings to the Gate at a time when, more than ever, the theatre needed the undivided energies of its director.

Even if Godfrey had been able to survive the physical strain of directing the Gate for nine years, it is doubtful if he would have been able to continue for much longer. His taste in plays was a comparatively limited one. The expressionistic play, at which as a producer he excelled, was by now outmoded. He was uninterested in plays which were historical or biographical or in plays dealing with subtle undercurrents of emotion. His interest was in the morbid and extraordinary, in violent, twisted characters, in abnormality of every kind. By this time the group of continental dramatists on whom Godfrey mainly depended for his plays had tired of the psycho-analytic treatment of sex which for years had been their favourite theme. They were returning once more to realism and to the detailed and delicate delineation of less abnormal but none the less interesting kinds of human emotion.

The theatre now provided little scope for Godfrey's particular gifts. After leaving the Gate, he worked for a time in the West End, rather unhappily, and then left the theatre to write for the radio. Realising there was more scope for this sort of work in America than in England, he settled in New York. His success as a radio playwright led to a Hollywood contract as script writer. Then he turned to directing dialogue. Now he is a fully fledged film director. The first of his pictures to be seen over here was Vicki Baum's *Hotel in Berlin*.

In 1944 he opened a Gate Theatre in Hollywood. The plays he chose for his opening productions showed that theatrically he still lingered regretfully in the 'twenties. They were *Maya* and *From Morn to Midnight*.

CHAPTER V

THE FESTIVAL THEATRE, CAMBRIDGE

IN the 1920's the theatrical theorists were busy putting the playwright in his place. The play was no longer the thing. It was merely one of the several elements of a theatrical performance. A favourite quotation was that passage in Gordon Craig's *The Art of the Theatre* where he declares that the theatre is "neither acting, nor the play, neither scene nor dance, but all the elements of which these things are composed: action, which is the very spirit of acting; words, which are the body of the play; line and colour, which are the very heart of the scene; rhythm, which is the very essence of the dance". All these arts were to be combined into a unity by the controlling mind of the producer. The producer was to be no longer the servant of the playwright but his master. The Commedia del Arte was cited as showing that it was possible to have a play without an author; the ballet, it was argued, proved that words themselves were not essential to the theatre; that it was even possible to have a play without actors was proved by the marionette shows. The conclusion was that only the producer was indispensable, and that to him should be given absolute power in the theatre.

It was about this time that in every capital in Europe theatres were being founded which frankly proclaimed themselves to be "producers' theatres". In London the theatre placidly went about its business as usual, undisturbed by these new theories. It was in Cambridge that the solitary English example of this type of theatre was founded.

The Cambridge Festival Theatre, which opened in 1926, was unique among English theatres because its policy was based not on the choice of plays but on the manner of their production. Its policy was one of aggression. The Festival was founded to wage war upon what its director, Terence Gray, described as "the old game of illusion and glamour and all the rest of the nineteenth century hocus pocus and bamboozle". In other words, its mission was to attack the realistic tradition of acting and production which in England at this time had been brought to a pitch of almost photographic perfection by Basil Dean at the St. Martin's. "The modern theatre", declared Terence Gray, "is weary of naturalism—naturalism is superficial and a limitation. We can no longer see any essential virtue in representing on the stage all the externals of life. Because the locality of the action is said to be the Tower of London, Lady X's drawing-room, or Epping Forest, must we really try to reproduce these localities on the stage? What for? Most of us can see the real thing when we want to, most of us can guess what they are like. To reproduce them is a laborious and not very relevant business, of no perceivable dramatic importance, conveying information for which the programme is an adequate and convenient medium. Aeschylus did not ask it, Shakespeare did not ask it, really modern authors do not ask it. There is, let us admit, something a little futile in such make-believe. The most it can achieve at its best is an independent work of art, architectural or pictorial, but what has this to do with the theatre? Is it not rather for painters and model-makers? Frankly we cannot conceive it as part of our job. We are the theatre theatrical. We don't want the wisest or the most foolish member of our audience to play at visual make-believe or ever to forget that the stage is only the stage. And what should the stage be? We think the stage should be a raised platform designed to give the greatest mutual relations of the actors playing their parts in each play, and accordingly for each play there should be a specially designed raised platform, the levels and angles of which fulfil a function in emphasising the dramatic relation. Beyond this platform all that is called for is a background against which the actors can be seen, and such objects architectural or otherwise as may be designed to emphasise some aspect of the play".

The Festival stage was so designed that conventional realistic production was almost impossible. The first essential to a photographically realistic production is a picture-frame proscenium isolating the actors from the audience. At the Festival it was difficult to find any definite point at which the stage ended and the auditorium began. There was no proscenium. The width of the stage was the width of the auditorium itself. The broad forestage merging into a great fan-shaped flight of steps extending to the feet of the audience sitting in the front row abolished any boundary line between actor and audience.

Working at the Festival as a producer gave one an extraordinary sense of elbow room. The several levels provided by the stage, the forestage, and the steps gave opportunities for innumerable new combinations of movement and grouping impossible in an ordinary theatre where the actors would be masking one another. It was easy to get the actors on and off the stage without the elaborate and unnatural manœuvres necessary on a picture-frame stage, as at the Festival in addition to the usual entrances there were two on the forestage, two more opening on to the steps from where in an ordinary theatre the stage boxes would be, and two more entrances down the gangways of the stalls on to the forestage steps. The upstage section of the stage was constructed so as to roll forward giving access to the understage where a flight of steps provided yet further entrances, so that it was possible for an actor to walk straight up out of the back of the stage and instantly dominate the scene. An actor on the forestage or the steps was literally playing among the audience, for the auditorium itself was on the old Regency horseshoe plan, with curving balconies stretching on either side as far as the forestage itself. In fact, the actual building, at the time of its conversion, was one of the few remaining Regency playhouses in England. It had been known as the Theatre Royal, Barnwell, and had enjoyed a long period of prosperity during which most of the great actors and actresses of the day had appeared there. But later it fell upon evil times and finally was let as a mission hall, re-opening with a function at which the advertised attraction was "Tea and Buns for 500".

Terence Gray did not content himself with remodelling the stage and equipping it with one of the most elaborate and up-to-date lighting systems in the world. Unlike most theatrical crusaders, he remembered that his audience would have bodies as well as minds, and he saw to it that his theatre was as comfortable as possible. In those days repertory theatres were notoriously spartan and uninviting. Liverpool and Birmingham, it is true, were no more uncomfortable than any other theatre, but the majority of the repertory theatres at that time were existing awkwardly and uncomfortably in buildings originally intended for very different purposes. One had originally been a big game museum, another a horse tramway stable, a third a mission hall, a fourth a lecture hall in an educational settlement. Terence Gray, starting with the advantage of premises originally built as a theatre, did everything in his power to make playgoing a social and civilised affair. The seating of the theatre was exceptionally comfortable, there were programmes which could be read in the dark, and special seats were provided for late-comers. The bar was the only theatre bar I have ever known which was large enough to make it possible for the audience to obtain their drinks without taking part in a wild scramble. At the beginning of the second year he opened a theatre restaurant where the food was the best obtainable outside London and the wine far better than anything that could be obtained at the prices anywhere else in England. Gray, himself a considerable connoisseur of food and wine, wanted to encourage the Cambridge undergraduate to drink intelligently. Beer and spirits were not to be had in his restaurant, but it was possible to order a pichet of wine for one-and-sixpence (or a half-pichet for ninepence) which was far better than anything I have drunk in a London restaurant at four or five times the price. The elaborately annotated wine list was both a delight to the connoisseur and a tactful guide to the novice. I have wistful recollections of a magnificent Richebourg on that list; and there was a delicious red Graves from Leognan; but the wine that I remember with particular affection was an Anjou Savienniѐres, a beautiful, fresh, invigorating wine which can seldom be drunk in this country because there is a superstition that it does not travel.

Neither Terence Gray nor his partner in founding the Festival, Harold Ridge, were professional men of the theatre. Gray was a young man of thirty who had already earned for himself a considerable reputation as an Egyptologist. Ridge, five years older, was a metallurgist. An amateur actor of exceptional ability, he had been a member of the Sheffield Repertory Company, at that time an amateur organisation. He had also published *Stage Lighting for Little Theatres*, which was the standard book of its kind. It was Ridge who was responsible for the design of the lighting system at the Festival, and later he was to become the leading authority in England on stage lighting, with the equipment of the Shakespeare Memorial Theatre at Stratford as one of his major achievements.

The first producer at the Festival was Herbert Prentice, a railway clerk who for some years had been producing for the Sheffield Repertory Company. A little while previously he had turned professional in order to devote the whole of his time to producing at Sheffield. After leaving the Festival, Prentice went to Northampton and then became producer at the Birmingham Repertory Theatre.

I joined the Festival as stage director. I had first met Gray when I was engaged to handle the preliminary publicity for the Festival in the London press. A week or two later he asked me if I would consider coming to the Festival to stage manage. I pointed out that I was totally inexperienced, a fact which he seemed to think unimportant. Besides being inexperienced, I was in other ways peculiarly unfitted for the job. I am a vague, absent-minded and altogether unpractical person. Fortunately my assistant stage manager was Rodney Millington, who abundantly possessed all the qualities I lacked. At that time he was fresh from the O.U.D.S. Now he finds plenty of scope for his immense energy and organising ability in editing *Spotlight*, the theatre's casting directory.

Even the company itself had very little professional experience. The leading man was an amateur who had gained his experience by acting for amateur societies in the evenings while working as a clerk in a music publishers during the day. He was Maurice Evans, who is now America's leading actor-manager.

All these strange appointments were part of a deliberate policy. The Festival was to be a theatre unlike any other, and Gray's ultimate aim was to collect round him a company of actors untainted by the conventions and prejudices of the ordinary theatre, who would be prepared to evolve a fresh technique of acting. Unfortunately, coming to the theatre entirely without practical experience, he had little natural ability for moulding or developing talent. Worse, he was a bad judge of raw material. At auditions he based his opinion of an actor almost entirely on an ability to read intelligently a complicated passage in verse or a long speech from Shaw. Too often he mistook half-baked intellectualism for intelligence. He failed to realise that an ability to talk intelligently about acting is not a reliable symptom of an ability to act. Acting is a matter of instinct and sensitiveness rather than intelligence. The result was that his companies usually contained a large proportion of excessively bad actors, though it also contained from time to time some extremely good ones such as Maurice Evans, Robert Morley, Hedley Briggs, Vivienne Bennett, Beatrix Lehmann, Margaret Rawlings and Jessica Tandy.

Fortunately the lack of acting ability among many of the members of the Festival company was not as obvious as it might have been, as Gray's highly stylised methods of production made little demand on personality, subtlety or technique. Although he was a bad judge of an actor, he had many other qualities to offset this—immense originality, great courage, a wide knowledge of the European theatre, a tremendous capacity for hard work, a superb sense of showmanship, and a vivid and delightful personality. Added to this he was a man of considerable wealth. Nevertheless, his seven years of ceaseless experiment at the Festival had in the end little practical effect upon the English theatre. His great weakness was that he had an infinite capacity for attacking people, but little capacity for gathering and keeping followers of his own. He was too extreme in his views, too violent in the expression of his opinions, too obstinately uncompromising. This lack of any ability to compromise or to accept and use criticism led him to surround himself too often with third-rate people who were prepared to follow him uncritically, faithfully carrying out his ideas undisturbed by inconvenient opinions of their own. He required disciples rather than collaborators.

Although he failed in what he set out to achieve, his failure was on a grand scale, and the record of these seven years is a magnificent one. Here, for example, is a typical programme covering a year's work, divided into three seasons of eight weeks, each coinciding with the University terms.

1928		
Jan. 16	Caesar and Cleopatra	Bernard Shaw
Jan. 23	Inheritors	Susan Glaspell
Jan. 30	The Carthaginian	Frank Taylor
Feb. 6	From Morn to Midnight	Georg Kaiser
Feb. 13	Cheezo	Lord Dunsany
	Dr. Knock	Jules Romains
Feb. 20	Richard III	Shakespeare
Feb. 27	The Passion Flower	Jacinto Benavente
Mar. 5	The Knight of the Burning Pestle	Beaumont and Fletcher
Apr. 23	The Pretenders	Henrik Ibsen
Apr. 30	The Devil's Disciple	Bernard Shaw
May 7	The Riding to Lithend	Gordon Bottomley
	A Royal Audience	Terence Gray
May 14	The Last Hour	George Graveley
	The Dreamy Kid	Eugene O'Neill
	Emperor Jones	Eugene O'Neill
May 21	Madame Pepita	Martinez Sierra
May 28	Adam the Creator	Karel and Josef Capek
June 4	The Birds	Aristophanes
Oct. 10	Heartbreak House	Bernard Shaw
Oct. 22	The Man Who Ate The Popomack	W. J. Turner
Oct. 29	The Show	John Galsworthy
Nov. 5	The Subway	Elmer Rice
Nov. 12	As You Like It	Shakespeare
Nov. 19	The Spook Sonata	Strindberg
Nov. 26	The Hairy Ape	Eugene O'Neill
Dec. 3	Marriage à la Mode	John Dryden

This is obviously a remarkable programme for any repertory theatre, still more remarkable when one realises that each play was produced in an entirely fresh manner, that an exceptionally high proportion of them are costume plays, and several of them have very long casts and big crowd scenes. Such a programme was only made possible by the elaborate equipment of the theatre, and by the fact that an eight-week season meant that it was possible to rehearse for four weeks before the season opened. Even so, the strain on the company was enormous. Rehearsals were far longer than those in normal repertory theatres, beginning at ten in the morning and seldom ending before six in the evening. Even on Sunday the company did not rest, as the first dress rehearsal of each play used to begin late on Sunday afternoon.

Obviously no one producer could have survived many seasons working at this pressure, so never less than three producers were at work each season. Usually Terence Gray produced about half the shows himself and the rest of the productions, after Herbert Prentice left, were in the hands of guest producers, of whom the most frequent were Peter Godfrey and myself.

It had not at first been Terence Gray's intention to direct any of the productions personally. The plan was for Prentice to work under the general supervision of Gray. His opening production of the *Oresteian Trilogy* of Aeschylus was a complete justification of this method.

The whole conception of the production was Terence Gray's. Working under him were Herbert Prentice in charge of the actual production work; Ninette de Valois producing the chorus; Doria Paston composing the scenery out of a permanent set of screens, steps and rostrums already designed by Terence Gray; Reginald Leefe designing the costumes; William Hampton designing the masks; Dennis Arundell conducting the music composed by Professor Donald Tovey and Gordon Jacob; Harold Ridge in charge of the lighting; and a cast headed by Maurice Evans, Miriam Lewis and Hedley Briggs.

This may seem an unwieldly band of collaborators, but actually it resulted in one of the most magnificently successful productions that I have ever seen. If only this method of collaboration under Terence Gray's supervision could have been maintained, the Festival would rapidly have become the most important theatre in all England. Unfortunately Gray's lack of any real ability for leadership soon became obvious. Within a year Prentice, Ridge and myself had all left and Terence Gray had assumed the role of producer, relieved by one or two guest producers each season.

The principle behind all Terence Gray's productions was his dislike of any form of realism. He hated it when a guest producer attempted to build a realistic looking room on the Festival stage. He wanted his stage always to remain to the audience just obviously what it was—a platform for the actors to act upon. But not merely a flat platform. In his own productions Gray made elaborate use of multiple levels as he thought that thus the relationship between the characters could be more easily emphasised. Believing that significant movement and grouping can mean almost as much as speech, he eventually developed this theory of production to the extent of producing a completely realistic play on a pile of platforms, steps and ramps built on a turntable isolated in the centre of a bare stage. It was a technique of stagecraft which came within a method then known as constructivism insofar as the raised platform (Gray called it a "podium", a term in use in the French theatre) was the essential object. But constructivism as normally understood implied a bare structure of which the constituent parts—the struts, boards, framework, and so on—were left visible, forming their own natural decorative scheme. Gray's podium settings were not strictly constructivist. He built them solidly, giving them a certain number of architectural features and decorating them according to the mood and period of the play. Sometimes these constructions failed to achieve any sort of form or design and merely looked like a higgledy-piggledy collection of steps and platforms, but more often they had a strange, unexpected beauty of their own. To-day I suppose they would be dubbed surrealist, but at that time the word was not yet in use. They had much in common with the functional style of architecture which at that time was being evolved in its most extreme form by Mendelssohn.

Even a realistic play often gained more than it lost from being produced on a podium setting. The multiple levels, the ramps and steps, often made possible an extraordinary variety of grouping and movement which continually drove home with great vividness the relations of the characters to one another at any moment in the play. The lighting, too, was used completely unrealistically to emphasise the changing moods of the play and to concentrate attention on essentials, leaving the inessentials relatively invisible. At its best the lighting continually achieved effects which were both dramatic and beautiful. The great weakness of this method of production, like all forms of expressionism in the theatre, was that it over-simplified the play. Subtlety ceased to exist and the attention of the audience was concentrated entirely on the broadest outlines of character and situation. The criticism of Jessner by Kenneth MacGowan and Robert Edmond Jones in *Continental Stagecraft* might with equal justice be applied to Terence Gray. "He appeared to worship the obvious, to believe that the theatre is a place of A B C impressions and reactions. He was daring enough in his technique but not in his ideas. He flung out symbols right and left, but they were symbols of the primer. He directed in words of one syllable."

Another stage in Gray's war against realism in the theatre was his abolition of props. His defence of this was convincing enough. "To hand a man a purse, to open and read a document on the stage, such things must be small when performed with the real objects in the actor's hands. The expressiveness of the action is confined by the dimensions of the object handled. Only by discarding the actual article can the gestures of giving or of reading be rendered really significant. Only then does it cease to be a waxwork reproduction of life and become artistic interpretation. To crown a king with a crown of lead can never be effective as theatre art: to crown him with a magnificent gesture might be exceedingly moving."

This method certainly was effective when applied to props of great significance, such as a crown or a document, but when used in a play by Ibsen the result became distractingly like a game of dumb crambo, and far too much of the attention of the audience was spent in guessing what props were indicated by the various gestures of the actors.

Another principle of Terence Gray's productions was his determination that the actors should not be withdrawn from the audience behind a proscenium. The Festival's forestage and flights of steps made it possible for the actors to act almost among the audience itself. To emphasise the freedom of the actor to move out of the picture, exits and entrances were constantly made through the audience down to the aisles of the stalls. This was occasionally effective when the entrance was a very rapid one made by a crowd of actors, as for example when in *The Oresteia* the Chorus of Furies rushed through the audience, but it was never effective when the entrance was a slow one, particularly if the play happened to be a costume piece. It destroyed all sense of illusion to see a group of actors dressed as Egyptians, or Elizabethans, or Florentines slowly promenading past rows of flannel-trousered undergraduates. It was for this very reason that Gray had such an affection for bringing his actors through the auditorium and often playing whole scenes among the audience. It seemed to him the most effective way of forcibly reminding the audience that they were *not* in ancient Egypt, or Elizabethan England, or in seventeenth century Florence, but in a theatre. Why he was so anxious to destroy all illusion in the theatre I could never understand, except that it was an extreme symptom of his obsession against realism. "Here", he declared, "we forswear the old-fashioned attempt to create an Illusion of Reality. We often largely forswear the more modern attempt to substitute the creation of an Illusion of Atmosphere. The present-day audience must adjust its values. In a London theatre the audience creeps in, listens to a play, claps ritually, and creeps out. It has remained utterly apart. In Cambridge the theatre demands a different attitude from its audience. The stage is open and the actors are all over the place, and this fact alone makes some people positively shy and uncomfortable as though they had been caught looking on at other people's tragedies. The audience must realise that old game is no longer being played. It is no longer asked to imagine that it is spying on reality. It is no longer being asked to believe in an impossible pretence; it is no longer being fed with illusion, glamour and all the other varieties of spoof."

One of his most extreme productions, done in collaboration with Peter Godfrey, was *The Oil Islands*. By this time he was so determined to make it as difficult as possible for his audience to play the game of make-believe that he removed the wings from the stage so that throughout the performance the audience could see the actors waiting to make their entrances, the stagehands standing about, the prompter with the book in his lap, the electrician at his board, the props for the next scene standing in a corner. At every moment during the evening the audience was being forcibly reminded that they were in a theatre and were watching, not people on a mythical island, but members of a repertory company doing their work upon the Festival stage. That was in the later days of the Festival when Gray, exasperated by criticism, was angrily pushing his theories to the farthest possible limit.

Gray was at his best as a producer of Greek tragedy, in which his anti-realistic theories could be applied with complete justification. There is every reason for stylising Greek tragedy. Nothing could be more incongruous than to attempt to impose any form of realism on plays in which the characters were never intended to be ordinary everyday people who talked or acted like the audience who watched them. Greek tragedy is not a drama of conflict of character but a drama of the conflict of abstract forces. Most producers attempt to humanise the characters in these plays by adopting a method of acting which is an uneasy compromise between realism and stylisation. The inevitable result is that the plays are reduced in scale and become sentimental rather than tragic. Gray's productions were frankly modern in conception without any attempt at a pseudo-Greek effect. For instance, in his productions of Aeschylus the actors wore masks, but these masks did not merely reproduce the human face on a bolder scale as did the traditional masks of Greek tragedy; they were designed to intensify the dominant emotional characteristics of each part. It was Gray's contention that a highly stylised production of a Greek tragedy without masks was as incongruous as a naturalistic production with masks, although when he came to produce the more humanised plays of Euripides he abandoned masks except for the chorus. Yet although they were expressionistic in manner his productions of Aeschylus were genuinely archaic in mood. They were heroic, declamatory and ritualistic. The settings, although frankly unrealistic, had a stern and massive magnificence exactly right for the plays.

Ninette de Valois' handling of the choruses was criticised because of the harshness and angularity of much of the movement. Certainly they had little in common with the soft flowing movements and gestures of the sentimentalised chorus to which audiences were accustomed at that time. They had the beauty of strength and power, and although so uncompromisingly modernistic in manner they reproduced with perfect faithfulness the essential ritualistic quality of the Greek drama.

Next to the Greeks, it was Shakespeare who provided Gray with his most legitimate opportunities for the application of his theories. Shakespeare, like the Greeks, never intended his plays to be presented realistically. A common defence of modern realistic productions of Shakespeare is that if he had been able to use elaborate scenery he certainly would have done so. Possibly, but he would have written his plays in a different manner.

At the Festival, Gray had the great advantage of working in a theatre which was almost ideal for the performance of a Shakespearian play. "The withdrawal of the stage from the auditorium", he wrote in a programme note, "and its seclusion behind a proscenium, placing the audience in a different world from that in which the actors are living on the stage, was a bad blow for Shakespeare. Shakespeare's plays are essentially three-dimensional: the West End picture stage is essentially two-dimensional. Shakespeare's characters live and move among the audience, they speak to the spectators, who are often nearer to them than to the fellow actors with whom they are in converse, whereas the picture stage actor is a specimen on a slide observed through a microscope. From behind a proscenium an 'aside' is an amazing absurdity which no realistic and no expressionist technique of production can justify.

"Something remains to Shakespeare when he is produced behind a proscenium but it is little more than an echo. I myself would rather produce Shakespeare in a barn, a cellar, a church, a concert hall, a boxing ring, a public square, or any architectural structure than in a traditional theatre. I KNOW that Shakespeare cannot be compressed within the arbitrary limits of a proscenium stage without losing his three-dimensional character.

"The Festival stage is not perfect for Shakespeare, perhaps I should rather have said the Festival auditorium is not perfect for Shakespeare, but the theatre on the whole is, in my view, more suitable for Shakespeare than any other theatre in this country."

Nowadays we are comparatively used to the "fresh" production of Shakespeare through the work of Tyrone Guthrie, Komisarjevsky and Michel Saint Denis; but in the 1920's Shakespearian production was still on conventional lines. For instance, the lavish productions of *Henry VIII* and *Macbeth* at the Empire under Bronson Albery's management were in the elaborately realistic Tree tradition. Gray's treatment of Shakespeare was, in 1927, revolutionary. It caused so much violent criticism that his reply, as always, was to push his theories far further than he would have done had criticism been a little more sympathetic. By the time he reached his last Shakespearian production at the Festival he had abandoned any pretence of respecting Shakespeare's script. The play was *The Merchant of Venice*. It was a play that had been repeatedly asked for, as it was a favourite for examination purposes, but it bored Gray, and in his opinion would bore all the more intelligent members of his audience. This is a point of view which at least has some justification. If Gray had produced *The Merchant of Venice* attempting to conceal his boredom, the production would inevitably have been dull. His method of avoiding boredom was, paradoxical though it may sound, frankly to confess his boredom. For instance, when Portia embarked upon "The quality of mercy . . ." speech, the entire court relapsed into attitudes of abject boredom and the judge whiled away the time by playing with a yo-yo, a toy which happened to be in vogue at the moment. The speech itself was deliberately delivered in a listless tone of voice as if the actress was repeating it for the thousandth time. The setting for most of the play was the banks of a canal in Venice with houses built up on either side. The middle of the stage was the canal, on which the characters moved to and fro in miniature gondolas. One scene was played with Shylock sitting on his doorstep fishing. In the final scene Shylock entered playing a barrel organ, and the whole treatment of this character as an object of ridicule, dirty, smelly and greasy, was probably very much in the Elizabethan manner.

Whether or not the result was Shakespeare's *The Merchant of Venice* is not the point. It was what it intended to be—Terence Gray's version of *The Merchant of Venice* and it is arguable that Terence Gray's version was much more entertaining to modern audiences than Shakespeare's. The production was perfectly in accordance with his own theories which he repeated again and again in the pages of the Festival Review—that the producer's aim was "not to interpret any author's text but to create an independent work of theatre-art. The producer is an independent artist, using other artists and co-ordinating their arts into a whole which is the composite art-of-the-theatre. The author contributes a frame-work, ideas, dialogue, the designer contributes line and colour and architectural form, the actors contribute sound and movement by means of the human body in speech and action, and the whole is designed and built up by the producer into what should be a work of theatre-art".

Gray's Shakespearian settings, although at first sight violently modern, were actually much more truly Elizabethan than anything which had been seen on the English stage since Shakespeare's day apart from the Maddermarket's reproduction of an Elizabethan

[Bertram Park

LYRIC THEATRE, HAMMERSMITH: *The Way of the World* with Edith Evans and Robert Lorraine. Setting by Doris Zinkeisen.

LYRIC THEATRE, HAMMERSMITH: *La Vie Parisienne.*

[Bertram Park

[*Campbell Press Studios*

LYRIC THEATRE, HAMMERSMITH: *The Would-Be Gentleman.* Nigel Playfair and Florence McHugh.

LYRIC THEATRE, HAMMERSMITH: *When Crummles Played.* Hermione Baddeley and Richard Goolden.

[*Lenare*

[Pollard Crowther

THE GATE THEATRE: *The Eater of Dreams.*

THE GATE THEATRE: *Uncle Tom's Cabin.*

[Pollard Crowther

[Pollard Crowther

THE GATE THEATRE: *All God's Chillun.*

THE GATE THEATRE: *Peer Gynt.*

[Pollard Crowther

[Scott & Wilkinson

FESTIVAL THEATRE, CAMBRIDGE: *Alcestis.* Setting by Doria Paston.

FESTIVAL THEATRE, CAMBRIDGE: *Antigone.* Setting by Terence Gray.

[Scott & Wilkinson

[*Scott & Wilkinson*

FESTIVAL THEATRE, CAMBRIDGE: *The Eunuch.* Setting by Hedley Briggs.

FESTIVAL THEATRE, CAMBRIDGE: *Twelve Thousand.* Setting by Terence Gray and Doria Paston.

[*Scott & Wilkinson*

THE AMATEUR THEATRE: *God Bless the Guv'nor* at Unity Theatre.

THE AMATEUR THEATRE: *The Arbitration* at the Questor's Theatre, Ealing.
[*Middlesex County Times*

[Angus McBean

THE GATE THEATRE: Hermione Gingold in *The Gate Review.*

[Angus McBean

THE OLD VIC: *Hamlet* in modern dress. Setting by Roger Furse.

THE OLD VIC: *The Taming of the Shrew.* Setting by Roger Furse.

[Tunbridge-Sedgwick

[Debenham

THE OLD VIC: *The Country Wife.* Setting by Oliver Messell.

THE OLD VIC: Lawrence Olivier and Ralph Richardson in *Richard III.*

[John Vickers

stage. Briefly, his method was to build up a frankly unrealistic set on a turntable in the middle of the stage. This setting, sometimes unfortunately bearing a resemblance to a Mappin Terrace, was his favourite construction of steps, platforms and ramps which pretended to be nothing more than a platform designed for the actors. It made no more attempt to represent time or place than did the Elizabethan stage, but by means of constant and elaborate changes of lighting it did attempt to represent to some extent the changing moods of the play. One of the essentials of a Shakespearian production is continuity, and on this setting continuous action was easily achieved. As the closing lines of one scene were spoken the set revolved to show another aspect to the audience with the actors already in place ready to take up their cue immediately upon the concluding lines of the previous scene. In conjunction with this permanent setting built upon the turntable, he used the Festival forestage and steps to bring the actor out among the audience for the passages which Shakespeare intended to be delivered direct to the spectators.

Gray's whole theory of Shakespearian production is summed up in one of his articles in the Festival Review:

"Fundamentally Shakespeare's characters are always conscious of the audience, they never pretend to be anywhere but on a stage, they welcome and use, rather than seek to deny, the theatre which is their life. All this I have sought to restore. My actors do not pretend, are not attempting the impossible task, insulting to your intelligence, of persuading you that they are in Bayard's Castle, Pomfret or the Tower of London. They are, as they were in Shakespeare's day, frankly on, in or beside a structure which stands as symbol for Bayard's Castle, Pomfret or the Tower of London.

"In Shakespeare's day this structure was simpler, often a mere placard, whereas here the structure serves greater purposes in the play; it raises the actors to varying levels, thereby emphasising their relationships and intensifying the drama of the situation; by its form it symbolises the spirit of the place or of the emotion of the scene, or in some way helps to reveal subtleties in the action. On these structures the actors can move on all three planes, longitudinally, latitudinally, and vertically; they can affect the spectators' vision in every dimension, and by revolving the structure the action of persons who have left the main scene can be observed, without a pause, simultaneously or consecutively with progress in the normal action of the play. This is the 'fourth dimensional' aspect of this method. Not least important, an essential requisite of Shakespeare's technique can be restored to him, the scenes can change often and quickly, almost every scene having its individual and significant setting, an impossibility with any other method."

In his productions Gray succeeded in carrying out these theories with complete effectiveness. Unfortunately Shakespearian producers have failed to profit by his example or that of Nugent Monck, but still break the continuity from scene to scene, so that the play is not allowed to sweep forward uninterruptedly but is constantly being arrested, perhaps for only a few seconds at a time, but long enough to break the essential rhythm which could be so easily maintained in the Shakespearian playhouse.

Admittedly in Gray's productions there was much which was merely wilfully eccentric—Sir Toby Belch and Sir Andrew Aguecheek on roller skates, Rosalind dressed as a Boy Scout and Celia as a Girl Guide, a Spanish *Romeo and Juliet*, the wrestling match in *As You Like It* done in slow motion. On the other hand, the unorthodox features of his best productions, such as *Richard III* and *Henry VIII*, were based on sound reason and scholarship. *Henry VIII*, which was, I think, the most satisfactory of all his Shakespearian productions, was played on a set of great beauty and dignity consisting simply of a tremendous aluminium ramp rising steeply in a great curve until it vanished out of sight high above the stage. The actors, dressed in formalised costumes suggesting the court figures in a pack of cards, made their entrances from above, down this ramp. The constantly changing lighting, glowing on the aluminium, was of extraordinary beauty and effectiveness, heightening the different moods of the play like an accompaniment of incidental music. Until the end of the play Wolsey wore stilt-like *cothurnoi* beneath his robes which made him tower above the other characters. This effect of height and dominance was further emphasised by constantly placing him on slightly higher levels than the rest of the characters; but when his fall from power came, he no longer wore the *cothurnoi* and literally seemed to wither in stature, an effect once more emphasised by clever grouping, so that he became a beaten and cringing figure delivering the "Cromwell, I charge thee, fling away ambition" speech not in the sonorous tones usual to that speech, but as a whining attempt at self-justification. In this production, as in all the others, there was, of course, a scene to outrage the susceptibilities of the audience. This time it was the christening scene which ends the play, and here Gray had perfect justification for his handling of it. The scene is barefaced flattery of Queen Elizabeth. It has neither point nor interest to a modern audience and is in any case an extremely poor scene. Gray treated it frankly as an epilogue to the play and emphasised its ludicrous insincerity by using a baby which was a lifelike caricature of what Queen Elizabeth might have looked like at that age and by producing the scene somewhat as it might be done in a Crazy

Show at the Palladium, with the stage revolving madly, until finally with a shout the company tossed the baby into the audience. Whereupon, on the first night, the curtain fell to a pandemonium equally compounded of cries of rage and shouts of delight.

During the seven years of Terence Gray's directorship of the Festival there were two periods during which he handed the theatre over to other companies. The first time was when Anmer Hall brought a company to Cambridge for a year and a half. The other time was when I myself took a company to the Festival for a season.

Anmer Hall came when Terence Gray after working for three years at the Festival decided that he needed a pause to overhaul his ideas and evolve new ones. At first the change was by no means popular with the audience. After Terence Gray's stormy seasons, Anmer Hall's policy seemed tame and academic. But his company was a fine one, headed by Flora Robson and Robert Donat with Tyrone Guthrie as producer. Gradually Anmer Hall won the confidence of Cambridge, although up to the end of his time he appealed more to the dons and the residents than to the undergraduates. A specimen season's programme at once makes clear the difference between Anmer Hall's policy and Terence Gray's.

Six Characters in Search of an Author	Pirandello
Woman's Honour	Susan Glaspell
Marriage	Gogol
The Mask and the Face	C. B. Fernald
All For Love	John Dryden
Iphigenia in Tauris	Euripides
Rosalind	Barrie
The Dover Road	A. A. Milne
Deirdre of the Sorrows	J. M. Synge
Dandy Dick	Pinero
The Rivals	Sheridan

What the audience were given was a reasonably varied programme with something to appeal to every taste, acted by a company far above the normal repertory standard and produced with distinction. Terence Gray summed all this up in an article written on his return to the Festival in which he said: "For three years the Festival Theatre worked experimentally, calling down approbation, execration, praise, pleasure and wrath. Then Mr. Anmer Hall came and with well deserved popularity kept alive our tradition, and gave Cambridge what a large part of Cambridge wanted. Now we return. I cannot give Cambridge what Mr. Anmer Hall gave it. It is not for me to fulfil academic expectations and maintain standards of tradition. I seek the unexpected reaction, the unanticipated pleasure, the irresponsible wrath, the readjustment of values."

In 1932 Gray again left the Festival for a season, during which I took over the theatre with a company of my own, presenting the following programme:

This World of Ours	Revue
Love for Love	Congreve
Bastos the Bold	Regis and De Veynes
Marco Millions . . .	Eugene O'Neill
Will You Play With Me? . .	Marcel Achard
Alison's House . . .	Susan Glaspell
In a Glass Darkly . . .	Hugh Ross Williamson
The Knight of the Burning Pestle	Beaumont and Fletcher

At first sight this is a programme strictly in accordance with the Festival tradition, as it was intended to be, but in one important respect it was very different from any of Terence Gray's programmes in that six of the eight plays were being given their first performance in England. It was a weakness of Terence Gray's policy that he very seldom gave a first performance of a play. More important to him than the play was the manner in which it would be presented, so his energies were devoted less to finding new plays than to finding new methods of presenting old ones. Ironically enough, it was the difficulty of finding plays which finally forced him to abandon the Festival. After seven years he had produced all the Greek and Shakespearian plays which interested him, and such other classics as seemed to him to provide opportunities for experiments in production. These production experiments had been so many and so varied and had been pushed to such extremes that there were no further variations to be made upon his theories. As a producer his work was degenerating into mere freakishness and eccentricity. Had he been more interested in plays for their own sake he would have had no reason for growing weary of the Festival.

The greatest condemnation of his whole policy is that having built a theatre on entirely new lines and made every possible experiment in production, he failed to encourage a single author to write a play for production according to the methods practised at the Festival. Had he from the beginning been more ready to encourage authors and to collaborate with them, a whole new school of playwrights might have grown up around the Festival.

So the Festival virtually came to an end in June, 1933, with a production of Edmund Rostand's *Chantecler*.

Terence Gray made his farewell to his audience in the following letter printed in the Festival Review:

"On 17th June, the theatre will have completed seven years' work and will cease to exist as the Festival.

"Founded by Harold Ridge and myself in 1926, contrary to the prophecy of all the theatrical people consulted, the theatre prospered from the first. Cambridge has supported our work magnificently, for we have compromised with none and pandered to nobody's prejudices. Whatever we believed to contain truth and to be worth saying or doing we have said or done without hesitation; for a theatre that considers everybody's feelings, seeks to please all and offend none, will get nowhere for it can have no policy.

"What will become of the theatre I cannot say. It belongs to a company composed of disinterested persons for whom I managed it. I have told that company that I have done all the work I wish to do, have devoted to the Festival theatre as much of my life as I intend to devote, and that on 17th June I withdraw.

"Perhaps the Festival will become what is termed a provincial repertory theatre, perhaps some enterprising person will use it for establishing high-class films as I have used it for drama of a similar kind, perhaps it will become just an ordinary cinema, a non-stop variety house, a cabaret hall, a skating rink. Its future lies open for any man of enterprise, and it should prosper—for it has tradition and it is a good place.

"TERENCE GRAY."

Afterwards the theatre carried on for a while under Joseph Gordon Macleod, who had been Gray's stage manager, but he had little success. The Festival then became what is termed "a provincial repertory theatre" with a programme even more ordinary than that of most repertories. To-day it is closed and derelict, infested by rats and falling into ruin and decay.

Reluctantly it has to be recorded that these seven years of ceaseless experiment had in the end practically no effect upon the English theatre. It is fascinating to speculate what might have happened had Terence Gray's most cherished scheme been realised. This was to go into partnership with J. B. Fagan, build a new theatre on the lines of the Festival to replace the Oxford Playhouse, and run the two theatres together in conjunction with a third theatre in London. For this purpose the National Sporting Club in Covent Garden was acquired. Eventually the whole scheme had to be abandoned owing to the opposition of the London County Council, whose requirements as to the building of theatres simply did not cover a theatre of so unusual a design as that proposed for the National Sporting Club site. Had the London County Council been willing to collaborate there is not the slightest doubt that a theatre could have been built which would have been as safe as any other theatre. Similar opposition was met with at Oxford, where the local council, openly unsympathetic, raised every possible objection to the proposed theatre.

Although Terence Gray's experiments had in the end so little result on the English theatre, there is much which we owe indirectly to the Festival. There is the Westminster Theatre, for example, which was built as a result of Anmer Hall's four seasons at Cambridge. The Vic-Wells Ballet too owes much to the Festival, which gave Ninette de Valois her early experience as choreographer and employed the small troups of dancers who afterwards became the nucleus of the Vic-Wells Ballet. Some of the actors and actresses who gained their experience at the Festival have already been mentioned. If the Festival had never existed they would presumably have developed their abilities in other repertory theatres, but no other repertory theatre could have offered them such a variety of great parts. It is doubtful if at least two of them—Flora Robson and Maurice Evans—would have had any career at all if it had not been for the existence of the theatre, as Flora Robson had left the stage in despair when Anmer Hall persuaded her to return as his leading lady at the Festival, and it is improbable that any other theatre would have been so crazy as to engage as its leading man the obscure amateur which Maurice Evans was at that time. Nor would any other theatre have appointed as one of its producers an untried young man in his early twenties. I owe an immense debt of gratitude to Gray. After trying me out on a couple of one-act plays, he gave me C. K. Munro's *The Rumour* as my first full-length production. In the seasons that followed, directing plays such as *Emperor Jones*, *The Insect Play*, *Beggar on Horseback*, *Dr. Knock*, and *The Shoemakers' Holiday*, I had opportunity for experience and experiment such as few young producers can ever have been lucky enough to enjoy. But the effect on me as a producer was not, I am afraid, quite what Gray intended. Working in a theatre where the producer was billed larger than anyone else and encouraged to consider himself the star of the show, I found how easy—and how dangerous—it is for a producer to call attention to his own cleverness. I soon grew bored with my exhibitionist tricks and stunts and capers. They were too easy. Ever since then I have had an almost morbid dislike of doing anything which might remind the audience of the existence of a producer.

What Cambridge itself owed to the Festival is best summed up in an open letter addressed to Terence Gray by one of the undergraduate papers:

"You have provided the undergraduate with a haven of refreshment from the banalities of the conventional stage, you have supplied the thinking man with endless food for thought, the critic with endless material for criticism and the disputant with much weighty matter for discussion. The artist, you have supplied with inspiration;

the journalist with copy; to the babbler you have given subject for decent conversation and to the philistine a target at which to scoff."

When Terence Gray abandoned the Festival he turned to his other love and became a wine-grower in France. At Tain l'Hermitage in the province of Drome he grew his own vines and produced a noble wine the like of which, according to connoisseurs, had not been known since the great days when Hermitage was a royal drink. When the Germans invaded France he escaped to his native Ireland, where now he breeds race horses with the same enthusiasm and efficiency that he devoted in turn to archeological expeditions in Egypt, running a theatre and cultivating the vine.

CHAPTER VI

THE SUNDAY THEATRE

MY FIRST production in London was for the Stage Society at the Prince of Wales, in those days a friendly sized theatre for straight plays. I was a young and almost unknown producer, so I was immensely flattered to be asked to produce for the Stage Society, especially as the play, Franz Werfel's *Paul Among the Jews*, was a big production with over forty speaking parts, a crowd, and many changes of scene. It was only after I had started rehearsing that I began to suspect the reason I had been offered the play was because it had been turned down by all the experienced producers as too elaborate a production for a Sunday night performance. I was never able to get the whole cast together at rehearsal, not even at the dress rehearsal. Every time I rehearsed a scene with more than three or four characters in it, someone was bound to be away broadcasting, or filming, or playing a matinee, or seeing a management about his next engagement. The only time the dress rehearsal could be held was on Saturday morning, and all through the last act the company grew smaller and smaller as actors had to hurry away to be in time for their matinees. The actual performance went off without mishap, but as a production it did not make much impression on any of the critics except St. John Ervine, who in *The Observer* advised me to abandon forthwith all hopes I might have of ever becoming a producer. He helpfully suggested the profession of a nonconformist minister as more suitable.

In spite of the difficulties and hazards of a Sunday night production, in the 'twenties the numerous societies never seemed to have much difficulty in getting together a cast. Many actors already playing in West End runs spent most of their spare time from October to May rehearsing for one Sunday night production after another. Perhaps there was more enthusiasm for experiment, more eagerness for variety of experience in those days. But there are other reasons why Sunday night adventuring nowadays makes less appeal to the theatrical profession. One is that the average period of rehearsal for a West End production has increased by at least a week in recent years, and the play almost invariably has a preliminary tour, so an actor is rarely asked to "open cold" in

London. In the 'twenties a single dress rehearsal was considered sufficient for any ordinary production; now it is usual to hold three or four. In spite of all this increasingly elaborate preparation, or perhaps because of it, actors seem more apprehensive than ever of facing a first-night audience in London. Consequently many of them are appalled at the idea of rehearsing a show for only two or three weeks and then playing it after the single rushed dress rehearsal which is all that a Sunday society can manage.

Yet the need for the Sunday societies is greater than it has ever been now that abnormally long runs and the shortage of theatres have reduced the number of new productions in London during the course of a year to so meagre a figure. Sunday societies are equally necessary to new playwrights who would otherwise have little hope of production in London, to actors growing stale in long runs, as well as to those out of an engagement and in need of a shop-window, to young producers in search of a chance to prove themselves, to managements incapable of judging the merits of a play in manuscript, and to playgoers looking for something to supplement the sparseness and monotony of the ordinary theatrical diet.

The Sunday societies to which I, as a playgoer, have been most grateful were not those which produced plays likely to be sold to the commercial theatre but those founded in a spirit of rebellion against the conservatism of London managers and audiences, and as a protest against the suffocating effects of the censorship. The oldest and most famous of this type of Sunday society was the Stage Society, founded in 1900. Had it expired on the outbreak of war in 1914 it would still be famous for its productions of the early works of Shaw, Granville Barker and Somerset Maugham, and for its persistence in producing Ibsen and Chekov in spite of every discouragement from most of the critics and many of its own members.

The Society managed to keep alive throughout the war of 1914–18 by doing an occasional production, and as soon as the war ended it returned to its usual custom of giving four productions each season. The first post-war programme consisted of Vanbrugh's *The Provok'd Wife*, H. F. Rubinstein's *The Spirit of Parsifal Robinson*, Masefield's *The Faithful* and Swinburne's *The Duke of Gandia* with Yeats' *The Player Queen* as a curtain raiser. This was hardly a typical Stage Society programme. In normal times revivals were not a part of the Society's policy, but immediately after the end of the war new plays were hard to find, especially plays of the type which appealed to the pioneering spirit of the Stage Society. By next season it was back in its stride with a production of Kaiser's *From Morn to Midnight*, the first example of the new expressionist drama, and the first German play to be produced in England since 1914. Later, in 1924, when expressionism had spread from Germany to America, the Stage Society gave Elmer Rice's *The Adding Machine* and in 1927 Eugene O'Neill's *The Great God Brown*. Less extreme examples of expressionist drama were the early plays of Ernst Toller. The Stage Society presented his *Machine Wreckers* in 1923 and his *Masses and Man* the following year. Other notable post-war German plays presented by the Society were *The Race with the Shadow* by Wilhelm von Scholz, Karl Schonherr's *The Children's Tragedy*, and Wolfgang Moeller's *Douaumont*: or *The Return of the Soldier Ulysses*.

Among the French plays given their first performance in England by the Stage Society between the two wars were Vildrac's *S.S. Tenacité*, Georges Duhamel's *The Mental Athletes*, Jean-Jacques Bernard's *The Unquiet Spirit*, Jules Romains' *The Dictator*, Giraudoux' *Intermezzo*, Cocteau's *Infernal Machine*, and an adaptation of Colette's novel *Cherie*.

From Italy the Stage Society brought to England Pirandello's *Six Characters in Search of an Author*, which for several years afterwards was refused performance on the public stage by the Lord Chamberlain unless it was played in Italian. The old Russian theatre was represented by productions of *Uncle Vanya* and *Ivanoff*, the new by Afinogenov's *Fear*, produced in 1932, the first Soviet play to be seen in this country.

Although importations of foreign plays were an important part of the Stage Society's policy, it by no means neglected English authors. The most famous, though not the best, English plays the Society produced were *Journey's End*, and *Young Woodley*, a play far below the Stage Society's normal standards, produced as a protest against its being banned by the Censor. It is hard to believe now that the Lord Chamberlain considered this sentimental little play about calf-love too shocking to be seen by the general public. Other Stage Society productions which afterwards had long runs in the West End were Ashley Dukes' *The Man with a Load of Mischief*, C. K. Munro's *At Mrs. Beam's* and John Van Druten's *After All*. But the success of the Stage Society must not be judged by the number of its productions afterwards seen in the ordinary theatre. Its policy was to produce plays of distinction which seemed otherwise never likely to be seen in England, either because they were banned by the Censor or because they had been refused production by all the ordinary managements. It may seem surprising that *Journey's End* was refused by every management in London before the Stage Society presented it, but in 1928 it was believed that the public still would not accept a war play. Even after it had opened for a run at the Prince of Wales Theatre, and the critics had praised it enthusiastically a second time, the libraries refused to do a deal. They were convinced that the public would not go to a play which, besides being about the war, had no women in the cast. Among the other English plays produced by the Stage Society were D. H. Lawrence's *David*, Beatrice Mayor's *The Pleasure Garden*, Herbert Trench's *Napoleon*, James Joyce's *The Exiles*, Eric Linklater's *The Devil's in the News*, Henry James' *The Reprobate*, and three more plays by C. K. Munro, *The Rumour*, *Progress* and *Bluestone Quarry*.

By the 'thirties the Stage Society had begun to lose strength. To a large extent the Gate was taking its place. It had the advantage over the Stage Society of being able to run a play for several weeks instead of only for two performances. The continental dramatists who had previously depended on the Stage Society for production in England now preferred to have their plays put on at the Gate for a run. The Stage Society found itself limited to plays which the Gate had to reject because the casts were too large for so small a theatre. This so restricted the Stage Society in its choice of plays that the annual programme had to be reduced from four productions to three and the Monday afternoon performances were abandoned. Unable to compete with the Gate for the latest continental plays, the Stage Society went back to the nineteenth century and in 1937 produced Strindberg's *The Road to Damascus* and *Queen Christina*. The Society's last season, 1938–39, included Lorca's *The Marriage of Blood* and Clifford Odets' *Paradise Lost*. The final production, in 1940, was Strindberg's *Easter*.

Those who remember the Stage Society in its decline, when it was giving its performances in small theatres which were often half empty, may have difficulty in realising the position it held for over thirty years. During the period between the two wars it brought to England the work of twenty-eight foreign dramatists of the first rank, many of whose plays were refused public performance in England by the Censor; it launched Van Druten, Sherriff, Ashley Dukes, and C. K. Munro into the commercial theatre; it introduced English playgoers to constructivism, expressionism and the Soviet drama; and it gave opportunities to actors and producers such as they would rarely have found among the stereotyped plays of the West End theatre. Many producers did their best work for the Stage Society. I remember vividly a series of brilliant productions by Komisarjevsky, which included *Uncle Vanya*, *Six Characters in Search of an Author*, Knut Hamsun's *At the Gates of the Kingdom*, *Ivanoff*, Arnold Bennett's *The Bright Island* and his constructivist production of Fernand Crommelynck's *Le Cocu Magnifique*. Other fine productions were Lewis Casson's production of *Masses and Man*, Nugent Monck's *The Machine Wreckers*, A. E. Filmer's *The Adding Machine*, Irene Hentschel's *The Unquiet Spirit*, Stephen Thomas's *The Children's Tragedy*, and Peter Godfrey's production of *Toussaint L'Ouverture*, C. L. R. James' play about the negro who made himself king of San Domingo.

An offshoot of the Stage Society was the Phoenix. When during the war the Stage Society was finding it difficult to get suitable plays for production, it revived Farquhar's *The Recruiting Officer*, as recruiting was a topical subject in 1915. Its success led to further productions of Restoration plays including *The Double Dealer*, *Love for Love* and *The Provok'd Wife*. While many of the Stage Society's subscribers enjoyed these plays, it was felt that the Society ought to devote its energies and its revenue to new and "advanced" work. So the Phoenix came into being "under the auspices" of the Stage Society, which advanced the initial capital and shared its offices and secretary. At first the Phoenix had very little success, but suddenly it found itself fashionable, perhaps because Lady Cunard became one of its most enthusiastic supporters. For three years the Phoenix enjoyed a period of prosperity when its performances drew a more distinguished audience than any ordinary first night. Then the fashionable contingent (what Desmond MacCarthy called the "snob rush") found a new hobby in the Film Society and there was an immediate decline in the membership. The genuine enthusiasts were not sufficiently numerous to keep the Society going. In 1926 it was wound up.

Its first production, in 1919, was *The Duchess of Malfi*. The remainder of the programme for the first season consisted of *Marriage à la Mode*, *The Fair Maid of the West*, and *Venice Preserv'd*. The list of its subsequent productions includes nearly every play by the Elizabethan and Restoration dramatists which is still stageworthy. Apart from the well known classics of the two periods, the most interesting productions were Dryden's *Amphitryon*, Ben Jonson's *Bartholomew Fair*, Wycherley's *The Gentleman Dancing Master*, Marlowe's *Edward II*, and Fletcher's masque *The Faithful Shepherdess* with music arranged and conducted by Sir Thomas Beecham.

The Phoenix did immensely valuable work in restoring to the stage the plays of a number of half-forgotten dramatists. They had been rediscovered in turn by Lamb and Swinburne, who, in the excitement of their discovery, had fantastically overpraised them. Then came the inevitable reaction. By the 'twenties most of the literary and dramatic critics had relegated the plays of the

Elizabethans and Restorationists to the library shelves. They were considered dull, unstageworthy and, by some of the critics, obscene. Typical of this opinion was William Archer's *The Old Drama and the New*, an attack on "the stifling malodorousness of the Elizabethan drama" and "that fetid fairyland, that insanitary Alsatia" which was his description of the Restoration theatre. He declared that the Elizabethan theatre was "the product of an age that was but semi-civilised", that its plays were "brutal, shambling and maladroit". One of his many complaints against the Elizabethan dramatists was that they expressed themselves "not in sober prose but in the incomparably easier medium of blank verse, substituting rhetoric for human speech". Max Beerbohm had also been attacking the Elizabethan and Restoration playwrights from a different angle. His complaint against them was simply that they were deadly dull. "Who, really and truly, in his heart of hearts, wants to see a performance of a play by Ben Jonson or any other Elizabethan or Jacobean, or by Congreve or any other Restorationist? These plays are interesting curiosities, and many of them may be read with enjoyment. But, as plays, they are dead utterly; and a theatrical production of any of them is a mere rattling of dry bones". The answer to Max Beerbohm's question is provided by the fact that of the twenty-five plays produced by the Phoenix (apart from its solitary Shakespearian production) eleven have since been played successfully in the ordinary theatre, and two of those "curiosities" by Congreve have each run for over a year.

The Phoenix productions had a continuity of style unusual in the work of Sunday societies. This was mainly due to the fact that nearly all the plays were produced by Allan Wade in a setting by Norman Wilkinson which ingeniously combined the balcony and inner stage of the Elizabethan theatre with the forestage, proscenium doors and boxes of the Restoration theatre. Although this set was devised to do duty for both Elizabethan and Restoration plays, when the Phoenix had more money to spend Wilkinson designed a set specially for the Restoration plays, magnificently spacious and dignified.

The chief feature of Wade's productions was their simplicity. Nothing was allowed to interfere with continuity of action and swiftness of speech. He reduced furniture and props to a minimum. He seemed at his happiest as a producer with a bare stage which gave him complete freedom to design bold movement and strikingly pictorial groupings. He never attempted to stunt or fantasticate the plays. He believed in allowing them to stand or fall on their own merits. In one of his letters he refers to the importance of the producer "sternly resisting all efforts to astonish, to scribble, as it were, his own name across the author's page". In the same letter he refers to "my long-held belief that what the good dramatist gives and what the intelligent public most eagerly acclaims in the theatre is, above all and before all, opportunity for acting". As he had a gift for casting and the ability to teach actors how to speak both verse and prose with rhythm and balance without subduing their performances to a recitation, the result was generally very satisfying.

Towards the end of its life the Phoenix had a rival in the Renaissance Society which only survived it for a short while. Among its productions were *Rule a Wife and Have a Wife*, *The Wild Goose Chase*, and *The Maid's Tragedy*, all by Beaumont and Fletcher, Wycherley's *The Plain Dealer*, and Webster's *The White Devil.*

With one exception the many Sunday societies which started during the 'twenties were founded by groups and directed by committees. The solitary exception was The Three Hundred Club, founded, financed and directed by Mrs. Geoffrey Whitworth. Lennox Robinson described the founding of the Club in an article in *The Observer:* " . . . Where two or three are gathered together—or not even two or three. One, if that one be a woman, seems to be enough. Here is Mrs. Geoffrey Whitworth, who has gathered herself together, multiplied herself by three hundred, christened herself the Three Hundred Club, elected herself President and Secretary and Reading Committee, and proceeded calmly to arrange for the production of the plays she wished to see performed. Being neither mad nor a King of Bavaria, she unselfishly allows the public to share her enjoyment, and you can become a three-hundredth part of her for the sum of two guineas."

When Mrs. Whitworth founded the Three Hundred Club in 1923 the Stage Society was devoting two-thirds of its programme to foreign plays, and the rest of the Sunday societies were busy either reviving the classics or trying out plays for the commercial theatre. Mrs. Whitworth saw there was need for a society which would produce the work of young English authors who were writing interesting plays of a sort which had little chance of production in the commercial theatre.

The foundation of the Three Hundred Club was given a very mixed press. Many of the theatrical journalists dragged out the old argument that the theatre is a popular art and that it is waste of time to found a society to produce plays which have been deliberately chosen because they are never likely to be commercial successes. According to this theory the only good plays are those which appeal to the taste of hundreds of thousands of playgoers. No literary critic would dream of suggesting that it is silly of a publisher to bring out a fine book knowing that it is likely to appeal only to a small section of the reading public, but in the 'twenties most of the lesser dramatic critics and theatrical journalists were openly hostile to any attempt to cater for the minority playgoer. This was a period when a large section of the press was fawningly sycophantic towards "the plain man". He was eulogised for his sound common sense. His opinions were always right, especially in matters of art. He knew what he liked and he was assured that his taste was far better than that of the highbrows, the minority, the "long-haired intellectuals" as they used to be called, who, according to popular belief, invariably lived in either Chelsea or Bloomsbury, had unwholesome ideas and probably practised what in those days was known as "free love". In the theatre any attempt by this minority to cater for their own tastes by means of theatre clubs and Sunday societies was apt to be resented by the popular press as an insolent declaration of superiority.

The first production of the Three Hundred Club was *The Discovery* by Frances Sheridan, adapted by Aldous Huxley. The productions which followed were *A Comedy of Good and Evil* by Richard Hughes, *Guilty Souls* by Robert Nichols, *Smaragda's Lover* by W. J. Turner, *The Prisoners of War* by J. R. Ackerley, *Mr. Godley Beside Himself* by Gerald Bullett, Flecker's *Don Juan*, *Confession* by W. F. Casey, *The Widowing of Mrs. Holroyd* by D. H. Lawrence and *Socrates* by Clifford Bax. Two of these plays, *A Comedy of Good and Evil* and *The Prisoners of War*, were afterwards put on for runs at West End theatres. Both failed, proving Mrs. Whitworth to have been right in believing that the plays she chose to put on had no commercial future. The ordinary playgoer was completely baffled by *A Comedy of Good and Evil*, a very un-English mixture of satire, mysticism, humour and fantasy. *The Prisoners of War*, one of the very few good tragedies written in England during the present century, was rejected by the public as "morbid".

By 1926 Mrs. Whitworth was finding it difficult to discover enough worth-while plays of the sort that came within the scope of her deliberately limited policy. Unwilling to eke out her programme with plays which seemed to her inferior to the standard she had so far maintained, she amalgamated the Three Hundred Club with the Stage Society.

The Stage Society, the Phoenix, the Renaissance Society and the Three Hundred Club were all founded by playgoers. There was another type of Sunday society which was founded by actors. The actors were much less adventurous than the playgoers in their choice of play. These actors' societies were not in revolt against the standards of the West End theatre; their main object was to sell a play, complete with most of the cast, to a commercial management, and as they sought to "give the managements what they want", they naturally chose plays cut to fashionable West End patterns. They could seldom get the rights of a play until it had been rejected by all the West End managers, so they were rather like someone who picks something useful out of a wastepaper basket and says: "Do you *really* want to throw this away?" It is difficult to believe in the commercial acumen of so-called commercial managements which rejected plays such as *George and Margaret*, *Rope*, *A Murder Has Been Arranged*, *If Four Walls Told*, *Many Waters*, *Petticoat Influence* and *Eight Bells*, all "discovered" for the managers by the Repertory Players.

The Repertory Players were founded in 1921 "to afford those connected with the Theatre an opportunity for furthering themselves in their profession". It was an odd name to choose for a society which never performs a play more than once and gets together a different cast for each play. To-day the Repertory Players are the only survivors of all the numerous Sunday societies which were busy between the two wars. The fact that most of these societies had short lives does not necessarily mean they were failures. Many of them packed up simply because they had finished their job. They had got a hearing for the particular dramatic cause that they championed. They had fulfilled the purpose for which they had been founded, and if they were wise they closed down. The Repertory Players have outlived all their contemporaries because they have based their policy on what changes least of all in the English theatre—the taste of the London theatre managers. During the nineteen years of their existence before the war they sold thirty-four of their productions to London managements, and seven more were sold for production in the provinces or in America. Actors are supposed to be poor judges of a play. This may be true of an actor picking a play for himself. If he sees a part that will give fine opportunities for his own particular talents he is apt to indulge in a good deal of wishful thinking about the merits of the rest of the play. But the success of the Repertory Players has proved that a small committee of actors not primarily looking for parts for themselves can pick plays far more shrewdly than most theatrical managers.

Not all the actors' societies were founded merely to provide shop windows. The Fellowship of Players, for instance, was founded to give opportunities for playing in Shakespeare to actors who during the week were appearing in plays which gave them little chance for real acting. So far as possible preference was given to actors who had never before been in a Shakespearian production. Often the casts were a rather odd mixture of rising young Shakespearian actors and raw recruits to Shakespeare from the musical comedies and farces. With rare exceptions, those without previous experience of speaking verse were at an obvious disadvantage compared with the others in the cast. Gradually casting became almost entirely limited to actors experienced in Shakespeare. The experiment had failed. There was no longer any reason for the existence of the Society, so it closed down. Whatever the faults of the performances, they were always lively and interesting, and the plays were mostly those one rarely has a chance of seeing.

The Pioneers were another Sunday society founded within the profession which aimed at being more than just a shop window. It was started in 1911 by the actress-producer Edith Craig, with her mother, Ellen Terry, as chairman. The Pioneers did valuable work in introducing Claudel to English audiences. Resuming their work in 1919 they only survived for a couple of years during which their most notable productions were Claudel's *L'Otage*, Duhamel's *The Children's Carnival* and Heijerman's *The Rising Sun*, a sombre, tragic play in which an unknown young actress, Meggie Albanesi, made her first success. All the plays put on by the Pioneers were directed by Edith Craig, a producer to whom the theatre never gave the opportunities she deserved, perhaps because in those days, when women producers were even rarer than they are now, there were too many prejudices to be overcome. Even to-day Irene Hentschel is the solitary woman among the established producers of straight plays in the London theatre.

An actors' society of a rather different type was the Play Actors'. The plays they chose to display to the managers in their shop window were more unusual than the "popular lines" which the Repertory Players put in their window, but they avoided the plainly uncommercial plays produced by the Stage Society and the Pioneers. Founded in 1907, the society continued after the war until 1926. The most memorable of its post-war productions were Monkhouse's *The Conquering Hero*, Benn Levy's *This Woman Business*, Chesterton's *The Napoleon of Notting Hill*, and *Ecole de Cocottes* by Paul Armont and Marcel Gerbidon in an English version by H. M. Harwood. Under the title of *Excelsior* it was afterwards put on at the Playhouse with Gladys Cooper in the lead.

The Ventures, which began in 1926, was a society founded neither by actors nor playgoers but by an author, primarily for the production of his own plays. The author-founder was Lord Lathom, whose play *Wet Paint* had been refused public performance by the Censor. It was not the sort of play to appeal to the Stage Society, and shop window societies were uninterested because the Censor's ban denied the play any commercial future. So Lord Lathom founded his own society and opened his first season with *Wet Paint.* It was an excellent play of its kind, considered by some of the critics to be better than *The Vortex* to which it bore a family resemblance. Two more of Lathom's plays, *Tuppence Coloured* and *Twenty Houses in a Row,* were produced by the Venturers, which during the five years of its existence put on a number of distinguished plays including Leonhard Frank's *Karl and Anna,* James Laver's adaptation of Sternheim's *La Marquise d'Arcis* and Lenormand's *Les Ratés*—all of them banned by the Censor.

There is no need to catalogue all the many Sunday societies founded during the 'twenties and the 'thirties. Some were merely commercial rackets, putting on plays which were financed either by the author or by some actress with more money than talent who was willing to pay heavily for a chance to display her imaginery gifts in a leading part. The promotors of these societies charged high management fees and stipulated that they should also get a rake-off in the unlikely event of any of the plays being sold for production in the ordinary theatre. But most of the societies, apart from those already dealt with, were founded by woolly-minded idealists who soon discovered that good plays are far more difficult to find than they had imagined, and that running a Sunday society needs experienced business management as well as ideals and enthusiasm. Herbert Farjeon voiced what must have been the feelings of most of the dramatic critics when in the late 'thirties he wearily protested that "play producing societies formed to present better plays in better ways are such an old story now that the advent of a new one hardly makes professional critics feel like jumping over five-barred gates for joy. These better plays, these better ways, rarely get beyond the statement of aims which say the same things with devious deediness".

There was one Sunday society founded during the 'thirties which varied the monotonous series of manifestos about "better plays in better ways" by announcing that its aim was "to develop and encourage available talent for ballet". This was the Camargo Society, founded by J. M. Keynes, Constant Lambert, Edwin Evans and Lydia Lopokova in 1930. At that time there was no such thing as "English ballet", and little future for any English dancer and choreographer unless he joined a foreign company. The Camargo's opening programme included the first performance of Frederick Ashton's *Pomona.* Other ballets produced by Ashton for the Camargo were *Facade, Lord of Burleigh* and *A Day in a Southern Port,* afterwards included in the Sadler's Wells repertoire under the title of *Rio Grande*. It was for the Camargo Society that Ninette de Valois produced her first important ballet, *Job*. Two years after its foundation the Camargo disbanded itself, not because it had been a failure but because it had succeeded in what it set out to do. It had called attention to the wealth of talent among English dancers, it had given Ashton and de Valois the opportunities to prove themselves as choreographers, it had persuaded English composers and painters to take a serious interest in the ballet, and by accustoming the critics and some of the ballet public to the idea of ballets performed almost entirely by English dancers it prepared the way for the foundation of the Vic-Wells Ballet and the Rambert Company. When these two companies were founded the Carmargo Society decided that its work was done, and that it could best serve the cause of English ballet by handing over its funds and its productions to the Sadler's Wells Company.

The only other Sunday society of any importance founded during the 'thirties was the London International Theatre, directed by Lady Playfair, Mary Hinton and Roma June. It was started in 1937 with the frank intention of replacing the Stage Society, which by that time had grown enfeebled and aimless. Instead of giving only a single performance of each production, the London International Theatre put on each of its plays for three consecutive Sundays. The opening production was *Susannah and the Elders*, one of Bridie's best plays which for some unexplained reason has never been produced commercially in London. The rest of the first season's programme consisted of Jean Anouilh's *Identity Unknown* which had been produced in Paris by the Pitoeffs, *Gentleman's Agreement* by the Hungarian author Eugen Haltai, Rosamond Lehmann's *No more Music* and Peter Blackmore's *Lot's Wife*. The second season opened with Rodney Ackland's *Remembrance of Things Past*, produced five years afterwards at the Whitehall in a revised version under the title of *The Dark River*. This was followed by Hans Rothe's *Night Arrival*, *Adults Only* by Reginald Beckwith and Andrew Cruickshank, *The Courageous Sex* by Mary Sheridan and *Scandal in Assyria* by Axel Kjellstrom. Then the outbreak of war put an end to the existence of a society which had proved that there were still plenty of original, intelligent and entertaining plays which were nevertheless not of a sort likely to appeal to a large public.

A brief account of the Sunday societies such as this has been must inevitably consist mainly of lists of plays. The names of these plays give some idea of the work of the societies, but it is difficult in a chapter of this sort to give any impression of the vitality of the acting. The productions may often have been patchy and uneven owing to insufficient rehearsal but the acting had a quality of excitement all too rare in the theatre nowadays. The fact that the play was usually being put on for a single performance gave a now-or-never spirit to the acting. The leading parts were seldom played by stars; they were played by up-and-coming actors, whose work was not yet inged by that anxiety, even timidity, which dulls the performances of many established stars, terrified lest they may do something to endanger their position at the top of the ladder and cause them to slip down a rung or two. Like Pinero's Duchess in *The Gay Lord Quex*, their constant thought seems to be "My reputation, Oh my reputation". Whatever the faults of these Sunday night performances, over-cautiousness was not among them. The actors were not bothered during the performance by anxious speculations as to the future of the play, whether they were "in for a long run" or whether in a few days they would be looking for a job again. Under-rehearsed though the performances often may have been, they had the kind of teamwork that comes from singleness of purpose. Everybody in a Sunday night show was there simply because they *wanted* to act, because even if they were already acting on the other six nights of the week, they preferred to spend the seventh in the theatre as well. I remember Sunday night shows seen years ago far more vividly than many famous West End productions because of the relish and the gusto and the adventurousness of the acting on these Sunday evenings, qualities which one can rarely detect beneath the gloss of the carefully polished, well-oiled productions that purr their way so smoothly through their London first night after having been running for months in the provinces.

CHAPTER VII

THE AMATEUR THEATRE

IN THE 'twenties I used to spend a good deal of time each winter acting as one of the adjudicators in the British Drama League Festival of Community Drama. Sometimes I toured for weeks on end adjudicating preliminary rounds, watching performances night after night all over the country in small towns and villages. Other times I adjudicated full-dress finals in the big cities. Each summer I used to spend a week or two lecturing and rehearsing at one of the Drama League's summer schools for amateur actors and producers. In those days I really did believe that "the future of the drama is in the hands of the amateur"—a phrase I used to hear with nightly regularity from the local dignitaries introducing the adjudicator to his audience. I believed that the development of the amateur movement was bound to have an invigorating effect on the professional theatre by providing an audience of enthusiastic playgoers with a working knowledge of acting and production. I envisaged playgoers' societies being formed among the amateurs in every town, societies which would demand a more progressive and adventurous policy from their local touring and repertory theatres, and would be able to influence the managements by guaranteeing large numbers of seats in the early part of the week for shows that might normally be considered risky propositions. I believed that the amateurs would provide an intelligent, enthusiastic and informed audience, intolerant of slipshod acting, production and scenery, able to appreciate the finer points of a performance, quick to recognise and applaud new talent, able to differentiate between a good performance in a difficult part and a mediocre performance in a fool-proof one, and not too easily bedazzled by stars irrespective of the merits of their performance.

It was only gradually that I began to realise how seldom is the amateur interested in the theatre as a whole. "Their cause", admits John Bourne, who used to edit *The Amateur Stage*, "is not truly that of the theatre, but the spontaneous and unconsidered desire to don the motley and have fun and games in doing so. They are too busy to support the commercial theatre, the repertory movement, or the National Theatre project. They do not study deeply, or read widely.

Publishers of books on drama would die if they had to rely on amateur actors who, unless they are actually concerned with a production, allow their interest to flag. When the light evenings come, they throw off the motley and turn to tennis with that same spontaneity and simplicity that prevents them ever reaching Wimbledon."

What puzzles me most about amateur actors is how seldom they go to the theatre. Even if they had no particular interest in the drama one would have thought they would be frequent playgoers if only to learn for their own sakes more about the craft of acting. But few amateurs believe they have much to learn from the professional. I have talked to many who sincerely believe that there is no reason why an amateur actor should not be just as accomplished as a professional. If one points out that it is hardly logical to expect someone to whom acting is simply a spare time hobby to be as good as those who make it their life's work, the argument generally produced is that though the amateur is naturally less experienced than the professional, he makes up for it by being much more sincere, the assumption being that anyone who acts for love must necessarily be more sincere than someone who does it for money. This is an argument that always bewilders me. I have never been able to understand why anybody should think that those who devote their entire lives to the most insecure and heartbreaking profession in the world should be considered less sincere than those to whom acting is merely a pastime for the winter evenings.

Another confident belief of the amateur is that he brings to the portrayal of ordinary everyday life a freshness and understanding which can never be achieved by the professional. Leaving aside the question of whether the portrayal of ordinary everyday life is a particularly important function of the theatre, this theory obviously limits the amateur actor to plays dealing with his own kind of life and environment. But it is, of course, a fallacy to suppose that the actor builds up character from his own experience and observation. Acting would have little cause to be reckoned an art if it did not call for more imagination and sensitiveness than this.

The growth of the amateur movement in the years before the war was awe-inspiring. According to *The Amateur Theatre*, at an extremely conservative estimate over five million people paid each year to see amateur performances in Great Britain. This in itself would seem to be sufficient proof that amateurs satisfy a very real need. But these figures are misleading. Spread over the thirty thousand amateur companies in the country, the average audience for each performance is an extremely small one.

It is the continual multiplication of societies which is the real weakness of the amateur movement. There are many provincial towns in which there are over fifty amateur societies. If these societies were to co-operate there would presumably be enough talent to put on half a dozen first-class shows each season. Still, one can hardly blame a mediocre amateur actor who is the leading man of his own little society vigorously opposing any attempted amalgamation likely to reduce him to parts more commensurate to his talents.

Whether or not the amateur is to be blamed for this reluctance to co-operate for the sake of better shows depends entirely on whether or not the amateur movement is to be taken as a serious branch of the theatre. The amateur has been given every possible help and encouragement, mainly as a result of the efforts of the British Drama League founded by Geoffrey Whitworth in 1919. There are the schools for amateur producers and actors which the British Drama League organises all over the country, some of them running for a fortnight, others limited to highly concentrated courses covering a long weekend. At many of these schools the amateur works under professional producers of the first rank. There is hardly a producer of note in England who has not produced or lectured at these schools. The British Drama League also provides the amateur with a magnificent library, a monthly magazine, advice of every sort, lectures and debates throughout the winter and a drama festival run on a gigantic scale which gives the amateur the opportunity to have his work criticised by professional producers.

With all this assistance, the amateur has only himself to blame if he has contributed little of importance to the theatre as a whole. On the other hand it is arguable that the main function of the amateur movement is simply to give as many people as possible opportunities for indulging in an extremely pleasant form of recreation. There are tens of thousands of people in England to-day whose lives are much fuller and happier because of the amateur societies. Acting gives them a chance of escape from their everyday environment; it stimulates them; it probably rids them of a number of inhibitions; it gives them confidence and poise and teaches them to move and speak with a certain amount of grace. Such is the glamour of the stage that some of it shines on even the amateur actor, giving him a new importance among his friends, and increased confidence in himself. Doubtless this leads to a certain amount of mild exhibitionism, but I doubt if the amateur actor is any more of an exhibitionist than his friend who enjoys showing off at the tennis club or displaying his figure on the diving board at the local swimming pool.

There are many amateurs who demand to be taken more seriously than this. They claim that they are doing experimental and pioneer work, and cite the amateur societies that are keeping the drama alive in small towns and villages where otherwise the cinema would be the only form of entertainment. This is true enough, but I am not convinced that there is any particular virtue in people spending an evening watching a bad amateur performance instead of a well acted film, though in fairness to the amateur it must be admitted that some of their performances are no worse, and sometimes considerably better, than those of the small, under-rehearsed, weekly repertory companies.

The professional on the subject of amateurs is inevitably suspected of prejudice and ignorance, so let me quote someone who by the nature of her work is in a position to speak with authority about the amateur. Here are the views of Miss Frances Mackenzie, who organises and directs the Drama League's many schools for amateurs and is the League's chief lecturer and adjudicator.

"Generally speaking, good amateur work has always been found in and around the industrial cities, particularly in the north and Midlands. London and the southern counties are not so good because the influence of London and its theatre seems to sap enterprise, but in the provinces there is a lot of good, lively and enterprising work being done, some of which, I think, could definitely claim to have artistic significance. These groups represent, however, a minority in the amateur movement as a whole. To a great extent the amateur movement is still content to tread the beaten track of out-worn West End successes, or machine-made one-act plays, and is satisfied with clumsy production and stereotyped acting, but then, could not exactly the same be said of, say, sixty per cent of the professional theatre? It seems to me that the English attitude to the theatre as a whole is reflected both in the professional and the amateur theatre. Judged from my angle, in the job I do, there appear to be a great many amateurs who are complacent about their own efforts. These just have not got the artist's approach to the job. They have no pride in wanting to make a thing good for its own sake, if they can 'get by' with something second-rate which demands less of them. (The worst of it is, they do 'get by', owing to the uncritical friendliness of their audiences.) The moment rehearsals begin to look like work they are apt to lose interest, and tend to be interested only in playing parts in which they feel they can easily be successful and in which they will have the sympathy of the audience. It is significant that when we have auditions of our students for parts in a class production, nearly all the girls will want the part of the attractive ingénue (however uninteresting it may be as a part) and there will be very few candidates for the more interesting character parts, from which they could learn something about acting. The men are more interested in tackling all kinds of parts, but often they will not bother to attend rehearsals. Here they are usually in a strong position because they know that they are not easily replaced. Amateurs do not work because they don't know *how* to work, owing to lack of skilled direction. Most of their producers are not sufficiently experienced to know how to work on a scene, and therefore the actors get bored. On the other hand, there is a goodly number of really enthusiastic amateurs, who are prepared to devote all their energies in their leisure time to the putting on of plays, and who really care for the theatre as an art."

Perhaps I am being unfair to the amateur movement in taking it too seriously as a branch of the theatre, and not seriously enough as a social force. It is significant that the amateur theatre has lately acquired official status as a "cultural and educational activity". Public money is being spent on it by Local Education Authorities—largely because of the demand for help which came quite spontaneously from the youth organisations, so insistent that "authority" was forced to recognise the demand and cater for it. A lead given by the Carnegie Trust in allowing funds for salaried drama instructors was quickly followed by the Local Education Authorities appointing full-time County Drama Advisors.

I doubt if official assistance of this sort is going to do much to raise the standard of amateur drama. Paid officials have to show results that look impressive on paper. Figures impress most; so quantity rather than quality becomes the goal. Nor am I convinced that lectures, schools and adjudicators are doing as much as might be expected in achieving a better standard of acting and production. These have taught amateur actors and producers to eliminate the more obvious faults, but the supply of talent among the amateurs is too small for it to be possible to do much to increase the number of companies whose work approaches anywhere near to even the lowest professional level. Sometimes I think the amateur has been taught too much. Most of the acting I have seen in the Festivals has been far too timid and careful. What amateur acting badly needs is more gusto, more attack, more signs of enjoyment. One would willingly sacrifice a little of the carefully learned correctness for the sake of a little more abandon.

That it is nevertheless possible for the amateur to achieve work of real importance when properly organised, and working under professional producers, is proved by the history of the Leeds Civic Playhouse, which was founded in 1925 and for eight years could claim to be one of the most distinguished theatres, amateur or professional, in the English provinces. Although in the end it became a professional organisation, it owed its whole existence and its early success entirely to amateurs. It was, like all successful theatrical organisations, the creation of one mind, and was only successful so long as it was directed not by a committee but by a dictator.

The theatre was founded by Charles F. Smith, a Leeds manufacturer with a remarkable flair for the theatre. He had already been one of the founders and financial guarantors of the Leeds Art Theatre, but withdrew from this because he disliked that theatre's dependence on the monied classes, who paid their guineas and lip homage to the theatre's aspirations, but only attended to see the lightest of comedies. The maids and housekeepers they sent in their place were, according to Charles Smith, "even more snooty".

So the Arts Theatre found itself in the strange position of playing to empty seats but with income unimpaired. It was this that gave Charles Smith the idea of a "free" theatre, where the audience would be charged no admission fee but would merely be asked to contribute to a collection. It seemed better to him to take £20 in pence from a packed house than £20 from twenty people.

To be a dictator was never Charles Smith's intention. But he was sole financial backer of the theatre as well as its director, and this inevitably gave him absolute power. Dictatorship in any form was against all his principles, so he was continually trying to form consulting committees, to delegate and divide responsibility, but he was too rapid in thought and too quick in action to find a committee anything but a hindrance. Despite his democratic leanings the theatre soon became an autocracy.

Very wisely he made no attempt to form a permanent company of amateurs. He drew his casts not only from all the amateur societies in Leeds and its suburbs but also from the neighbouring towns including Huddersfield, Bradford and York. Naturally the Civic was not popular with the local amateur societies, who might at any moment be deprived of their best actor, but such was the theatre's prestige that it could always call upon the most suitable actor in the district for any particular part.

A "free" theatre requires a large auditorium, so the Albert Hall with a seating capacity of over a thousand was acquired. Although the players were amateurs, the producers were not. In addition to two resident professional producers, James R. Gregson and A. E. Paine, there were frequent guest producers including Komisarjevsky, Edith Craig, Nugent Monck, A. E. Filmer and myself.

The policy of the Civic, like all satisfactory theatrical policies, was largely dictated by the personal tastes of its director. Although his audience was mainly a comparatively uneducated one, he made not the slightest attempt to play down to them and gave them Sophocles, Skakespeare, Shaw, Romain Rolland, and Chekov, and packed the house. As his actors in the early years were unsalaried, he could afford to put on plays with long casts and big crowds. When I went up to Leeds to produce Romain Rolland's *Danton* I was given a crowd of two hundred and fifty for the trial scene. Perhaps the best idea of the vitality of the theatre and its audience can be gathered from a list of those productions which were the biggest box office successes: *Oedipus Rex*, *The Dybbuk* (which was produced in Leeds long before it had ever been heard of in London), *Good Friday*, *The Adding Machine*, *The Knight of the Burning Pestle*, *The Marvellous History of Saint Bernard*, *Danton*, *The Tempest*, *The Unknown Warrior*, *Back to Methuselah*, *The Showing-up of Blanco Posnet*, *The Father*, *Peer Gynt* and *The Cenci*. In addition to the theatre's ordinary programme, a number of outside productions were given, including *The Kirkstall Miracle Play*, produced by Nugent Monck in the ruins of Kirkstall Abbey with a cast of over a thousand; *Everyman* produced by Edith Craig on the steps of the Leeds Town Hall; and the tercentenary production of *The Pilgrim's Progress* which I produced in a church with a company of over two hundred.

As the theatre prospered it gradually became professionalised. At the outset a play a month was given during the winter for a run of four or five days. Audiences steadily increased until the Civic was playing continuously for six or eight months of the year with each production running at least a fortnight. It was no longer possible to rely on amateur companies. Rehearsing and acting for the Civic became a full time job, though the theatre still relied on unpaid assistance for stage management, scene designing and front of the house management, and occasionally a play was staged with a purely amateur company to retain the interest of the original actors and to make it possible to produce plays with large casts.

The next step was the opening of the Bradford Civic Playhouse and the interchange of plays and players. Although at first this extension of activities was highly successful, it was eventually one of the causes which led to the closing of the Leeds Playhouse. The Bradford Civic began to resent the Leeds' dictatorial control. They demanded, with justice, more say in the selection of plays and players than it was possible to grant. In the meantime a trade slump had set in with the result that collections shrank. Charles Smith, harassed with his own business worries, was left with less and less time to devote to the theatre, so that the cumbersome committee meetings which would probably have satisfied the Bradford Civic were out of the question.

Even if these practical difficulties had not arisen I doubt if the Civic would have existed for much longer. The hundred or so plays that had seemed important to Charles Smith to produce had been produced. His business, like so many at that time, was fighting for its existence and demanded all his attention, so he had little time for play reading. Because he was a dictator, there was no play reading committee to help him. He was forced back upon revivals or inferior plays. Tired, a little stale, he lacked the energy to combat the decline. This theatre which for long had flourished because it had been ruled by a dictator, now suffered the inevitable results of dictatorship. It could not be handed over to a successor, for no successor was apparent. The theatre began to lose money. There was no alternative but to close it.

I have a letter written to me by Charles Smith about this time. "I feel now", he wrote, "that if slower and more democratic methods had been used, the progress of the theatre would have been less rapid but perhaps more enduring. A despotism is essential in the beginning, but a wise despotism should pave the way for its own abdication."

The Maddermarket Theatre in Norwich may some day come to an end for the same reasons, because this theatre, too, is ruled by a dictator.

The Maddermarket owes its origin to a group of young men sitting round a fire in an old house in Norwich, deploring the fact that they would never have a chance of seeing performed the plays which they had read and liked—certainly not in 1911 in an out-of-the-way cathedral city. They had no means and not much leisure, as all of them worked during the day, most of them as clerks; but among them there happened to be one professional actor, Nugent Monck. "At least", says Monck, "I called myself a professional but my acting ability was small and I seldom had any work to do." But if Monck was not a particularly good actor, at least he had stage experience. He had stage-managed several of William Poel's Elizabethan revivals, and had also been stage manager at the Abbey Theatre in Dublin. To these young men who wanted to see unusual plays he pointed out that the only way was for them to act them themselves.

This little group of idealists considered their resources. Between them they could muster £12. It was decided to spend £3 3s. on the hire of a hall, £2 on a curtain background, £3 on the costumes, eked out by some borrowed clothes, leaving thirty shillings for printing circulars and ten shillings in hand towards sundry expenses. Monck decreed that the only kind of play that could be produced under these circumstances would be an early religious drama. This at least would not require a drop curtain, which was more than the budget could afford. Besides, in a miracle play the characters are easy to act and there would be no standards of comparison with other performances. The performance succeeded. It took some twenty odd pounds and had cost fifteen. It was thus that the Norwich Players were launched.

Most amateur societies are content to muddle along in some local hall for years, but the Norwich Players immediately set about acquiring premises of their own. What they found was the upper floor of what had once been a medieval banqueting hall attached to an inn called The Old Music House. It had been a carpenter's shop and builder's store, but the magnificent chestnut roof still remained. "Under the cobwebs and neglect", wrote Monck, "I could see it was a very nice room, if not in the least suitable for plays; but that did not matter, the entertainment must be made to fit the room."

At the cost of a few pounds it was converted into a theatre holding an audience of ninety-nine, and opened on Twelfth Night, 1914, with a group of Nativity Plays. Two more performances given in the spring and early summer of 1914 encouraged the Players to make more ambitious plans for the autumn, but by September 1914 they had all gone their different ways to France, Salonika and Egypt. Of the original group of players none of them ever returned to perform again in their little theatre.

After the war, Nugent Monck came back to Norwich, collected a new group of players, and re-opened the theatre in September 1919 with Shakespeare's *Much Ado About Nothing*, giving altogether nine productions that year. During the next year ten productions were given, opening with *Romeo and Juliet* and including the *Hippolytus* of Euripides.

Monck attributes the financial success of these seasons to the fact that the productions were guaranteed, not by one or two wealthy patrons, but by a long list of guarantors promising a guinea each. "It is better", according to Monck, "to have a hundred poor patrons at a guinea each than one rich man who is willing to throw away a hundred guineas. For the rich man does not mind if he loses his money. He almost expects to do so, for it makes him a patron of the arts, but the guinea guarantor has not the slightest intention of losing his, and will see that his friends, enemies, and relations are buying tickets first. He is an active and excellent publicity agent so long as his guarantee money is in danger of being touched."

As up to now the guarantors had lost no money and more and more guarantors were coming forward, Monck felt justified in moving to a larger building. He found, in the middle of one of those networks of back alleys so typical of Norwich, an old Georgian building with a gallery running round it. It had been built as a church, converted into a baking powder factory, and afterwards acquired by the Salvation Army. At first sight it was hopeless to attempt to convert it into a theatre, as there was no space for offstage room. It was then that Monck had the inspiration of keeping the gallery as it was and building at one end an Elizabethan stage modelled on that of the old Fortune Theatre. It was christened "The Maddermarket" because it was situated by the side of the medieval market where the madder roots were sold for dyeing turkey red the once famous Norwich wool.

When the Maddermarket was finally opened it had cost £3,300, and it took Monck seven years of hard work and brilliant business management to free the theatre from debt.

Since he opened his theatre Monck has presented there all the plays of Shakespeare, played for the first time since the days of Elizabeth under the conditions which ruled in the theatre at that time. Apart from Shakespeare, the authors most popular with Norwich audiences have been Sheridan, Shaw, Chekov and Euripides. According to Monck, "Greek tragedy plays to a young audience, bent I suppose on educating themselves; comedy to the middle-aged, who refuse to be educated". Among the other authors whose plays have been produced at the Maddermarket are Webster, Ben Jonson, Congreve, Dryden, Farquhar, Vanbrugh, Etheridge, Wycherley, Goldsmith, Molière, Ibsen, Flecker, Cervantes, Alfieri, Pirandello, Gogol, Turgenev, Goldoni, Schnitzler, Masefield, Wilde, Eliot, Mauriac and the Japanese playwright Seami.

The Maddermarket is a perfect example of an amateur theatre doing something which under professional conditions would be impossible. In a city of some 130,000 inhabitants there can obviously be only a small number of people interested in a theatre which sets itself a relentlessly high standard in its choice of plays. The Maddermarket holds 220, and in the course of a week's run probably plays to most of the people in Norwich who care for this type of play. It gives only eight productions a year. Were it to give more than this it would inevitably have to lower the standard of its plays. Under professional conditions, with a cast and stage hands to pay, such a theatre would be impossible. Surely every city in England of similar size ought to have a theatre like the Maddermarket which would supplement the ordinary professional theatres, and cater for the two or three thousand connoisseurs of the theatre which there must surely be in all these cities. Why then are there not more theatres like the Maddermarket? Simply because there are not more Nugent

Moncks. Like the Leeds Civic Playhouse, the Maddermarket is governed by the taste of one man, not by a committee. Still more important, that man is not an amateur but a highly skilled professional producer who is also a brilliant man of business.

Monck at his best deserves to be ranked among the first half-dozen producers in England. His interpretation of a play is subtle, fastidious and exact. Trained as a musician, his productions have infinite variety of tone and tempo. His theatre is exceptionally intimate, not merely because of its size but because the platform stage has not barriers of any kind between actor and audience. Monck takes full advantage of this to achieve effects of great delicacy, using subtle touches of detail in expression and gesture which would be wasted in an ordinary theatre. Sometimes this delicacy of method betrays him into work which is lifeless and anaemic. "I have always tried", he remarked to me once, "to make the Maddermarket a 'gentlemanly entertainment', without fuss, with a maximum of taste and the minimum of vulgarity. It is very difficult not to be vulgar in a theatre, and even the fear of it makes one suburban."

He is the most successful pageant producer in England, and can handle a huge crowd with tremendous effect. At the Maddermarket he takes full advantage of the excellence of the amateur as a crowd player. His production of *Coriolanus* contained the best crowd scenes I have seen in any theatre. His weakness as a producer is that his work is extremely uneven. I have seen some of the best productions in England at the Maddermarket and also some of the worst. Perhaps the bad ones may have been due to the fact that Monck is easily disheartened if his cast is unsatisfactory. Although his casts are not drawn from one small amateur company but from all over the district, the difficulties of casting plays satisfactorily in Norwich are obviously very much greater than they were in Leeds, which is geographically so much more fortunately situated. A great many of the players one sees at the Maddermarket have obviously little natural talent, and I have seen shows at the Maddermarket which were so feebly acted that one could hardly blame the producer for having lost heart. On the other hand, I have seen shows there so well acted that they could stand comparison with any professional performance of the same play.

Apart from Shakespeare, Monck is at his best in the production of a Chekov play. The mood of these plays is perfectly in tune with the gentle melancholy of his own character. In his handling of other plays his streak of melancholy often leads him into mere sentimentalism. His production of *From Morn to Midnight* was an astonishing example of this. He managed to transform this angry, noisy, violent play into something sad, gentle and pointless.

The great virtue of his Shakespearian productions is their speed. *Twelfth Night*, for example, is played in an hour and three quarters. Much of this speed is achieved by the pace at which the lines are spoken, but there is no gabbling. It is remarkable how fast an actor can speak without becoming inaudible in a theatre like the Maddermarket where he is playing almost among the audience. Monck, even in cases where it has not been possible to teach his players to act, has almost invariably succeeded in teaching them to speak rapidly, simply and clearly. Another explanation for the speed of the Shakespearian productions at the Maddermarket is that Monck uses his Shakespearian stage exactly as Shakespeare intended it to be used, each scene following on the other without even an instant's pause. The closing lines of one scene are the immediate cue for the opening lines at the beginning of the next scene. As a scene closes upon the balcony or the inner stage, the actors in the next scene are already walking on to the apron speaking the opening lines of their scene as they appear. In the normal Shakespearian production it is amazing how much time is wasted between the innumerable scenes—half a minute here, a minute there, often still longer pauses while the orchestra is given the unnecessary task of attempting to create the atmosphere for the next scene. Until one has seen a production by Monck it is difficult to realise how essential it is for the full effect of any Shakespearian play that it should flow along without the slightest interruption.

There are other characteristics of Monck's besides his talents as a producer which help to explain the continued success of the Maddermarket over so long a period. One is that he is a shrewd man of business, although he hates to admit this, preferring the pose of the unworldly and innocent artist bewildered by figures. Another is that he is a born diplomat, delighting to meet intrigue with intrigue. It is extremely difficult for one man to hold together a large, loosely defined body of amateurs, particularly if he refuses the aid of any sort of committee. He is like a dictator ruling without ever summoning parliament. The amateur, unlike the professional, is not bound by any form of contract. He has no obligations beyond moral ones, and if he does not receive all the flattery and cajolery which he expects, he is very apt to desert the company for some smaller organisation where he can be an acknowledged star. Monck holds his company together with something of the skill of Diaghileff, who played each member of the ballet against the other. Just as Diaghileff's ultimate power over his company was that each of his ballerinas knew that there was a dancer almost equally as good to take her place, so Monck has never allowed any of his actors to believe themselves indispensable. The practice of not printing the names of the cast on the programmes helps this policy. It was first done because the opening production was a religious play and it seemed more fitting that it should be thus. It has been continued (although I do not know if Monck would admit this) because it is a very good method of ensuring that the name of the Norwich Players shall be very much more important than that of any individual player. This method is even carried so far that at the end of the performance the company does not take a call. As a member of the audience, I personally dislike this. It always seems to me arrogant and ungracious for the actors not to respond to the applause of the audience by bowing their thanks. It is absurd to say that calls destroy the illusion. The whole essence of the theatre is that it is a game of make-believe. Not even a small child in the audience believes that the actor who dies in the play is really dead. When the final curtain falls the game of make-believe is over and it is right and proper that the actors and the audience should thank one another.

In Manchester the Unnamed Society, founded in 1915, follows much the same policy as the Maddermarket in catering for a small public whose tastes are not fully satisfied by the ordinary theatres in the town. Here, too, is another theatre which owes its success to the fact that it admits to a dictatorship. The ruling genius of the Unnamed Society is Sladen Smith, originally an amateur producer who gave up his post as a designer to a firm of Manchester manufacturers in order to devote himself entirely to the theatre.

The policy of the Unnamed Society is to present plays otherwise unlikely to be seen in Manchester, which, apart from a small suburban repertory theatre, is entirely dependent on tours sent out from London. But for the Unnamed Society Manchester would not have been able to see plays such as T. S. Eliot's *Family Reunion* and his *Murder in the Cathedral*, Mauriac's *Asmodée*, Saroyan's *My Heart's in the Highlands*, *The Way of the World*, *The Beaux' Stratagem*, Bernard's *Invitation to a Voyage*, Gilbert Murray's version of Menander's *The Rape of the Locks*, Goethe's *Faust*, Ben Jonson's *Epicene*, O'Neill's *The Hairy Ape*, Flecker's *Don Juan*, Ludwig's *Versailles*, and George Moore's *The Making of an Immortal*.

The Newcastle People's Theatre is another amateur organisation with a similar policy to that of the Unnamed Society. It began as the Clarion Dramatic Society in the days when the *Clarion*, the first socialist newspaper in England, was organising social activities of all sorts, including cycling clubs, debating societies and dramatic groups. One of its founders was Colin Veitch, the English International, who was captain of Newcastle United. Later the society dropped the name of Clarion, and ceased to have any political bias.

In 1921 it acquired a theatre of its own seating 200 and in 1928 moved into its present premises, a converted church seating 300. Among the achievements of this theatre have been the production of every full length play of Shaw, twenty plays by Shakespeare and all the major plays of Ibsen and Chekov. Hundreds of local societies hire costumes from the theatre's wardrobe and books from the library. The more experienced members of the People's Theatre companies are sent out to the neighbouring counties to help new societies.

One of the most recently built and best equipped amateur theatres in the country is the Bradford Civic Playhouse opened in 1937. When the Bradford group broke away from the Leeds Civic Playhouse in 1932 productions were given in the Jowett Hall. In 1935 the hall was burnt out; no other suitable accommodation could be found in the town so with the last of their ready cash the committee bought the site of the Jowett Hall and set about planning the building of a new theatre. The rest of the money was raised by subscriptions and by the personal efforts of the players. Only members of the Society are eligible to take part in the productions and as there are now over two thousand members, drawn not only from Bradford but from all the neighbouring towns, the Playhouse can cast almost any part at least adequately. Although the casts are amateur, they work under a professional producer—Miss Esmé Church. A new production is put on every third week running for ten days. The odd week is used for showing films of the type seen in London at the Academy, the Curzon and Studio One. In the summer there is a ten day drama school, and there are plans for starting a professional training school in connection with the Playhouse. It is felt that there is a good deal of wastage of talent in the district because youngsters cannot afford to go to London to train. The theatre runs a first-rate theatre magazine, published quarterly, which has a rapidly growing circulation not only in England but also in the United States. The Playhouse programme for the 1945–46 season gives a good idea of the theatre's policy. It consisted of Leo Walmsley's *Sally Lunn* (for the first time on any stage), Jean-Jacques Bernard's *The Springtime of Others*, *A Bill of Divorcement*, *The Druid's Rest*, *I Have Been Here Before*, *The Italian Straw Hat* (Thomas Walton's version of the play by Labiche and Marc Michel), *No Time for Comedy*, *Juno and the Paycock*, *The Kingdom of God*, *The Master Builder*, *The Tempest*, Norman Nicholson's play in verse *The Old Man of the Mountain*, *The Bells Are Ringing* by Ted Willis, and the first English production of *Yellow Jack* by Sidney Howard.

In London before the war The St. Pancras People's Theatre did valuable pioneer work not only as a local repertory theatre with a weekly change of programme, where plays could be seen at prices far less than even the cheapest seats in a West End theatre, but also as a training ground for young would-be actors and actresses who could not afford to go to one of the ordinary dramatic schools. At the St. Pancras theatre they were able to do their training and acting in the evenings while earning their livings during the day. The theatre had a huge number of amateurs competing to appear in the productions, and as standards were high there was little hope of anyone getting good parts unless he was prepared to regard acting not just as a pastime but as a craft to be studied and learned. Maurice Evans is among the many professional actors who owe their training to the St. Pancras People's Theatre. To-day it no longer exists. It was destroyed in an air raid. But a similar organisation, the Tavistock Little Theatre, also founded before the war, still flourishes.

There must be something about the Borough of St. Pancras particularly conducive to dramatic activity, as nearly all the small amount of really serious amateur work in London seems to be done in this district. It was in Goldington Street that Unity found a derelict building which had once been a mission hall, later a doss house, and converted it into an exceptionally well equipped little theatre seating 320. It was built by voluntary labour. Bricklayers, joiners, plumbers, painters and electricians worked in their spare time. Some spent their holidays on the job. "Thus", proudly records Unity's handbook, "was the agitational theatre born."

Unity began as The Rebel Players, a band of amateurs formed in revolt against "the escapism and false ideology of the conventional theatre". In 1936 the sixty active members of the Rebel Players, together with the three hundred associate members who were the backbone of their audience, formed themselves into the Unity Theatre Club and rented St. Jude's Hall in King's Cross. At the end of 1937 they moved into their present theatre. Unity proclaims itself "a people's theatre, built to serve as a means of dramatising their life and struggles, and as an aid in making them conscious of their strength, and of the need for united action. Its aim is to help in the vitally urgent struggle for world peace, and a better social and economic order, by establishing a drama which deals with realities, and reflects contemporary life, instead of plays which merely provide a dream world of escape, and at best depict false ideas of life".

It is a fallacy that art and propaganda are incompatible. Any serious play has ideas to propagate. If we don't like the ideas we contemptuously dismiss the play as propaganda. If we approve the ideas, we call it a play with a message. There is no reason why a play should not be at the same time good art and good propaganda, but the so-called "propaganda play" is more often than not a poor play because the author has concentrated on ideas at the expense of characterisation. His play, instead of being peopled with human beings, merely contains puppets with a point of view. Even the point of view expressed by these puppets is apt to be flatly and uninterestingly expressed. There is no freshness of impact. The author is merely repeating in slightly altered words the ideas and slogans of his cause without adding to them anything personal of his own. In any form of art ideas are only persuasive if the artist has made them his own and filtered them through his own mind and personality.

On the other hand, propaganda usually has an extremely healthy effect on acting. An actor who lays claim to being an artist ought in theory to be able to sink his individuality in his part to the extent of playing a communist with complete conviction even though in private life he may himself be a staunch conservative. In practice, however, there is inevitably an added reality and conviction in the performance if the actor is expressing ideas which he himself feels deeply and sincerely. It is this which so often lifts the acting at Unity Theatre to an extremely high level in spite of the fact that much of it is technically raw and clumsy. Its strongest point is its teamwork. This is quite different from the teamwork of a professional company which is largely a matter of technique. The teamwork of Unity's players goes deeper than that. It is the result of a group of people united by the same beliefs and the ideals working together to express ideas in which they have absolute faith.

Among the most notable plays produced by Unity in its Goldington Street theatre have been Pogodin's *Aristocrats*, Clifford Odets' *Waiting for Lefty*, J. L. Hodson's *Harvest of the North*, Afinogenov's *Distant Point*, Lope de Vega's *Spanish Village* and O'Casey's *A Star Turns Red*. In addition to producing plays such as these by established authors, part of Unity's policy has been "the nurture of working class dramatists from the ranks of people". Among these "nurtured" playwrights are Herbert Hodge and Buckley Roberts, two London taxi drivers who wrote *Where's That Bomb?*; Leonard Peck, author of *Green and Pleasant Land*, a play about Chartism; David Martin, author of *The Shepherd and the Hunter*, which deals impartially with the Arab-Jewish conflict in Palestine; and Jack Lindsey whose *Robin of England*, a play in verse, portrays Robin Hood not as the carefree outlaw of the story books but as a man struggling for the rights of the people against the oppression of the landowners. But it was with an American play, Ben Bengal's *Plant in the Sun*, that Unity won the British Drama League Festival in 1939. So far the only one of Unity's playwrights who has advanced from promise to achievement is Ted Willis. *Sabotage* deals with the work of French patriots during a British raid on the French coast; *Yellow Star* with the Nazi oppression of the Polish Jews. But personally I much prefer his two London plays —*Buster*, the story of a Cockney air raid hero, and *All Change Here*, about clippies in war-time.

As a means of political satire, Unity has made entertaining use of the old-fashioned pantomime in its Christmas shows, *Jack the Giantkiller*, *Babes in the Wood* and *Alice in Thunderland.* These entertainments are still perhaps somewhat over-ingenuous, depending mainly on burlesque of well-known figures. The general effect is reminiscent of those end-of-term concerts at school which were successful chiefly because of their topical jokes and their caricatures of the housemaster and the matron. Compared with *Pins and Needles*, an amateur revue put on by the Garment Workers in New York, which achieved a phenomenal run, Unity's musicals seem too easily pleased with themselves, lacking the wit, satire and drive which the American show possessed. But it must be remembered that in England political satire and burlesque have been practically non-existent on the stage since the days of Fielding, who in his plays directed his wit against the Government with such effect that it led to the imposition of the censorship, which ever since then has been increasingly vigilant in suppressing any attempts at political satire on the stage. In New York, where there is no censorship, the theatre has always prided itself on its power to ridicule, so that topical satire comes much more naturally to the American writer. If the satire of *Babes in the Wood*, *Jack the Giantkiller* and *Alice in Thunderland* is school-boyish, it is at least a beginning which may eventually produce a genuine school of satirical writers, provided Unity's audiences do not remain content with mere political slap-stick. So far Unity's most successful musical production has been *Winkles and Champagne*, a cavalcade of English music-hall. The cast put over the racy Cockney humour of the old songs with immense gusto, helped by an audience much more akin in spirit to the real music-hall audience than the self-conscious hearties at the Players Club.

Unity's most interesting experiment in playwriting has been its "living newspapers", a method of collective authorship borrowed from the W.P.A. in America. The first of these dealt with the London busmen's strike of 1937. During the crisis of 1938 a living newspaper was written in thirty-six hours and put on the stage the following day. The technique has since been developed for the radio, and the army adopted it for its A B C A productions, using some of Unity's authors to write them.

Unity has not confined its activities to its own theatre. For instance, during the season of 1936–37, over three hundred performances of *Waiting for Lefty* were given in innumerable small halls in London and farther afield. The company has acted in places as different as the People's Palace, the Phoenix Theatre, the Cambridge Festival Theatre, on lorries at street corners, in shelters during air raids, in the London parks during "Holidays at Home", in factory canteens, in army camps, and even on the plinth of Nelson's Column.

All over the country amateur companies with aims similar to those of Unity have become affiliated to it and are helped with advice on choice of plays, loan of scripts, and correspondence courses on production. In the summer there are schools for actors and producers, and in London classes are held in conjunction with the L.C.C. There is a National Organiser to encourage and assist the formation of new companies.

To-day Unity has, in its own words, "left behind the rather narrow propaganda play, apt in its day but no longer adequate for the time. Artistically and politically so far as resources allowed, we have taken our place in the people's struggle against fascism. These phases have been successfully concluded and neither the narrow nor the negative will take us further. The people have developed a breadth of interest and confidence which demands a new expression. This breadth of interest is truly national but not exclusive. It is still somewhat naïve but will respond readily to the best". Its company is no longer amateur. This manifesto goes on to point out that if the people are still artistically naïve yet they have been nurtured on the cinema and demand technical competence. "Therefore the amateur theatre must raise its standards. Unity Theatre means to do this. Amateur actors and producers can reach a high standard but the professional can reach higher. Therefore, Unity Theatre aims at creating a professional theatre alongside its amateur companies."

Its aim was achieved at the beginning of 1946 when professional companies were established in London and Glasgow. The personnel of these companies was chosen from among the amateurs who had been working for Unity. They were given two-year contracts, with guaranteed employment, children's allowances and holidays with pay. At the same time dramatic schools were set up in these towns to provide a training not only for amateurs affiliated to Unity but also for the members of the professional companies. Unity did not make the mistake of imagining that the mere fact that their actors were now being paid for their work converted them into fully qualified professionals. Their training continues side by side with their professional appearances, a method which should be more widely adopted. At the Royal Academy of Dramatic Art and similar schools, a pupil does not begin acting before ordinary audiences until he has finished his course, and once it is finished he assumes that his training is complete. The only really satisfactory method of training an actor is in a school attached to a theatre where the pupil can gain stage experience, starting with crowd work and graduating to small parts, his class-room work growing less as he is employed more in the theatre company, so that there is no definite line of demarcation at which the pupil ceases to be in training and becomes a fully fledged professional. Unity, by adopting the apprentice system instead of the student system, is making it possible for would-be actors without financial resources to adopt the stage as a career. Under present conditions, it is difficult for anyone without private means to obtain a sound stage training unless he wins a scholarship such as one of those to the R.A.D.A. provided by the L.C.C. which not only defray the cost of tuition but also add a maintenance allowance. Consequently the stage draws its recruits from far too narrow a class. Dramatic schools are comparatively recent institutions. (The R.A.D.A. was founded in 1904.) Before then the normal way of getting on the stage was by joining an actor manager's company as a complete novice, playing walk-ons and small parts. The older actors in the company were expected to do their share in training any beginner who showed promise. So Unity's method, which at first sight seemed an innovation, is merely a return to the old practice when the only capital a young actor needed to start in his profession was talent.

The importance of Unity to the theatre as a whole is that it has adopted new methods to break down the barriers between the amateur and the professional. There are repertory companies which use both amateurs and professionals in the same cast but it is makeshift arrangement to combine full-time professional actors with amateurs who can only rehearse in their spare time. There are, too, the amateur companies which employ a permanent professional producer and technical staff. But Unity's method is different from either of these. It is creating entirely professional companies recruited from its amateur companies without calling in ready-made professionals to give them support. The Unity amateur turned professional is not segregated from the non-professionals. He continues his training with them as a pupil-teacher. When he is not being used in a production by the professional company he is sent out to affiliated societies to attend their discussion groups, to coach, to give lessons in make-up and to advise during rehearsals.

In Russia this liaison between professional and amateur is firmly established. It usually takes the form of supervision by professionals of amateur societies in the big factories. For instance, actors from the Moscow Arts Theatre give their spare time to lecturing and teaching at the Krasny Vogatyr factory group, the Kamerny Theatre is in charge of the amateur company at the Stalin Auto Plant and the Maly Theatre sponsors the Hammer and Sickle Plant. It is not only the amateur that benefits from this scheme. As André van Gyseghem points out in his book on the Soviet Theatre, "it helps to build up the sympathy of the actor for his audience, and enables him to slip with greater ease into the playing of parts which, if he lived the isolated life of the English actor, would be way outside his comprehension".

The system is more easily workable in Russia where all theatres play a nightly change of repertoire so that most actors have some evenings in the week free. As the repertoire system develops in England and when at last we have a National Theatre, perhaps it will become a normal part of the work of an actor in a repertoire company to give practical help to worth-while amateur organisations; but it will remain to be seen how many amateur societies are willing to submit to professional direction. I have a suspicion that most amateur societies would regard it as "outside interference" in what perhaps, after all, should be allowed to remain just a pleasant recreation for the winter evenings.

CHAPTER VIII

BACK TO THE GATE

ONE day in the spring of 1934 I gloomily emerged from the Underground at Charing Cross. I was on my way to return the script of a singularly unfunny farce which I had been asked to produce with a world famous lawn tennis player (who had never acted before) in the leading part. I had just finished a year's engagement with the Stoll management, during which I had produced at the Alhambra a Viennese musical comedy (fashionably disguised as "A Romantic Comedy with Music") called *A Kiss In Spring*. Although this elaborate entertainment achieved very little success, seemingly I was now accepted as a producer of musical comedies and farces. At least, I was offered nothing else. Even the Sunday societies would not give me a play to do. The sort of plays they put on were not, they politely suggested, quite in my line.

As I crossed the road from the station I saw Peter Godfrey standing outside the Gate Theatre looking as dejected as myself. If he had been looking even moderately cheerful I would probably have nodded to him and passed on, but I was in that mood when one takes a morbid pleasure in the company of other people equally depressed. So I went over to talk to him. He listened sympathetically while I bemoaned the fact that nobody would offer me a decent play to produce. When I had finished I noticed that he was looking at me rather thoughtfully. "Why", he said, with a hopeful gleam in his eye, "don't you buy this theatre? Then you could put on any damned play you liked." Fumbling in his pocket he produced a couple of rather crumpled sheets of typing which with all the dignified optimism of a house agent's advertisement described the many amenities of the Gate Theatre and the financial rewards likely to be reaped by anyone fortunate enough to become its owner. Slightly embarrassed, I accepted this somehow rather pathetic document and went on my way.

I knew the Gate was in low water. It was anything but a going concern. It had lost all its old prestige and the building itself was grubby and dilapidated. On the other hand I saw little future for myself as a hired producer. At the Gate, as Godfrey said, I could put on "any damned play I liked" instead of waiting to be asked to produce plays which had been turned down by all the established producers. To me the Gate represented that most difficult of all things to achieve in the theatre, independence. I decided to buy the lease, and the goodwill, such as it was.

I calculated that it would need a capital of £2,500 to buy the theatre, refurbish it, re-equip it, and have enough money in the bank for the year or so I expected it would take to build up a new audience. This sum was no more than the amount of capital required to put on a single inexpensive production at a West End theatre, but all the available capital that I possessed amounted to £250. My brother Ian contributed another £250 and was gratefully elected the other director of the reconstituted "Gate Theatre Limited".

Where the remaining £2,000 was to come from I had not the slightest idea. I knew few people in the London theatre and fewer still with any money to spare. Those whom I approached not unnaturally considered the Gate a decidedly risky investment. I was contemplating various wild-cat schemes for raising the money when I suddenly thought of two cousins of mine living up in Aberdeenshire. I saw no particular reason why they should be expected to back me at the Gate apart from the somewhat irrelevant one that they had been bridesmaids at my mother's wedding. However, I wrote them a long letter in which with typical Scots pessimism (the English call it Scottish caution) I set forth all the reasons why I was almost certain to fail at the Gate and warned them that they could hardly make a more dangerous investment. By return of post I got a letter saying that it all sounded most interesting, that their cheques would follow within a day or two, and that the rhododendrons were looking particularly lovely.

"The little Miss Gate Theatres", as they came to be affectionately known at the Gate, proved to be model backers. Their active participation in the affairs of the Gate began and ended with their each writing a cheque for £1,000. They offered no advice, they made no criticisms, they persistently refused to accept any return on their money, they even insisted on paying their annual subscriptions as members of the Gate, and it was only with the greatest difficulty that they were restrained from buying their seats when they came to the Gate on their occasional visits to London.

My next headache was to find a business manager, a stage director and a stage manager. It was hardly reasonable to expect people of experience to tie themselves down to work for a long period at the Gate where remuneration would be altogether inadequate for the amount of work involved. Then I had another stroke of luck. Three people from the Cambridge Festival Theatre with whom I had worked very happily in the past offered to join me at the Gate.

They were Enid Collett, Scobie Mackenzie and Michael Morice. In spite of my gloomy prophecies as to the future of the Gate and the tiny salaries which were all the theatre could afford at that period, they were undeterred. They became my business manager, stage director and stage manager. The four of us made a perfect team. One of the many drawbacks of being a hired producer is that one is constantly adapting oneself to different managements, stage directors and stage managers. Far too much time is taken up with asking and answering questions, holding conferences, checking up on what has been done or left undone. At the Gate the four of us became so used to one another's methods, and had so much confidence in one another, that shows went on with the minimum of talk and discussion. In time it seemed as if we could have put on a production without ever needing to speak more than a few sentences to one another from beginning to end.

When I announced that I was taking over the Gate nobody was very encouraging. The Gate, I was told, was finished; it had outlived its purpose. One paper referred disapprovingly to the Gate's "dank, darksome dramas". Another declared that "the drama is a popular art and would seem to be denying its own nature by a deliberate appeal to the few". This writer—I don't think he can ever have been to the Gate—went on to decry what he called "the coterie audience" of the Gate, "with its affected sensibility, childish sophistication, its bibble-babble of art and letters, its ludicrous pretensions to superiority of taste and understanding to which it has no claim". Not even the Gate's own members seemed particularly anxious that it should continue to survive. Of the twelve hundred members who were still on the register when I opened my first season, five hundred discontinued their subscriptions.

I began with Ernst Toller's play on Mary Baker Eddy entitled *Miracle in America* with Dorothy Holmes Gore in the leading part. It proved, as I had hoped, a safe choice as Toller was well known to Gate audiences and his play was controversial enough to create a good deal of discussion. The second play of the season was one which everybody assured me was a very unwise choice. It was Jean-Jacques Bernard's *The Sulky Fire*. I was warned that it was far too delicate and unsensational a play for the Gate. Besides, the production of Bernard's *Martine* had already proved that the Gate audience did not care for his plays. Still, it was a play which I personally liked very much, and as there seemed little point in owning a theatre if I did not put on the plays which I liked, I decided to go ahead with the production. I cast Donald Wolfit for the leading part. My ever encouraging friends warned me I had made another mistake. Wolfit's style and personality, they pointed out, were completely unsuited to a theatre as intimate as the Gate and an author as subtle as Jean-Jacques Bernard. But Wolfit adapted his style to the Gate with great skill and understanding, giving a performance of remarkable sensitiveness and controlled power. Contrary to all expectations, *The Sulky Fire* filled the theatre for most performances.

As *The Sulky Fire* had been included in the programme simply to please myself, I had chosen as the next play one which everybody assured me was a "Gate play". It was a dramatisation of Sarah Salt's novel, *Strange Combat*, a story of an out-of-work boxer and a woman journalist, as raw in its language and as sordid in its setting as any of the plays seen at the Gate in the past. It was a complete failure and only survived for a run of ten days. So short a run did not give time enough to get a new production ready. Frank Birch gallantly came to the rescue by offering to produce a play which he had already done at the Cambridge Festival Theatre—*Nichevo* by Scobie Mackenzie and Clinton Baddeley. It was a pleasant amusing play, but the sort of play which could perfectly well have been put on at an ordinary theatre. The Gate members very properly showed their disapproval of this obvious lack of policy by staying away. At one performance there was only £3 in the house and the takings seldom reached double figures.

Of these four productions, only *The Sulky Fire* had made any money. The losses on the other three had been heavy, for although *Miracle in America* had drawn good houses, it was by Gate standards a very expensive production owing to the size of the cast, the number of scenes and the many changes of costume. Financially the Gate was in an extremely precarious position, but at least the lesson I had learned, though costly, had been extremely valuable. I had learned that it is safer to please one's own taste than to attempt to please the supposed taste of one's audience. This was the principle on which I henceforth ran the Gate, and the success of the policy was simply due to the fortunate fact that there were a few thousand people in London who happened to like the same sort of plays that I like myself.

Everything turned on the next production, *This Year, Next Year*—the first of the Gate Revues. It was a time when intimate revue was "presumed dead". The long line of brilliantly successful intimate revues produced by Charlot and Archie de Bear had come to an end. Cochran had abandoned intimate revue for a more spectacular form at the London Pavilion. To re-create the type of show put on by these masters of revue was obviously impossible at the Gate. We had neither the space nor the money for constant changes of scenery or for even the smallest chorus. Nor could we follow the usual method of building the show round one or two star personalities.

What we could do—or at least try to do—was to be topical, witty and satirical. Revue writers at that time were humorists rather than wits, and the Lord Chamberlain had successfully cured them of any ambitions they might ever have had of being satirists. The one exception was Herbert Farjeon who for years had been engaging the Lord Chamberlain in single combat. I was able to get from him two numbers in his most mordant style which had been banned by the Lord Chamberlain, and he contributed a third specially written for the revue. Apart from Farjeon, there was no established revue writer who had the bite for the sort of show I was planning. A year earlier I had done a revue at the Cambridge Festival Theatre which was the work of some very young authors and composers. I gathered together the best of them to write the Gate Revue. They included Diana Morgan, Robert MacDermot, Ronnie Hill, Geoffrey Wright and Walter Leigh, who started his professional career as musical director at the Festival Theatre. Walter Leigh had had two of his operettas produced in London, at the Savoy and the St. Martin's, but the rest of the group were completely unknown in the London theatre. Henceforth there were to be few revues in London which did not include contributions from some of these writers, and it was as a result of this Gate Revue that Farjeon and Walter Leigh teamed up together to write the Farjeon Revues for the Little Theatre, designed and produced by Hedley Briggs who was responsible for the decor, dances and ensembles in the first Gate Revue. Walter Leigh's death in action in North Africa deprived the theatre of a musician with an exceptional understanding of the difficult and highly specialised art of composing for the stage. He could be both witty and tuneful, and besides composing operettas and scores for intimate revues, he was the best composer of incidental music since Norman O'Neill.

The cast was headed by Hermione Gingold, a name at that time almost unknown in the theatre. Incidentally, she was always being warned by her friends that she would never be a success until she changed her name.

Nobody had much confidence in the show during rehearsals. In fact, two members of the cast were so depressed by the material that they left the company. Everybody was very kind and helpful in suggesting alternative numbers, but I hung on obstinately to the material I had collected. *I* liked it, and at least it seemed worth while trying to discover whether there was an audience for the sort of revue which I liked myself.

On the first night, to everybody's surprise, the show was a huge success. In spite of this, on the second night there was only £7 in the house, and very little more on the third night. It looked as if audiences had lost confidence in the Gate. But gradually the show began to be talked about round the town. By the third week business was good. By the fourth week the theatre was packed, and long before the end of its eight weeks' run not a seat could be bought for any performance.

This revue was followed by another success, Hugh Ross Williamson's *The Seven Deadly Virtues* which had been specially commissioned for the Gate. The next two plays were Maurice Watkins' *Chicago* and Richard Hughes' *A Comedy of Good and Evil* which were only moderately successful from the point of view of the box office. Then came *Victoria Regina.*

This play, which was afterwards to make a fortune for its author in New York, London and Paris, made a profit at the Gate of exactly £5. Although the critics were enthusiastic, a large proportion of the Gate audience stayed away. At that time interest in Queen Victoria was at its lowest ebb and those who came to see the play were mainly people old enough to remember the Victorian days. I think the play was seen at its best at the Gate. It is essentially a chamber play, ideally suited to the intimacy of the Gate where Roger Furse succeeded brilliantly in suggesting the palace settings in spite of the smallness of the stage.

I offered the part of the Queen first to Gwen Ffrangcon-Davies, who was not free to accept it. For a long time I could not think of any other actress equal not only to the extremes of youth and age which the part demands, but also to the far more difficult period of middle-age. An added difficulty was that it was essential to have someone not much taller than the Queen herself. At last I fortunately thought of Pamela Stanley, then an almost entirely unknown young actress.

The part of the Prince Consort proved even more difficult to cast. Here again the choice was limited by physical appearance, as the Prince Consort was an exceptionally tall man. In the end I gave the part to a young and almost totally inexperienced American called Vincent Price, who had not only the height and looks for the part but was able to put on an extremely convincing German accent. His only other appearance on the professional stage had been at the Gate as an American policeman with a dozen lines in *Chicago.* Six months later he was playing opposite Helen Hayes in Gilbert Miller's production of *Victoria Regina* in New York.

The final production of the season was to have been Maurice Rostand's *The Trial of Oscar Wilde* with Frank Pettingell as Wilde. This was described by the *Evening Standard* as "the most extraordinary piece of casting in recent years". Pettingell was known to London audiences, as the *Standard* pointed out, "chiefly as a portrayer of the kind of clownish bumpkin with which every Londoner imagines every town north of Watford is exclusively populated". But it took only a very few rehearsals to show that this very fine actor was going to give the most brilliant performance of his career in the part.

After we had been rehearsing for about a fortnight, I received a telegram several pages long from Lord Alfred Douglas vehemently protesting against the production of the play. In the play as originally written and presented in Paris, Alfred Douglas was one of the characters, but he did not figure in the English adaptation made by Hugh Ross Williamson. Nevertheless he still objected to the play on the ground that it implied he had deserted Wilde as soon as the scandal broke. I went down to Hove to see Alfred Douglas who showed me many letters written by Wilde during the last years of his life which were conclusive proof that this was not the case. I agreed to withdraw the play from rehearsal, and the season came to an end with the last performance of *Victoria Regina*.

The season showed a profit of £17. That there was any profit at all was due to the fact that the whole of the permanent staff at the Gate—manager, stage director, stage manager, and so on—had been working twelve hours a day for a salary of £4 a week. There was no salary for myself during that first year.

When the next season opened many of the original Gate members did not renew their subscriptions. These were mostly the sensation-hunters who had found the programme altogether too tame for their liking. Five out of the nine plays on the season's programme could have been described as "banned plays", but with the exception of the disastrous *Strange Combat*, they were banned not because they were plays about sex but because they were plays about people and events within recent memory.

The first two plays of the next season were Leonhard Frank's *Karl and Anna* and Schnitzler's *Anatol* (a bad mistake as the whole spirit of the play was too essentially Viennese to be handled by English actors). Then came Jean-Jacques Bernard's new play *National* 6 which was produced at the Gate during the same week as its first production in Paris at the Théatre de l'Oeuvre.

I found the leading part extremely difficult to cast. It needed an actress who was youthful and unsophisticated without being girlish and ingenuous. Most young English actresses are, on the stage, either too old or too young for their years. They lack the genuine simplicity of youth because they have either tried to grow up too fast or refused to grow up at all. After interviewing dozens of young women the only hope seemed to be to find a girl of the right type who had never been on the stage before. At Miss Fogerty's School I found Jill Furse. She was at once recognised by the critics as an actress of rare and exquisite quality.

In these days when young actors and actresses on the London stage have no continuity of work, moving from one management to another as a suitable part presents itself, it is rare for a producer to have the opportunity of guiding and developing young talent over a period of years. With Jill Furse I had this opportunity. During the seven years of her tragically brief career she played in all eleven parts; eight of these were in productions of mine. I don't think I have had any more rewarding experience than that of watching her genius begin to unfold. Her reputation grew with every part she played. As a person she had a withdrawn quality; she was never quite of the world about her; certainly not of the world of the theatre. It was this air of withdrawal into a world of her own that gave her acting its clear rarified quality. It also made her difficult to produce. The producer's task was to help and encourage her to project her personality without losing anything of her own peculiar individuality. Projecting a withdrawn personality may seem a hopeless contradiction in terms, but in her case it was made possible by a personality which a critic, writing of her very first performance, described as having "the true magnetism from which great acting sometimes springs". It was often said of her that she would take the place in the English theatre which Meggie Albanesi had seemed destined to fill. But Jill Furse too was fated never to fulfil her destiny. She died in 1944 when she was still in her twenties.

National 6 was followed by Sarah Gertrude Millin's *No Longer Mourn* played by a cast headed by Gwen Ffrangcon-Davies, Marda Vanne and Walter Hudd. As I was in New York for the American production of *Victoria Regina*, it was produced by Margaret Webster, then almost unknown as a producer but soon to become one of the most successful directors in America. At Christmas there was another revue. It became almost a tradition at the Gate that the annual revue should bring to light some new young player of star quality. This year's discovery was Googie Withers.

The revue was followed by Hugh Ross Williamson's *Various Heavens* in which Beatrix Lehmann gave an exciting performance. Then came the first really big success of the season—an adaptation by Reginald Beckwith and Andrew Cruickshank of Aristophanes' *Lysistrata* with Joan Swinstead magnificent in the title role. This is the first anti-war play ever written. There had been productions of *Lysistrata* in London before, but always in versions so filleted by the Censor that little of the real quality of the play remained. "The writers of this new version of the *Lysistrata*", reported *The Times*, "have not considered it part of their duty to expurgate Aristophanes and those who prefer him expurgated had better look elsewhere.

The rest of us may enjoy his wit in the happy knowledge that these translators, rightly perceiving that the play itself strides easily from 412 B.C. to this year of peace, have nowhere pressed his moral or paraded themselves in smart anachronisms. They have translated freely, but they have, in spirit, translated. The result is a pointed and dashing comedy, and not what might so easily have been thrust upon us—a shabby little *revue*, masquerading under a great name."

Earlier in the season, when I was over in New York in connection with the American production of *Victoria Regina*, I saw Margaret Rawlings in *Parnell* at the Ethel Barrymore Theatre. The play had originally been intended for production in England first, but had been banned by the Censor on the grounds that it dealt with people and events of too recent a date. I went round to see Margaret Rawlings after the performance wondering whether I dare suggest to her the idea of playing the part of Katie O'Shea at the Gate. She forestalled me by immediately asking whether I liked the play enough to put it on at the Gate with her in the lead. At the end of the New York run, during which her salary had been a thousand dollars a week, she returned to England to play the same part at the Gate for a salary which did not even reach double figures. With Wyndham Goldie as Parnell, Arthur Young as Gladstone and James Mason as Willie O'Shea, the play was an immediate success. It was unanimously praised by the critics, nearly all of whom protested in their notices against the banning of the play. *The Times* devoted no less than three leading articles to demanding that the ban should be lifted, and it was largely due to the determination of the press that after many weeks of discussion between myself, the Lord Chamberlain and representatives of the families of the various people portrayed in the play the Lord Chamberlain at last granted a licence. The play was transferred to the New Theatre.

The last production of the season was Ernst Toller's *No More Peace*, a satire with music by Herbert Murrill and lyrics by W. H. Auden. "I must thank England for one thing," said Toller when making a speech on the first night, "I have learned to see the very bitter things of life from the angle of comedy."

We ended the season with almost exactly the same number of members as at the end of the previous season, but the average attendance at each play had been much higher and the financial position was more satisfactory, though the membership was still too low to give any feeling of financial security. But the fortunes of the Gate were about to take a sudden change. Within two months of the opening of the next season the membership had more than doubled itself and it was decided to accept no more members for the time being, as otherwise the run of each play would have had to be prolonged to an extent that would have made it impossible for the Gate to continue its policy of producing at least seven plays each season. The two plays responsible for this sudden change of fortune were *Oscar Wilde* and *The Children's Hour*.

When I agreed with Lord Alfred Douglas to call off the production of Rostand's play, he told me that he would raise no objections to a play about Wilde which was true to fact. Accordingly I suggested to Leslie and Sewell Stokes that they should undertake to write another play on Wilde for the Gate. When the script was submitted to Lord Alfred Douglas, he readily agreed to its production, and raised no objections to himself being portrayed on the stage.

We had been rehearsing for over a fortnight when the actor cast as Wilde decided that he was not suited to the part and asked to be released. Here was another part, like that of the Prince Consort, where one was limited in casting by the necessity for physical resemblance. Frank Pettingell, whom the authors had had in mind when writing the play, was not available. It was then that somebody suggested Robert Morley for the part. I had known him as a member of the company at the Cambridge Festival Theatre when nobody had thought very highly of him as an actor. Although he had been on the stage for eight years he had never played a part in London, where he was known only as the author of *Short Story*, in which Marie Tempest appeared. But he bore a striking resemblance to Wilde, so at least it seemed worth while hearing him read a scene. Before he had read more than a page or two it was obvious that here was the ideal casting for the part. His performance was hailed as one of the most remarkable seen in London for a long time. Later this performance was to be still more enthusiastically acclaimed by the New York critics.

That actors are born and that actors are made are both equally true. The two stars the Gate created in America proved both theories to be right. Vincent Price was born an actor. He stepped on the Gate stage a complete amateur and played as if he had years of experience behind him. When he repeated his performance at the Broadhurst Theatre in New York he instinctively adapted it to suit an auditorium twenty times larger than that at the Gate as if he had been accustomed for years to playing in theatres of every size and shape. Robert Morley, on the other hand, was certainly not born an actor. In his early days on the stage he was as unpromising an actor as ever I have seen. He spent years in the repertories and on tour learning his job. His reward for these long years of apprenticeship was that when he played Wilde at the Gate most people were of the opinion that his performance was a triumph of casting rather than of acting. It was generally agreed that he was a personality rather than an actor. This myth about Morley still persists in spite of the fact that he has adapted his personality to parts as different from Oscar Wilde as the Prince Regent in *The First Gentleman*, Louis XVI in *Marie Antoinette*, Sheridan Whiteside in *The Man Who Came to Dinner*, Dumas in *The Great Romancer*, Higgins in *Pygmalion* and Undershaft in *Major Barbara*.

Oscar Wilde ran for six weeks at the Gate, selling out at every performance, and was followed by Lillian Hellman's *The Children's Hour*, a play which was, I think, most unreasonably banned by the Censor. Its success at the Gate with Valerie Taylor, Ursula Jeans and Glynis Johns (making her first appearance on the stage) was so great that we had to ration the seats, allowing no one member to buy more than two.

Although these two plays were the outstanding successes of the season, the remaining five productions drew big audiences. They were *Your Number's Up*, a musical satire about a very up-to-date public school, by Diana Morgan and Robert MacDermot with music by Geoffrey Wright; Jean-Jacques Bernard's *Invitation to a Voyage*; another play by Leslie and Sewell Stokes entitled *Out of Sight*, which dealt with prison life; Dunsany's *Lord Adrian*; and finally, *Tobacco Road*. This deeply shocked most of the critics. One of them stated in his notice that he felt so polluted that he had to go straight home and have a bath. *The Times* was of the opinion that the skill of the cast would have been much better employed in giving a good rousing performance of *Charley's Aunt*. The garbage heap and the muck-rake were the favourite similes for describing the play. But there were a few critics, less obsessed than the others by the play's lurid detail, who recognised it as sincere and full of pity, streaked with a strange, sombre beauty and written in language often comparable to Synge in its rhythm and eloquence.

After the end of the Gate season I produced *Victoria Regina* at the Lyric where Gilbert Miller and I presented the play in partnership. Why the Censor suddenly changed his mind and decided to grant a licence to this play I do not know. The rumour was that Edward VIII was responsible for the lifting of the ban.

The new season at the Gate opened with Hugh Ross Williamson's *Mr. Gladstone*. During the run of *Parnell* I had received many letters protesting that the portrait of Gladstone in that play was unfair and prejudiced. Knowing that Williamson was among those who shared this view I commissioned him to write a play giving a more historically accurate account of Gladstone's handling of the Home Rule issues. His *Mr. Gladstone*, with William Devlin in the part, was so successful at the Gate that I decided to transfer it to another theatre. But the Lord Chamberlain refused a licence because of two scenes in which Queen Victoria appeared. Admittedly Williamson was more critical of the Queen than Housman had been in *Victoria Regina*, but he limited himself as far as possible to the actual words of the Queen, taken mainly from her published letters. The Lord Chamberlain by his action thus granted official sanction to Housman's portrait, while protecting him from competition by any other playwright who was disposed to take up a more critical attitude.

"Is the objection to the stage impersonation of the Queen or any great public figure reasonable?" asked St. John Ervine when writing about *Mr. Gladstone* in the *Observer*. "If I am asked how I would like to see my mother put on the stage, I shall reply that I might not like to see a waxwork figure of her exhibited in Madame Tussaud's, but that I do not know of any way of preventing the exposure other than by an appeal to the good nature of the people who own that remarkable exhibition. If a novelist or a biographer or an essayist or a journalist decides to use my mother in a book or a newspaper article, I cannot prevent him from doing so. The single writer who can be prevented from using in his work people who lived recently, or are still alive, is the dramatist, and even he, though he may not have his play publicly performed can have it published. It seems to me monstrously unjust that one author should be forbidden to do what may be done by all other authors without even asking for permission." Pointing out that a large number of books on Queen Victoria have now been published and lives of almost all the characters included in Williamson's cast are obtainable in any public library, St. John Ervine went on to ask why people may "reasonably or unreasonably prevent a performance of a play about their celebrated or notorious relatives when they cannot prevent the publication of a book or a newspaper article about them". He ended his article by wondering what were the *reasonable* grounds on which the consent of the surviving relatives of Queen Victoria was withheld from the licensing of Williamson's play. "That sovereign lady is part of our history. She belongs to this nation, and not to any individual in it. What she did and said affected profoundly the lives of vast multitudes of men and women, and it is absurd that any effort to increase our knowledge of her should be frustrated merely because somebody objects in general to her impersonation on the stage. Those who occupy great positions must accept the responsibilities of them as well as the privileges, and be as prompt to discharge their duties as they are to enjoy their rights."

Ivor Brown expressed himself even more strongly on the matter. "The matter is one of principle. If Gladstone and Queen Victoria have once been legally staged, what are we to think of a censorship which permits the idealising of the Queen and the traducing of Gladstone and suddenly says 'No' when something different is said about Queen Victoria, and Gladstone is rescued from a mockery which is undeserved?

"To forbid a play favourable to Gladstone and less kind to Queen Victoria, after a less favourable picture has been allowed, puts the Lord Chamberlain's Office in a most unbecoming light. The Lord Chamberlain is a Palace official but that is no reason for his being a Victorian partisan.

"The treatment of the Gladstone play might suggest that the censorship is simply an asset of the Tory party and exists to keep historical truth off the stage. I do not for a moment allege that the Lord Chamberlain or his assistants are actuated by this motive. But it is very foolish of them to give their opponents of censorship, a liberal-minded people in general, any opportunity to hold this view."

After *Mr. Gladstone* came another Bernard play, *The Unquiet Spirit*, in which Catherine Lacey gave an exquisite performance. It was followed by Hubert Griffith's adaptation of Afinogenov's *Distant Point*.

For a long time I had been looking for a Soviet play for production at the Gate, but none of those I had read seemed to be written for adult audiences. Their melodrama, their humour and their propaganda were all too elementary. *Distant Point* is probably still the best play written in Russia since the revolution. Although at the Gate this play was only moderately successful, it was, I think, one of the best plays I put on there. It has poignancy, is written with a magnificent sense of the theatre, and is full of brilliantly drawn characters. "It is a refreshing reminder", said the *Daily Telegraph* in its notice of the play, "that Russians, whatever their political prejudices, can still be extremely charming."

At Christmas there was another revue with Hermione Gingold and Billy Milton leading the cast. Among the high spots of the show were two individual turns of real genius. One was Richard Haydn as "The Only Living Fish Mimic"; the other was Reginald Beckwith's performance as the frightened little man deputising for a strip-tease artist and agonisedly removing his garments one by one as he pathetically jigged up and down to the music.

After the revue came another play by Leslie and Sewell Stokes, *Frozen Glory*. It was not as successful as their other two plays, and I personally did not think it nearly as good a piece of work.

André Josset's *Elizabeth, La Femme Sans Homme*, which was the next play, was notable for a grand performance by Lilian Braithwaite. For years Lilian Braithwaite had been poorly served by West End managers and playwrights, who continually called upon her to conceal the weaknesses of some trivial little play with her brilliant sense of comedy. The attitude was: "It's not a very good play, but it would be a success if we could get Lilian Braithwaite". Again and again the Gate, without being able to offer any sort of financial inducement, was able to call upon the services of distinguished actors and actresses because at the Gate they could play parts other than those for which they were "typed" in the West End; nevertheless, for an actress of Lilian Braithwaite's standing to give up a profitable engagement, brave the discomforts of the Gate and play a part of exceptional length and difficulty was a gallant gesture. That it was a gesture which was appreciated was shown by the first night audience. When the curtain rose, showing the Queen, a golden figure against the dark background, playing cards with Essex, the audience burst into the most prolonged applause ever heard at the Gate, where it was not usual for the audience to applaud the entrance of any player however distinguished.

This play, which had been refused a licence, was the cause of further embarrassment to the Censor. The *Evening Standard* referred to "our extraordinary custom of dictating to men and women which plays they shall see or not see". The *Star* remarked that it was difficult to understand why the play had not been licensed "as it deals with a pathological and psychological problem with extreme discretion". In the *Daily Telegraph*, Sydney Carroll declared that there was no passage in the play "to which any adult audience should or could object. Why is it not possible to give a licence, such as is often given to films, of a limited character?" he asked. In the end the Censor once more yielded to public opinion and licensed the play, but only after so heavily blue-pencilling it that it had lost most of its point. It was transferred to the Haymarket where in its mutilated condition it survived for only a few weeks.

On the same night that *Elizabeth* opened at the Haymarket, *The Masque of Kings* opened at the Gate. This was the first play by Maxwell Anderson to be seen in England. I had originally intended to produce his *Winterset*, but when I saw it in New York the acting, the production and the settings were so good that I was filled with a sense of inferiority. It seemed hopeless to attempt to do anything as good with the play in England. The New York production of *The Masque of Kings* on the other hand gave me no such feelings. American actors, directors and designers are not at their happiest with costume plays, and I felt that the play could be done very much better. I think that the Gate performance with Eric Portman, Milton Rosmer, Mary Hinton and Jill Furse in the leading parts justified this feeling. It was one of our biggest successes.

The season was to have ended with Behrman's *Serena Blandish; or The Difficulty of Getting Married*, adapted from the novel by "A Lady of Quality". During rehearsals Vivien Leigh, who was to play Serena, was taken ill and the production had to be postponed until the beginning of the next season. By then I was in America producing *Oscar Wilde*, so *Serena Blandish* was produced at the Gate by Esme Percy. Playing opposite Vivien Leigh was Stewart Granger, making his first appearance on the London stage. I arrived back in time to see *Private History*, a play about school life by James Courage. It was produced by Reginald Beckwith, who had already been responsible for a number of productions at the Gate including *Invitation to a Voyage* and *Lord Adrian*.

Incidentally, *Private History* and *Lord Adrian* were the only English plays accepted for production out of the hundreds submitted every season. The other English plays were all commissioned. Paris and New York provided us with the rest of the programme. An average of two plays a day arrived at the Gate all through the year. Most of them were hopelessly unsuitable for the requirements of the Gate—farces, detective plays, drawing-room comedies, plays with a cast of forty or fifty speaking parts, and so on. I was once sent a play in which at one point a pack of wolves rushed across the stage.

Private History played to packed houses for the whole of its run and was offered a transfer to a West End theatre, but the Censor, who seems to regard the susceptibilities of public school headmasters as coming under his special care, refused a licence. It was followed by another English play, which had been commissioned from James Laver, entitled *The Heart Was Not Burned*, a fantasy on what might have happened to Byron, Shelley and Keats had they not died young. It was a play which I personally liked more than some of the audience and critics.

At Christmas another revue. Hermione Gingold was partnered by Walter Crisham and among this year's discoveries were Michael Wilding and Carole Lynne. It is typical of the difficulty of estimating the effect of a revue on an audience that during rehearsals everybody including myself thought that this was the weakest of our revues. It turned out to be the best. Several managements made offers to transfer it to the West End, but always on the condition that they could make various alterations. It was regarded as too sophisticated, too lacking in popular appeal for an ordinary audience. According to these managements the revue needed strengthening by the addition of an orchestra, a troupe of dancers, a star or two, and a lot of new material. What none of them seemed to realise was that a successful revue is a delicately balanced show which depends on the mixture being exactly right. Above all, if a revue is to have any style of its own it must be the expression of a single person's taste, not an indigestible hotchpotch resulting from a dozen people's suggestions and prejudices. In the end it seemed that the only way to preserve the essential quality of *The Gate Revue* was to put it on myself, so I rented the Ambassadors Theatre and transferred the show there, where it ran for nearly two years.

It was replaced at the Gate by Francois Mauriac's *Asmodée*, beautifully translated by Basil Bartlett, with Mary Hinton, Veronica Turleigh and Joyce Redman in the leading parts. Raymond Mortimer in *The New Statesman* described this as one of the four or five best plays seen in England since the war. It was one of our biggest successes at the Gate but I was surprised when Bronson Albery decided to take it to Wyndham's Theatre under the title of *The Intruder*. The first night there was the most unpleasant experience I have ever had in the theatre. It was the beginning of the London season; there had been no first night of importance for some weeks, and the audience consisted mainly of the worst sort of first-nighter who regards a first night purely as a social function. Few of the more intelligent first-nighters were present as most of them had seen the play during its run at the Gate. A certain section of the audience, fairly evenly distributed over all parts of the house, behaved with incredible stupidity, tittering, sniggering, whispering and guffawing throughout the evening. Next day the critics, almost without exception, commented acidly on the behaviour of the audience, one critic describing them as "a collection of mental degenerates". The play was praised unstintingly, and the courage of Bronson Albery in presenting it was rewarded by an eight weeks' run, which in those days was a reasonable one for a play which made little concession to popular taste.

The Intruder was soon joined in the West End by another Gate production, *Of Mice and Men*, with John Mills and Claire Luce. This play had been a great success in New York but every London manager who saw it decided that it was too strong meat for London audiences. I did not see it in New York, but I read it and thought it a fine play. Whether or not it was a play for the West End was no concern of mine. The Gate was not a try-out theatre. The plays put on at the Gate were put on solely for its own audience. If by some accident a Gate play happened to prove acceptable to a wider public, then that was pleasant and profitable for the Gate, but West End productions were merely a side-line. Had I started putting on plays with an eye to a transfer, then the Gate would have lost its purpose, its integrity, and finally its audience.

The season ended with the sixth play by Jean-Jacques Bernard to be produced at the Gate—*The Springtime of Others*, with Veronica Turleigh and Robert Douglas in the leading parts. It was produced by Irene Hentschel who had directed it at the Everyman in 1926. That was the first time a play by Bernard had been seen in England.

The Gate now had four productions running simultaneously in London while in New York *Oscar Wilde* had just come to the end of an eight months' run.

The future outlook was very satisfactory. I was planning to stay on at the Ambassadors and make it the permanent home of a series of Gate Revues. For the Apollo I had an option on *Ladies in Retirement* to follow *Of Mice and Men*. The Gate was, of course, to continue with its policy unchanged. As a result of the success of *Oscar Wilde* in New York, negotiations were afoot for taking other Gate productions to America. Obstinately refusing to believe in the possibility of war breaking out in the near future, I had the Gate re-seated and re-decorated at the end of the season.

There is an old theatrical superstition that if the curtain of a theatre is changed its fortune is changed. A new curtain was one of the improvements made to the stage when the Gate was being re-decorated. A week or two after it had been hung war broke out and the Gate was requisitioned as an Auxiliary Fire Station. So there was no next season at the Gate.

In the spring of 1940 the A.F.S. moved out of the Gate to other premises. It was decided to run a brief summer season of three plays. The first of these was *The Jersey Lily*, a play about Lily Langtry which just before the outbreak of war I had commissioned Basil Bartlett to write. Apart from his abilities as a playwright he was particularly fitted to write this play as his wife is Lily Langtry's grand-daughter. It was a play which could not have been produced in a public theatre as Edward VII was one of the characters. The part was beautifully played by Leo Genn. Hermione Hannen was Lily Langtry and the other leading part was Prince Louis of Battenberg, very finely played by Paul Henried. The second play of this brief season was Jean Cocteau's *Les Parents Terribles*. It is quite unlike the rest of Cocteau's plays; written completely realistically, it is a magnificently theatrical melodrama requiring something in the nature of a pyrotechnic display from the cast of only five characters. Mary Hinton, an actress who is much more versatile than she is usually allowed to show herself to be, gave what was perhaps the best of her many fine performances at the Gate as the slatternly, hysterical, bed-ridden mother, and the rest of the cast, consisting of Martita Hunt, Vivienne Bennett, Cyril Cusack and Henry Oscar, made this one of the most excitingly acted plays seen at the Gate. The season ended with another play specially commissioned—

Reginald Beckwith's *Boys in Brown,* a picture of life at Borstal, with John Carol and Derek Blomfield in the leading parts.

By now the Germans were sweeping across France and it was obvious to all of us that this would be the last play at the Gate for a long time to come. The day after it ended its run, Michael Morice joined the army (four years later he was killed on the Burma front), and within a few weeks Mackenzie and myself were also in uniform.

All through that winter when raids came night after night, the Gate escaped serious damage, although Kipling House on the other side of the street, where we had our offices, was hit, our scenery and costume store destroyed, and the billiard saloon adjoining the Gate demolished. In the spring of 1941 I was sitting after dinner in an army mess listening to the news when I heard the announcer say that among the buildings hit in the previous night's raid was "one of London's smallest but not least famous theatres". Next day I got leave and came up to London. As I walked down Villiers Street from Charing Cross I saw the ruins of the Little Theatre. Evidently this was the theatre that had been referred to in the news. But when I reached the Gate, it too was a casualty. The roof had been blown off.

As I stood ankle deep among the rubble and slush which littered the stage, I reflected that never again was I likely to work in a happier theatre than the Gate. It was singularly free from all the jealousies and heartburnings so usual in the theatre. Perhaps this was chiefly due to the fact that it was the most democratic of theatres. Everybody, whether they were a famous star or a young unknown actor with only a few lines to say, were paid the same small salary. There were only two dressing-rooms for the whole cast, so nobody could feel hurt because they had not been given the dressing-room to which they considered they were entitled. The vexed question of billing, which can embitter an actor for the whole run of a play, did not arise at the Gate. There was no billing to be vexed about, as the Gate's only form of advertisement was a post-card sent out to the members. Above all, the Gate was a theatre in which nobody acted for any other reason except that they were enthusiastic about their job. The Gate was obviously too small to pay anything but a token salary, so it was no place for the humdrum actor for whom the stage had become no more than a means of livelihood. This type of actor may sometimes play for a nominal salary because he believes the play has a commercial future. The Gate held out no such bait. It was no part of the Gate's policy to try-out plays for the West End theatre. The Gate's policy was simply to present plays which would not normally be seen in any other theatre, either because they were too sophisticated to appeal to a large public, or because they dealt with subjects frowned upon by the Censor, or because they needed a smaller and more intimate auditorium than any West End theatre possessed. Admittedly the Gate had its transfers, but no actor in his senses would have taken a part in plays such as *Victoria Regina*, *Parnell* and *Oscar Wilde* in the hope that they would eventually achieve long runs on the public stage. I remember the Censor assuring me before I produced *Parnell* that never in his lifetime or mine would a play on this subject be allowed in a licensed theatre. Perhaps one of the most important services which the Gate performed for the theatre as a whole was that it proved again and again that a play considered by the Censor unfit to be seen in public offended no canon of good taste when seen in performance.

To the actor one of the attractions of playing at the Gate was the audience. It had the reputation of being the best audience to play to in London. It differed from the ordinary West End audience in being on the whole a younger audience. Partly this is explained by the nature of the plays and partly because of the very low cost of theatre going at the Gate. The most expensive seats were five shillings and the cheapest two shillings and fourpence, so that it was possible for the young and impecunious to see a play at the Gate in much greater comfort than was possible at the same price in a West End theatre. The low prices, combined with the fact that there was no obvious division between the various priced seats, made the Gate a thoroughly democratic theatre. One went to the Gate in a pullover or a white tie and felt equally at home.

From the actor's point of view one great merit of a Gate audience was that it became an entity as soon as the curtain went up. The mere fact of paying an annual subscription had a subconscious effect on a member of the Gate. He felt to some extent that it was *his* theatre. Coming to the Gate eight or nine times a year, he got to know the various members of the staff; the whole atmosphere was comfortably informal and friendly. He knew that the play he was going to see was fairly certain to be the sort of play he would like because it would have been chosen to suit the taste of a permanent audience who belonged to the Gate to see the sort of play that was put on there. So there was no need for the actor to spend the first twenty minutes of the play "settling" his audience. The audience was disposed to be "with" the actors from the beginning.

I believe there will always be a need for a theatre like the Gate in London, a theatre where plays will be chosen not because they are likely to appeal to nearly half a million people (the number required to keep a play running for a year in an average sized theatre) but because they are plays of originality and distinction which the minority playgoer is entitled to have an opportunity of seeing. Our choice of books would be appallingly limited if publishers were only willing to print those which they considered had a reasonable chance of achieving a sale of half a million copies within a year of publication date. I believe there will always be actors for a theatre like the Gate, a theatre where established players are allowed to play parts different from those for which they are "typed" in the West End theatre, and young and untried players can be given important parts because the audience does not necessarily require the bait of a star name. I believe there will always be playwrights willing to write for a theatre like the Gate in spite of the fact that the financial rewards are infinitesimal compared with those to be earned in the ordinary theatre.

Whether the Gate itself can ever re-open again I do not know. I can only hope that in a year or two it will be possible to rebuild the theatre, making it a little larger and more comfortable while still retaining the old atmosphere and the friendly contact between actors and audience.

CHAPTER IX

LILIAN BAYLIS AND THE OLD VIC

LILIAN BAYLIS is one of the strangest figures in the whole history of the English theatre. "Strange" may seem a curious word to apply to that homely, dumpy, spectacled figure with her cockney accent, her deep sense of religion and her rough, humorous tongue; nevertheless it is very strange that a woman in every way so ill-equipped for her task should have succeeded in doing so much.

According to St. John Ervine, in an article published a few days after her death, she was ill-educated, stingy, domineering, rude, prudish, and an extremely bad business woman. All this was true enough, but it did not explain how such a woman succeeded in creating, in the face of every possible difficulty, permanent companies, housed in their own theatres, for the performance of opera, ballet and Shakespeare.

What advantages did Lilian Baylis possess to balance against those disadvantages enumerated by St. John Ervine? Very few. She had qualities such as great courage and an immense capacity for hard work, but these in themselves were not sufficient to make up for all the qualities she lacked. The best explanation of her character is to be found not in the innumerable enthusiastic eulogies which were published after her death, but in Father Andrews' description of her as "a simple woman, with some knowledge of music and very great faith in God. . . . God had called her to do a certain work for Him and for His children—to provide the education of true art for those who had hitherto been starved in the artistic part of their nature. It was His will that she should run first one theatre and then another, and, if it was His will, the work must be done without the slightest tampering with her own integrity".

A sense of vocation has led many women into attempting something for which they were unfitted by temperament and education. Fortunately Lilian Baylis was a woman who recognised her own limitations. She realised how little she was capable of doing on her own. As a manager, she possessed the most important of all qualifications—the gift for finding the right collaborators. She bullied them, she was rude to them, and she underpaid them, but she gave them her confidence and—provided they did not spend too much money—a free hand. Often she infuriated them, but they worked for her with complete loyalty, not out of personal affection (except to those who knew her intimately she was not a particularly likeable woman) but because they respected her and the intensity of her belief in the importance of the Vic.

As a person she was neither selfish, nor inconsiderate, nor unkind, but she had the ruthlessness that goes with singleness of mind. With anybody who got in the way of the aims she had set before her she was merciless. The theatre is the most sentimental of professions; incompetence is often tolerated out of sheer kindness of heart. Not at the Vic. If an actor or anyone else failed in what was expected of him, out he went.

I first met Lilian Baylis many years ago. I had gone down to the Vic to get the script of a play by a contemporary author recently produced there, as we were thinking of doing it at the Cambridge Festival Theatre. While I was looking through the press notices of the show, she came into the office. On discovering what I was doing, she at once proceeded to advise me against the play with extreme vehemence. She spoke of it as if it were a wicked and immoral work, and of the author as if he had been an evil schemer. All this merely because the play had lost money at the Vic. For that she could not forgive the play or the author. She hated them both.

To understand Lilian Baylis as a person, one must realise that she was an intensely shy woman. For someone as deeply and genuinely shy and reserved as she was, the theatre is a difficult profession. Anybody running a theatre is constantly dealing with people who are seldom on an even emotional keel. They are in turns depressed, exuberant, jealous, dissatisfied, unreasoningly optimistic or equally unreasoningly despairing. In a theatre such as the Vic where first nights were frequent and rehearsals unending, the company were apt to be nervy, excitable, over-tired and quick to exaggerate every thought and emotion that passed through their minds. So far as their emotions are concerned actors have no sense of modesty; on the slightest provocation they will fling aside the reticence which ordinary people use to cloak their uglier emotions and show themselves naked without any shame or embarrassment. It is painfully difficult for a shy person to have to cope with people so uninhibited. To protect herself, Lilian Baylis invented what was really an elaborate disguise. She became "a character", half comic, half frightening. Her brusqueness of manner was accepted as one of her eccentricities and she made full use of it for cutting short every interview. She knew she had no tact. She had none of the ordinary theatrical manager's elaborate technique for dealing with an actor, making suggestions gently and soothingly, carefully avoiding cracking the veneer of self-confidence with which the actor, usually very unsure of himself, protects his self-esteem. Lilian Baylis's method was to deliver her criticisms and decisions as if they were blows from a hammer. In two or three sentences she left the unfortunate actor so crushed that there could be no argument. Sometimes a nervous or diffident actor was ruined by the Vic. His confidence was broken for ever. But on the whole there was a rough, bracing quality about her criticism which angered the actor rather than depressed him; and anger is an invigorating emotion. He cherished no bitterness or resentment against Lilian Baylis. Because she was a "character", it was almost worth while incurring one of her crushing rebukes in order to have a new Lilianism to recount, even if it was at one's own expense.

It is difficult to estimate how much real knowledge, taste or flair for the theatre she possessed. There is no doubt that if she had felt God had called her to run a girl's school, or a Salvation Army hostel, or a society for the prevention of something or other, she would have done so with equal conviction and enthusiasm. She has often been praised as a good business woman, but I think her greatest weakness was the lack of a real business sense. For many years she handicapped the growth of the Vic by her reluctance to spend money. Her idea of business was always to scrape and stint, never to spend. She begrudged every penny so much that for a long time she refused to invite the press to her performances because she hated having to give them free seats. She would not spend money on publicity, and although in her later days the Vic did achieve very wide publicity, it was in spite of Lilian Baylis rather than because of her. Evelyn Williams, who was Lilian Baylis's secretary at the Vic, has described her as having the shrewdness of a French peasant woman, determined, and able, to make three sous do the work of as many francs.

Her great value to the actors and producers at the Vic was that she looked at a play from the point of view of her "dear audience". She wanted them to be given performances that were honestly theatrical. She demanded clear, vigorous speech, and productions which concentrated less upon subtle effects than upon making the play plainly understandable. She herself enjoyed Shakespeare chiefly for his humanity and his humour and she saw to it that her producers and actors made the most of these qualities.

Unfortunately, towards the end of her life she committed the fatal managerial mistake of not trusting her own tastes and opinions. At a time when theatre business was bad everywhere and receipts were falling at the Vic, she lost confidence in her own policy. In the hope of restoring the finances she began to compromise between catering for her permanent audience and attempting to attract a West End public willing to pay higher prices for the stalls. Her old, faithful audience resented both the increase in the price of seats and the importation of ready made stars to lure the West End theatregoers across the river. The Vic audience liked to make their own stars, not to have West End stars thrust upon them. The season Charles Laughton, Flora Robson, Athene Seyler and Ursula Jeans were all appearing together at the Vic under Tyrone Guthrie's direction provided several exciting first nights but something had gone from the theatre. There was not the same contact between stage and auditorium, there was a different note in the applause. Lilian Baylis herself quite frankly disliked many of the productions but she put up with them because they filled the Vic.

Much of the acting that season was below the level which the Vic audience was used to in the leading parts. Charles Laughton gave two magnificent performances in *Measure for Measure* and *The Cherry Orchard* but was unhappily cast in his other parts. The true Vic audience resented the fact that an actor inexperienced in Shakespeare, speaking verse atrociously, should play the parts they had already seen better played by their own favourites.

The worst feature of this season was that the control of the theatre passed out of the hands of Lilian Baylis into the hands of the actors concerned. Athene Seyler, in her article entitled *A Fellowship of Players* in *Vic-Wells*, records that "the choice of plays was finally decided by five of us in friendly conclave, who picked from possible productions those most suited to give each of us in turn a good part". In fairness to Athene Seyler it must be added that she writes of this period at the Vic without any pretence of having made a sacrifice in the cause of art. "To an actress bred in the West End system of precarious employments at different theatres, the prospect of eight months' continuous work in one theatre, with one company, under one management, and to do at least six classical plays was happiness undiluted. The modest salary was in every way balanced by the rich rewards of the work itself." When in *The Tempest* Charles Laughton cast himself not as Caliban, for which he was ideally suited, but as Prospero, it was to many people an indication that all was not well at the Vic. In the old days Laughton would have been cast as Caliban because he was obviously the right actor in the company for the part and that would have been an end of the matter.

That season lost the Vic many of its permanent audience. The West End, having found their way to the Waterloo Road, were

[Debenham

SADLER'S WELLS BALLET: *Douanes*, one of the Company's earliest ballets, with Robert Helpmann, Ninette de Valois and Frederick Ashton.

SADLER'S WELLS BALLET: *Job*.

[Debenham

[Tunbridge-Sedgwick

SADLER'S WELLS BALLET: *The Rake's Progress.* Drop curtain by Rex Whistler.

SADLER'S WELLS BALLET: *Dante Sonata.* Setting by Sophie Fedorovitch.

[Debenham

[Lenare

COURT THEATRE: *Macbeth* in modern dress.

THE MALVERN FESTIVAL: *Gammer Gurton's Needle.* Setting by Paul Shelving.

[Edwards & Jordan

BIRMINGHAM REPERTORY THEATRE: *The Winter's Tale.*

BIRMINGHAM REPERTORY THEATRE: *Czarina.*

[*Midland Press Agency*

[Ernest Daniels

STRATFORD ON AVON: *Cymbeline.* Setting by Gower Parks.

STRATFORD ON AVON: *Doctor Faustus.* Setting by Riette Sturge-Moore.

[Angus McBean

[Ernest Daniels

STRATFORD ON AVON: *Two Gentlemen of Verona.* Setting by Gower Parks.

[Angus McBean

STRATFORD ON AVON: *Love's Labour's Lost.* Setting by Reginald Leefe.

THE PLAYHOUSE, LIVERPOOL: *Street Scene.*

GLASGOW CITIZEN'S THEATRE: *A Babble of Green Fields.*

J. T. Stevenson

[Henry Bale

NORTHAMPTON REPERTORY THEATRE: *Androcles and the Lion.* Setting by Osborne Robinson.

Passion Play at the Maddermarket Theatre, Norwich.

[Angus McBean

WESTMINSTER THEATRE: *Mourning Becomes Electra.* Beatrix Lehmann and Robert Harris.

GROUP THEATRE: *The Ascent of F 6.*

[*Angus McBean*

ARTS THEATRE CLUB: *The Constant Couple.* Setting by Rolf Gerard.

[*Hulton Press*

[John Vickers

HAYMARKET THEATRE REPERTORY SEASON: *The Duchess of Malfi.* Setting by Roger Furse.

THE COMPANY OF FOUR: *The Trojan Women.* Setting by Michael Weight.

[Angus McBean

[John Vickers

THEATRE ROYAL, BRISTOL: *Twelfth Night* (Old Vic Company). Setting by Tania Moiseiwitch.

THE MERCURY THEATRE: *This Way to the Tomb.*

[Derek Beck

prepared to return there whenever there was a performance sensational enough to be talked about; they were not prepared to make the journey simply to see sincere and straightforward acting and production. The Vic found itself forced to depend on something which looked dangerously like the star system. Worse, the policy of a permanent company was abandoned and each play was cast from among the actors and actresses available at the moment. On more than one occasion productions were transferred in their entirety to the West End. It looked very much as if the Vic were descending to the level of a try-out theatre. It had lost its individuality, it had lost its policy, it had lost its audience, and was becoming a mere shop window for any West End actor who wanted to brush up his Shakespeare.

An instance of the extent to which the Vic had come to depend on a merely fashionable audience was provided by the fate of *A Midsummer Night's Dream* when it was revived for a second Christmas. When it was produced originally the theatre was packed for every performance. The décor was by Oliver Messel, the production was fashionably "amusing", the Titania was Vivien Leigh, and Robert Helpmann was the Oberon. It was impossible to get a seat without booking many days ahead. The revival of the production the following Christmas was a fiasco. It was no longer a subject for dinner party conversation. To see it was no longer the thing to do. Although the cheaper parts of the theatre were packed, there were rows and rows of empty stalls.

The history of the Vic up to the outbreak of the last war divides itself into six periods, each taking its character from the producer in charge. So much publicity was given to the experiments at the Vic under Tyrone Guthrie that many people have the impression that until he took charge the Vic was conventional and old fashioned in its methods. On the contrary, the Vic instead of following fashions in Shakespearian production, often led them. Robert Atkins, the first producer at the Vic after the war of 1914–18, inaugurated a style of production which was almost entirely new to London apart from a few special performances given by William Poel, to whom Robert Atkins has always acknowledged his indebtedness. Atkins adopted a method of production similar to that which Bridges Adams inaugurated at Stratford about the same time. He concentrated on speed and simplicity. Scenery was cut down to a minimum in order to facilitate quick changes. The verse, instead of being mouthed slowly and impressively, was spoken quickly and incisively. It is one of Atkins' greatest gifts as producer that he has always been able to teach his actors how to speak verse rapidly and clearly without either gabbling the lines or obscuring the rhythm.

He was greatly handicapped by lack of rehearsal time in those days when the Vic was seldom able to run a production longer than a fortnight. There was no time for subtleties. But Atkins has never been a particularly subtle producer. He works on broad, definite lines. At the Vic his productions were boldly outlined. They were always thoroughly understandable. They had clarity, force, vigour and speed. For his purpose he recruited a capable company, led by Ernest Milton whose genius often inspired the rest of the company to performances which were more than merely capable.

In 1925 Andrew Leigh took over from Robert Atkins. With Baliol Holloway as his leading man, he gave the Vic audiences orthodox, workmanlike productions in the Bensonian tradition. It was during his régime that Edith Evans established herself as one of the leading English actresses, playing in the course of a single season Portia, Cleopatra, Beatrice, Rosalind, Mistress Page, Kate Hardcastle, Margaret in *Richard III*, Mariana in *Measure for Measure*, Dame Margery in *The Shoemakers' Holiday* and the Nurse in *Romeo and Juliet*.

Andrew Leigh was followed in 1929 by Harcourt Williams with a company headed by John Gielgud. Harcourt Williams advanced the Vic to a more "modern" style of Shakespearian production. With longer time for rehearsal he concentrated on newer and more subtle readings, on "psychological" interpretation of character. Sometimes his productions were confused. His interpretations were not always logical or all of a piece. He lacked Atkins' vigour and drive, but often he made up for this by an imaginativeness and a sense of poetry which Atkins lacked. His own policy as a producer is to be found in a sentence of his *Four Years at the Old Vic* in which he describes the Vic audience as wanting "intelligent, well thought out, careful performances of good plays in a genuine theatre not given over to the slickness of showmanship".

Then in 1933 came the season with Guthrie directing what was almost an all-star cast, a season in which the showmanship Harcourt Williams so much disliked was the dominating note. After a year Guthrie was followed by Henry Cass, who was presumably appointed as an antidote to the uneasiness caused among the Vic's supporters by the previous season. Cass's productions were straightforward and efficient, but his work lacked the individuality of his predecessors. Sometimes he spoiled his productions by an occasional piece of stunting which had the air of being pushed in willy-nilly as if he feared people would suspect him of being dull. The chief feature of this season was the acting of Maurice Evans, but the Vic would have taken him more warmly to its heart if they had not felt that here was another "outsider", another imported, ready made star.

The Vic entered on its sixth phase with the return of Guthrie. It was during this period that Olivier joined the company, playing Hamlet, Toby Belch, the King in *Henry V*, Macbeth, Iago, (with Richardson as Othello), and Caius Marcius in *Coriolanus*. Those who dislike Guthrie as a producer accuse him of being an exhibitionist, determined to draw attention to his production by means of ingenious stunts, startling groupings, over-elaborate business and far-fetched interpretations. His admirers justly claim that he is easily the most original and lively producer of Shakespeare to-day. James Agate has summed him up as "an arch producer, nearly as arch as the Old Vic proscenium. He is a master clutterer, and his best defence is that his archness is exquisite and his cluttering bold and noble". His great virtue is that he is not the slightest bit over-awed by Shakespeare or any of the traditions that have grown up around the plays. But I have a feeling that this may be because in his heart he often doubts that the play he is producing, even when it is one of the great masterpieces, is really as good as it is supposed to be. He seems to think Shakespeare needs a lot of help from the producer if his plays are to interest present day audiences, so he gives his actors plenty of lively and unexpected business, thinks of more new tricks to play with the lighting, uses all his ingenuity and fine pictorial sense to compose new and fanciful groupings, in fact does all he can to make sure that the audience will at least have something interesting to look at if they get tired of listening. Guthrie's Shakespearian productions always give me the impression that he thinks the audience may very easily grow tired of listening. He seems to have little confidence in the power of poetry to hold the audience's attention unaided. Judging from his productions, he has little feeling for verse. It is his greatest weakness as a producer of Shakespeare. Under his direction the standard of verse speaking at the Vic was abominable. Like Robert Atkins he believes in verse being spoken speedily, but he lacks Atkins' ability to teach his actors how to speak speedily without spoiling the verse. His production of *A Midsummer Night's Dream* was a typical example of both his strength and his weakness. It had originality without freakishness, it was beautifully grouped, inventive, gay and amusing; but it was plain that the producer thought the poetry boring and hackneyed. The loveliest passages were scurried through with an air of apology. It was a grand theatrical entertainment; if only the poetry had been given its due, it would have been a great production.

As a producer Guthrie may sometimes irritate you but he will never bore you. He is determined that you in the audience will never have a dull moment. Like an over-anxious hostess, he may occasionally exasperate by distracting your attention from what Shakespeare is saying to show you some striking stage effect or some amusing piece of business that he has invented for your entertainment, but what he has to show will always be worth looking at. His productions are superbly theatrical. Everything is done with tremendous gusto. He takes endless trouble over the smaller parts, and he can make a scene or character which previously one had thought dull come vividly to life. You can go to his productions of Shakespeare's comedies certain that they will be far livelier and funnier and more entertaining than you have ever seen them before, but if you go to see a Guthrie production of one of the tragedies, you may be disappointed to find that full value has not been given to the greatest moments of the play, for Guthrie seems to shy away from a big emotional scene almost as if he found it faintly embarrassing.

In November 1937 Lilian Baylis died and Tyrone Guthrie became Administrator of the Vic-Wells organisation. At the time when he took over, the Old Vic drama company was much less flourishing than either of its two sister companies at the Wells. It had lost both its audience and its policy and was heavily in debt. Guthrie's policy was to inaugurate a system of genuine repertory. For the 1939–40 season a programme was chosen consisting of *Romeo and Juliet*, *The Good Natured Man*, *St. Joan*, *The Devil's Disciple*, and *Viceroy Sarah*. Instead of being performed for three or four weeks and then thrown on the scrap-heap, each production was to be kept in being throughout the season, but none was to be performed more than two or three times in uninterrupted succession. This was a bolder plan than it seems to-day when the success of the repertory seasons at the Haymarket and the New have at last definitely disproved the obstinately held theory that English audiences will not tolerate a nightly change of programme except for opera and ballet.

One of the many advantages of this plan was that it ensured a return to the Vic's old policy of a permanent company. But the fact that Robert Donat was engaged to lead the company showed that Guthrie was still clinging to his belief that it was necessary to have stars in the Old Vic company to draw the public. Donat would have been an admirable addition to the company if only he could have been a permanent member of it, but his film commitments made it impossible for him to sign a contract for the whole season. The rest of the company included Constance Cummings, Marie Ney, Sonia Dresdel, Stewart Granger, Andrew Cruickshank, Hubert Harben and Esmé Church.

It had been arranged for the company to break in its repertoire at a preliminary Festival season at Buxton in September. They were playing there when war broke out, and it was decided that the Vic should go on tour instead of returning to London. At Christmas Donat had to leave, and as it was considered that without him the company had not sufficient drawing power, it was disbanded. In April of 1940 the Old Vic was re-opened with an obviously temporary "all star" company including John Gielgud, Lewis Casson, Nicholas Hannen, Jack Hawkins, Robert Harris, Stephen Haggard, Harcourt Williams, Cathleen Nesbitt, Fay Compton, Alec Guinness, Marius Goring, Renée Ascherson, and Andrew Cruickshank. Only two plays were given—*King Lear* and *The Tempest*. On July 6th the season ended and the Old Vic was closed.

In August another Festival was held at Buxton limited to ten days. The plays were *She Stoops to Conquer* and Sierra's *The Kingdom of God*, retitled *The World is Yours*. The new company was headed by David Horne, Esmé Church, Alec Clunes, Renée Ascherson and Curigwen Lewis. After Buxton the company went on tour in the north of England, making history by being the first theatrical company to appear under the auspices of C.E.M.A. Meanwhile London was being heavily raided and in November 1940 the Governors decided to transfer the headquarters of the Vic and Wells to the Victoria Theatre, Burnley.

This decision was much criticised. It was felt that the Old Vic was essentially a Londoners' theatre. In fact the constitution of the Old Vic did not actually allow the company to undertake any tours, so the assistance of C.E.M.A. and the Carnegie Trust had to be invoked to make this breach with tradition financially possible. It is regrettable that for so much of the war London was without its own Shakespearian company, especially at a time when it was thronged with service men fom the Dominions, the colonies, the United States and the continent. Had it not been for Donald Wolfit, whole years of the war would have gone by without a single performance of a Shakespeare play in London. At the height of the blitz when nearly every London theatre was closed, Wolfit gave a series of lunch-time performances of Shakespeare at the Strand. Although the dressing-rooms were bombed and the costumes in them destroyed, the company continued to play one hour excerpts from Shakespeare for more than a hundred consecutive performances to an average audience of four hundred people a day.

Meanwhile the Vic, from its headquarters at Burnley, was sending out a series of companies all over the country. Sybil Thorndike and Lewis Casson went to Wales under the auspices of the Miners

Welfare Association with a fit-up production of *Macbeth*, playing in miners' halls, cinemas, parish halls and sometimes—but very rarely—in a real theatre. Ernest Milton and Sonia Dresdel were sent round an ordinary touring circuit with *Trilby*. The success of the Welsh tour led to a demand for a similar tour from miners in the north, so *The Merchant of Venice* was sent to them with Ernest Milton as Shylock. Later the part was taken over by Frederick Valk, and Ernest Milton joined Sybil Thorndike and Lewis Casson on a tour of *King John*. Meanwhile a special company was being recruited for the performance of modern plays, headed by Walter Hudd and Rosalind Atkinson. This company opened a tour of the north-west and midland towns with the first performance in England of Saroyan's *The Time of Your Life*. In July the Vic Company was seen in London for the first time for over a year when *King John* was produced for a brief season at the New Theatre. In August another Old Vic company appeared for four weeks at the New playing *The Cherry Orchard* with Athene Seyler, Nicholas Hannen and Walter Hudd heading the cast. That autumn *The Cherry Orchard* began a long provincial tour at Brighton; Sybil Thorndike and Lewis Casson went to South Wales in the *Medea* and *Candida*; and *The Merchant of Venice* resumed touring the north of England.

Seemingly the Old Vic saw itself in the role of a kind of universal provider of The Better Drama to the provinces. "We have never been busier", boasts a note in one of its 1942 programmes, "we have conducted no less than fifteen tours in two years, carrying productions of ancient and modern classics all over England, Scotland and Wales." But the Vic showed no sense of duty towards its London audience. The fact that the Old Vic had been destroyed by bombing in May of 1941 was not sufficient excuse for shrugging off its responsibilities so easily. There were other available theatres in London. Besides, the Old Vic had assumed the role of Lady Bountiful in the provinces at a time when its own theatre still stood undamaged and empty. So London was more than ever grateful to Donald Wolfit when from time to time he brought his company back to London for a season. Much of the acting surrounding him was poor in quality, but many of his own performances, particularly his Lear, Richard III, Shylock and Volpone, came near to greatness. With fifteen plays in his Shakespearian repertoire, he was able to vary his programme on each of his visits. Had it not been for his courage and enterprise a whole generation of young theatregoers would have grown up during the war without having seen a Shakespearian play on the stage.

Even if one were able to approve the Vic's newly discovered sense of responsibility to the provinces at the expense of London, it is doubtful whether the best course was to spread their available resources so thinly all over the country instead of aiming at the establishment of the best possible company obtainable in war-time for the performance of Shakespeare and the classics.

By 1942 there were signs that the Vic had come to some such conclusion, as the companies were reduced to two. One toured in Housman's *Jacob's Ladder* with Clemence Dane and Lewis Casson in the leads; the other, under the title of The Old Vic Shakespearian Company—a title which did at least give some indications of a definite policy—went on tour with *Othello, The Merchant of Venice*, and *The Merry Wives of Windsor*, including a brief season at the New Theatre in London. In November of that year the Old Vic re-opened the Liverpool Playhouse and installed a resident company there.

In 1943 the Old Vic company reappeared in London at the Playhouse, presenting *Abraham Lincoln, The Russians* and Peter Ustinov's *Blow Your Own Trumpet*. In the same year a company was provided to fill the first four weeks at the re-opened Theatre Royal, Bristol, giving *She Stoops to Conquer* and *Queen Bee*, a new play by Judith Guthrie. In the spring of 1944 the Vic presented *Hamlet* at the New with yet another hastily assembled company. By now the Vic seemed to have lost all sense of continuity and to have abandoned any attempt at maintaining its own company or any sort of tradition. The Helpmann *Hamlet* might just as well have been put on by any of the ordinary London managements.

The press was becoming increasingly critical of the Vic's haphazard policy and nomadic habits. At last the Governors began to realise that unless they made drastic alterations in their policy, the Vic's reputation as the leading English classical theatre would soon vanish for ever. So in conjunction with C.E.M.A. it was decided that, apart from continuing to maintain a company at the Liverpool Playhouse, the Vic should concentrate on founding a permanent repertoire company for the performance of the classics. Tyrone Guthrie, while remaining Administrator of the Drama, Opera and Ballet companies, relinquished any active direction of this new company for which a trio of directors was appointed consisting of John Burrell, Laurence Olivier and Ralph Richardson.

Ever since the beginning of the war there had been a complete break with the policy on which Lilian Baylis had built up the Old Vic. It was a simple, clear-cut policy. She founded a theatre where Londoners could see the classics in vigorous, straightforward performances at prices low enough to make theatre-going possible for everybody. During her régime the Vic had undertaken one or two brief provincial tours in the early summer after the Vic had ended its season, but the audience for which she worked was a London audience. It was not, as some writers on the Vic have tried to make out, an audience drawn mainly from the district around the Old Vic. The audience came from all over London, and it was mainly a young audience. Having left them in the lurch by going into the provinces for most of the war, the Vic made no attempt on its return to London to keep faith with its old audience. Full West End prices were charged at the New. The Vic had been a "popular" theatre, a People's Theatre in the broadest sense. Now it was merely following the lead of a West End management which had already instituted a repertoire season of the classics at the Haymarket, with John Gielgud, Peggy Ashcroft and Leslie Banks heading the company. Had the Old Vic not associated itself with Olivier and Richardson, it is very likely that these two actors would have performed much the same repertoire under their own management aided by a guarantee from the Arts Council. One wonders whether the Old Vic has sacrificed its traditions without giving the public anything they would not have had in any case. But what could the Vic have done to maintain its traditions when its own theatre was a ruin? It ought, I think, to have been more far-sighted. At a time when theatres were easy to acquire on reasonable terms, it should have obtained a lease of a much larger theatre than the New (the Princes Theatre would have been ideal) where it would have been economically feasible to present their plays at more popular prices.

The Vic is nearing the end of its life. When the National Theatre is built, the Vic will be the company to occupy it and then the name Old Vic will cease. But the need for an Old Vic will continue. A National Theatre, so far from making a theatre such as the Old Vic unnecessary, will make it more than ever essential. The National Theatre will enormously increase the audience for fine plays and one theatre alone will not be able to satisfy the demand, any more than the Vic seasons at the New, which include at the most two Shakespeare plays a year, can satisfy the demand at present. It ought to be possible for the young theatre-goer in London, discovering Shakespeare for the first time, to see at least eight or ten of his plays in the course of a year. When I first came to London as a young man it was mainly due to the Old Vic that I was able to see thirteen Shakespearian productions in a single season. Obviously it is impossible for a company operating on the scale of the present Vic company to put on more than three or four productions a year. Nor is there any point in attempting to do so when they pack the theatre every night and by the end of the season have by no means exhausted their audience for any of the plays. We can only hope for a successor to Lilian Baylis who will give us another theatre where a young and eager audience will be able each season to see a thoroughly representative Shakespearian repertoire at prices considerably below those in the West End theatre. If the repertoire is to be large enough, productions will obviously have to be simple and inexpensive and rehearsals limited to a maximum of three weeks for any one play. Professor Dent, one of the Governors of the Old Vic, argues in his book *A Theatre for Everybody* that a theatre run on these lines with a large number of inexpensive seats, would have to content itself from the first with an ensemble devoid of famous stars. According to him, "here we come at once to the fundamental difficulty of running any kind of 'idealist' theatre. . . . The best one could hope for would be that new stars would gradually emerge from the school of acting which that theatre would be, and after they had won their way to fame in other theatres they would occasionally come back for a certain period at a nominal salary out of loyalty to 'the old school' and in the same spirit in which eminent physicians and surgeons give their services gratuitously to certain hospitals".

But why this assumption that stars are essential, that only stars can act well enough to play leading parts? Neither John Gielgud nor Edith Evans were stars when they were at the Old Vic, but was their acting so very inferior to what it is now that they are famous stars? It is different perhaps, but not necessarily better. What they have gained in experience and technique and authority they have inevitably lost in youthful freshness and vigour and enthusiasm. And where are the new stars to come from if the theatre which will one day take the place of the Old Vic is not prepared to help in creating them?

Perhaps I seem to underrate the importance of stars. On the contrary, a dazzling star performance is, for me, the greatest of all the thrills that the theatre can provide. It is sheer nonsense for anyone to pretend that he would prefer to see at the New a well-balanced team in place of a company of uneven talent completely outshone by two great actors. The regular playgoer may grumble that he is crowded out by those who have only gone to see the stars, not the plays, but he goes too far when he protests that this is unhealthy for the theatre as a whole. If a star can bring into the theatre people who otherwise would not go to see a great classic, he is making the best possible use of his fame. Many of those who went to the New merely to stare at a star found themselves, rather to their surprise, enjoying Shakespeare. But the larger the public created by star performances of the classics, the more often they have to be repeated, so the repertoire is inevitably a very limited one, especially in a theatre as small as the New. London needs another theatre for those for whom a few star productions of the classics are not enough; a theatre for the still comparatively small audience who want to see great plays even when there are no big names in the cast; a theatre where the audience will be able to watch the rise of new stars; in fact, a theatre such as the Old Vic used to be.

CHAPTER X

NINETTE DE VALOIS AND THE ENGLISH BALLET

BEFORE I ever met Ninette de Valois I had decided I was not going to like her. I was young and intolerant in those days. I found it much easier to discover reasons for disliking people than for liking them, so I had no difficulty in making up my mind in advance about a young woman who had chosen to take the name of a line of French kings, rechristen herself Ninette, and start a dancing school in Kensington under the appallingly pretentious title of "The Academy of Choreographic Art". I don't think the word phoney was then in use, so I probably thought of her as bogus.

When she arrived at the Cambridge Festival Theatre to work on the opening production—it was the Oresteian Trilogy of Aeschylus—I was relieved to see that at least she was not the arty looking woman I had expected her to be. She looked rather like a young schoolmistress who made a point of dressing neatly and sensibly to set the girls a good example. At rehearsals her way of dashing about the stage, scolding, goading and exhorting, was so reminiscent of a hockey practice that the company nicknamed her The Games Mistress. One of the actors who had a habit of getting out of position remarked that at any moment he expected her to blow a whistle, admonish him for being offside again, and send him off the field. Perhaps her method of rehearsing in those early days was not unconnected with her own description of herself as "a Dubliner tamed at the age of nine by an English hockey field and an East Wind".

Never had I met anyone so desperately earnest. Her manner was abrupt and dictatorial. She always appeared to be in a hurry, as if she had already made up her mind about all the work she had to do in the future and had no time to waste. She was serious to the verge of pomposity.

In self-defence, in case I make myself seem a more foolish and intolerant young man than I really was, it is only fair to say that in those days Ninette de Valois made much the same impression on other people. Arnold Haskell, for instance, found "something a little smug and ridiculous about this young dancer who disapproved of the direction that the greatest of all companies was taking, and who formed her own Academy. It must have required an almost overpowering self-confidence".

I doubt if she was quite as self-confident as she appeared. It was, I think, stubborn determination rather than self-confidence that carried her through those first years after she left the Diaghileff company. When she came to the Cambridge Festival Theatre she was totally inexperienced in the work to which she had dedicated herself. I suspect that her brusque, school-marmish manner at rehearsals concealed a good deal of apprehension. She had yet to satisfy herself that she was a choreographer, that she had the ability to work creatively in the theatre. All her fantastically ambitious plans depended on that.

Her share in the production of the Oresteia provided immediate proof of her abilities. There are three separate choruses in the play. The chorus of Argive Elders, the chorus of Trojan Bondwomen, and the chorus of Furies. Both the opportunities and the difficulties for the choreographer were immense. What Ninette de Valois achieved reduced one's memories of all other Greek choruses one had ever seen to a series of pretty posturings by comparison. It was not until five years later, when she created *Job*, that she again displayed the strength, the depth of feeling, the originality and dramatic force which characterised her handling of these choruses.

The greatness of Ninette de Valois' achievements has been largely due to a rare combination of imagination and emotion allied to a fine intellect, but at first the alliance was an uneasy one. The mind tended to chill the emotions. The ballets she produced at the Festival with the tiny company she was training at her school were apt to be dry and impersonal. The first, *Rout*, inspired by a poem of Ernst Toller's and danced to music by Arthur Bliss, was a harsh, angry, rather pretentious work in which the dancers seemed to have been deliberately and ruthlessly drained of individuality. It was only in brief divertissements, in which she danced herself, that she revealed another side of her character—the gaiety, the wit and humour and gusto which gradually became more apparent as her ambitions began to be realised and the anxious uncertainty of those early years gave way to a sense of achievement.

It is many years now since I have worked with her and I see her rarely, but because of what she has achieved I have grown to admire this woman above all other people in the English theatre of to-day.

Creative genius in the theatre is rare. There is comparatively little scope for it. Actors and producers are not creators; they are the interpreters of their authors. During the period covered by this book the theatre discovered a number of intelligent, efficient authors, but since Shaw there has been none who could be described as a creative genius. One of the few figures which the theatre has produced during the period between the two wars to whom I would apply that description is Ninette de Valois. Choreography is a creative art, but I am not thinking of her as a choreographer when I describe Ninette de Valois as a creative genius, although creations such as *Job*, *The Rake's Progress* and *Checkmate* might with some justification be described as works of genius. It is of her work in creating a great English ballet company that I am thinking.

Writing of Massine, Ninette de Valois declared that to her "this man spells the word 'genius', not the genius of fiction but the genius of fact; that infinite capacity for taking pains, power of analysis and concentration, and, further, imagination and judgment as opposed to originality and flair". This might equally well have been written about Ninette de Valois herself. Very self-revealing too is her defence of Diaghileff against the charge of being uncreative because he never himself produced a ballet, or designed a piece of scenery, or put a company through an inspiring morning lesson. "Such troublesome analytical searchings have ended by confusing two issues, namely, creation in an objective sense and creation in a subjective. The writers and orators on this point overlook his persistent safe-guarding of each artist, his endless criticisms, his plans for everybody stretching months ahead, his conception and collection of all facts pertaining to a new production and his handing over of this matter complete to the choreographers, his endless visits to the rehearsals of new ballets, his exit with a grave shaking of the head, and the choreographer's entirely new effort, mysteriously started the next day, coupled with infinitely better results. There is no vision without creative stimulus, and we are discussing a man of infinite vision."

In this chapter we are discussing a woman of infinite vision. A woman who twenty years ago, when she was a young dancer in Diaghileff's company, had already decided on her aims, and at the moment when she was on the verge of becoming one of Diaghileff's stars left the company to begin her real work in a stern Victorian house in Kensington where in 1926 she started her "Academy of Choreographic Art". It was here she trained the little company of dancers which worked at the Cambridge Festival Theatre and later began to give an occasional brief ballet at the Vic or the Wells before some of the shorter operas. In 1931 she offered the entire school to Lilian Baylis in return for rehearsal facilities at the newly built Sadler's Wells Theatre and the promise that the company would sometimes be allowed to give an occasional evening of ballet. All that she asked for herself was a very modest salary. I suspect that what induced Lilian Baylis to accept was not so much an enthusiasm for ballet (I doubt if she had ever seen a ballet in her life) as the lure of the considerable fees from the now very prosperous school. These Ninette de Valois proposed should be paid to the Vic-Wells organisation instead of to herself. But although Lilian Baylis may have known nothing about ballet she knew a great deal about human nature. The development of the Vic-Wells ballet owed much to her absolute faith in Ninette de Valois and the freedom she allowed her to develop the company according to her own ideas.

By the end of that season the company had given three full evenings of ballet. These were so successful that it was decided to give programmes of ballet fortnightly during the following season. The growth of that little company of only eight dancers into a great organisation appearing in London and the provinces all through the war years for forty-eight weeks out of the fifty-two, and then most deservedly achieving the honour of being the company to re-open Covent Garden Opera House, has been described in so many books and articles that there is no need to recount the facts yet again. But the story reads so smoothly, the progression is so steady and orderly, that perhaps one is apt to underrate the difficulties surmounted, the courage and faith and toil needed to achieve aims so ambitious that in those early days Ninette de Valois alone believed them to be possible.

When it began to be realised that a serious attempt was being made to form an English ballet company there was little encouragement. The balletomanes, still mourning the loss of the Diaghileff company, were wittily contemptuous. Compared with the Russians they found these English dancers woefully lacking in glamour and temperament. The critics, when they gave any attention at all to this new enterprise, were either patronising or facetious or so morbidly afraid of being accused of artistic jingoism that they were ferociously super-critical. Only the audience gave the company real encouragement. They were mainly the everyday audience of the Vic and the Wells. They enjoyed the ballet without being self-conscious devotees. Their applause was enthusiastic, but without that note of hysteria which was to come later when the bulk of the audience were no longer theatre-goers but ballet fans.

To-day the Sadler's Wells company is surrounded by so much frantic enthusiasm, personality worship, uncritical adulation and general ballet-hoo that there is a danger that it may not be sufficiently realised that this over-written, over-photographed and over-applauded company is the sanest and healthiest organisation in the whole of the English theatre.

Under Ninette de Valois the company has proved itself to possess all those qualities most pitifully rare in the English theatre; complete artistic integrity, a long term policy, belief in tradition combined with the courage to experiment, and, above all, a sense of permanence. The Sadler's Wells company is the only theatrical organisation in England which can offer security to its artists, impose on them an absolute discipline, and count on their unfailing loyalty and enthusiasm. In a country where the theatre is so organised, or rather disorganised, that there is no permanent employment and no permanent artistic policy, Ninette de Valois set out from the first to build up a company and a policy both of which would be permanent, realising that the one cannot exist without the other.

It is this intense belief in the necessity for permanence that explains why Ninette de Valois continually backs out of the limelight and refuses to take her fair share of publicity and acclamation. This self-effacement is not a pose. It is not due to shyness or to any morbid dislike of publicity. It is part of a deliberate policy. When she was with Diaghileff she learned from watching him the necessity for an absolute dictatorship over a ballet company, but she also saw that while Diaghileff was right in not allowing a single star to become greater than the ballet as a whole, he was making a fatal mistake in allowing himself to become more important than the company itself, so that when he died it never occurred to anyone that it could continue without him.

In the early days of the Vic-Wells Ballet (it was not until later that it became the Sadler's Wells Ballet) Ninette de Valois was content to appear to the public simply as an able lieutenant of Lilian Baylis. Devoid of any desire for personal glory, she did not resent the fact that it was Lilian Baylis who got the credit for creating a ballet company to make a trio with her Shakespearian and opera companies. On the first nights of a new ballet it was Lilian Baylis who took the stage. One remembers affectionately the spectacle of that dumpy figure dressed in her academic robes, complete with mortar-board, waddling across the stage to embrace the leading dancers, taking off her pince-nez to wipe them and then roundly scolding the audience because there were some unsold seats in the house. Ninette de Valois' appearances to take a curtain were confined to the first nights of her own ballets. No speech, no showmanship. Superficially just an ordinary young woman in a very plain evening dress, obviously tired and over-worked.

All this was according to plan—Ninette de Valois' plan. It was essential for the ballet company, if it was to become a solidly permanent organisation, that it should be associated in the minds of the public with the Vic and the Wells rather than with the name of an individual. Lilian Baylis was more than an individual. She was a symbol. She was the Old Vic—and Sadler's Wells.

Another essential condition for a permanent theatrical company is a school of its own from which it can draw a constant supply of new talent already accustomed to the traditions and methods and environment of the company. Many theatre and ballet companies on the continent and in America which had a superficial air of permanence disintegrated because they realised too late the necessity for a school. The Sadler's Wells school, instead of being an afterthought when the ballet had become established, was the source of the company. Had Ninette de Valois not begun by founding a school instead of a company, the ballet could not have survived the loss of Markova in 1935 without engaging another star to replace her.

Markova and Dolin joined the company when it was decided to risk a short continuous season of ballet, followed by a provincial tour. During the next year or two Dolin appeared with the company from time to time when his other engagements permitted, but Markova became a permanent member from 1933 to 1935. Many of the ballet's supporters, less far-sighted than its director, disapproved of the engagement of this great dancer. They considered it a confession of weakness. It *was* a confession of weakness, and greatly to Ninette de Valois' credit that she had the courage to make this confession. She knew that Markova's dazzling personality and superb technique would expose the rest of the company to ruthless comparisons. She expected to be told—as she was, again and again—that one great ballerina does not make a ballet company. But she had realised that if the company was to continue its development it was essential that they should dance the classical ballets with a great ballerina in the leading roles to set the highest possible standard, even if it were a standard far beyond the capabilities of the rest of the company. Besides, Markova's name would ensure full houses at every performance. (The policy was now one evening performance a week with a matinée once a month.) For the first time the company had a feeling of financial stability.

When Markova left it was taken for granted that another star would be engaged to replace her. Ninette de Valois' decision to rely solely on the permanent company seemed at the time a decision of doubtful wisdom. The company was not yet really strong enough to do without a star personality. The fact that there were empty seats on the first night of the new season made it plain that many of the audiences which had packed the theatre on ballet nights during the past two years had come only to see Markova, and that the company had not yet gathered a sufficiently large and faithful audience of its own. But for some years now the school had been providing the company, as it grew in size, with a steady supply of new recruits. The time had arrived to prove that what had formerly been merely a group of dancers supporting guest stars was now a fully fledged ballet company with a personality of its own stronger than the personality of any individual dancer.

The personality which the company revealed during that season of 1935–36 was not, at first sight, a particularly interesting one. It was formal and reserved and self-consciously correct. There was a lack of warmth, an absence of gaiety. The standard of technique was good, but it seemed to have been achieved at the expense of any air of spontaneity. The ensemble was better than anything London had seen for years, but the blank, impassive faces of the corps de ballet made it difficult for one to enjoy the excellence of their team-work.

The criticism that the company lacked glamour and temperament was renewed, more loudly than before. Glamour is a vague attribute, dependant on an air of remoteness and a touch of the exotic, qualities which it was hardly reasonable to expect from those hard-working English girls in Rosebery Avenue. As for temperament, it is a misused word, too often applied in the theatre to splurgy emotionalism, or unrestrained exhibitionism, or mere lack of self-control resulting in silly tantrums. The best description of temperament I know is Arnold Haskell's definition of it as "the ability to suggest that the dancer is performing spontaneously and for pleasure, and not running through a set piece".

If one accepts that definition it is undeniable that the Sadler's Wells dancers at this period were lacking in temperament. The more informed critics of the ballet began to wonder if Ninette de Valois' methods of training were at fault. It looked as if she was over-drilling her dancers. But, as usual, she was more far-sighted than her critics. Her long term policy enabled her to take her time. She believed that individuality and personality should only be allowed to develop after fundamental weaknesses had so far as possible been eradicated.

The fundamental weakness she found in the English dancer was sentimentality. "Sentimentality is the tragedy of the English dancer", she declared in her book, *Invitation to the Ballet*, written in 1936. "It results in the frustration of his temperament, simply because it is the weakness to be found in the Englishman's domestic upbringing. Indeed, this tiresome and confused question cannot be taken too seriously. The Hollywood film star in the largest and most banal of close-ups is preferable to the bric-à-brac aesthetic feelings the English dancer is known to display. One can be tolerated for the sheer and genuine force of its positive vulgarity, but the other is beyond toleration because of its negative refinement. It is as misleading as that 'sense of humour' we are so often subjected to, which has a habit of proving itself to be nothing more than an indifferent wit shaped painfully into a form of fun that demands another name. Temperament is a dangerous word to use persistently to the English dancer at the present moment; rather suggest to him the necessity of developing an acute sense of characterisation, and aim at eradicating his misplaced sentimentality quietly and diplomatically."

Perhaps in her determination to root out "misplaced sentimentality" Ninette de Valois may have sometimes mistaken genuine emotion fumblingly and awkwardly expressed for mere sentimentality. Perhaps her early experience as a dancer in musical comedy gave her such a distaste for cheap and easy showmanship that she has sometimes misunderstood and misinterpreted a young dancer's crude but genuine sense of the theatrical. Perhaps her own fine seriousness of mind has communicated itself to some of the company only in the form of a too obvious earnestness. Or perhaps the fault is in the English character, its diffidence, its fondness for understatement, its exaggerated respect for sober competence. Whatever the reason, the Sadler's Wells company, with a few exceptions, could do with more élan, more emotional vitality, less distrust of genuine theatricality, more confidence in their own personalities.

In fact, there is still a good deal of truth in the old criticism that the company lacks temperament. It is a quality which few English actors and actresses possess. Most of them stroll down from their dressing-rooms each evening to perform their parts carefully and conscientiously, but with little gusto; only a few of them step on to the stage feeling that recurring excitement and nervous tension so essential if the actor is to give the impression that he is "performing spontaneously and for pleasure and not running through a set piece".

The dulling effects of long runs, more mercilessly drawn out than ever during recent years, inevitably make acting a humdrum business for the cast of a successful piece. The ballet dancer has the advantage of appearing in a large and varied repertoire of ballets, and the nightly stimulus of an audience keyed up to a pitch of excitement and anticipation rare in the ordinary theatre. But perhaps the ballet's audience has been more of a hindrance than a help to the development of the dancers. The excitement and enthusiasm is at times unhealthily akin to idolatry and hysteria. The company has had the integrity to withstand the temptation to play down to its audience and please them with cheap little tricks of showmanship and exhibitions of personality; but it is unhealthy for a company to have to react against its audience. The effect on the Sadler's Wells company has been to make them audience-conscious in the wrong way, to make them perhaps a little priggishly aware of their own good sense in not being unduly influenced by the indiscriminating howls of approval with which their performances have invariably been received in recent years. This feeling of superiority to the audience, even if it is largely subconscious, may explain the dryness and lack of warmth and excitement which is noticeable in many of the dancers. If the company could have more confidence in the taste and discrimination of its audience, then the collaboration between performer and spectator, which is the basis of all forms of theatre, would develop more freely and naturally, and the performances would gain in size and warmth.

It would be good for the company if they more often played to apathetic audiences who had to be roused and battled with. The ready-made enthusiasm in the auditorium before the curtain has gone up results in the dancers being more experienced in guiding and controlling the enthusiasm of the audience than arousing it. Less automatically enthusiastic audiences would force the dancers to project their performances more strongly. I am inclined to think that the weakness of the company, usually vaguely described as lack of temperament and personality, is not due to any fault of training or character but to the fact that they so seldom have to make that extra effort to "get" their audience.

William Chappell, who was for many years a member of the Vic-Wells company, complains bitterly, in an article on the ballet which appeared in *New Writing and Daylight*, of "the revolting edifice, fashioned from adulation and sentimental hysteria that has been built up round the ballet by its fans in the last ten years". He pleads for a proper understanding of the ballet's place in the theatre "as a natural part of national entertainment, as usual and satisfactory as Shakespeare". That will only be possible when the ballet audience ceases to be so proud of itself because it can appreciate something so "artistic" as the ballet.

"If one asked the ever-growing ballet audience, 'Why do you come?'" wrote P. W. Manchester in an article in *Arabesque*, "a completely honest answer from about ninety per cent of the audience would be something like this: 'I come from a respectable, comfortable and extremely dull home, and I work at a dull job and nothing ever seems to happen to me. I come because Ballet is not anything like that. It is beautiful and exciting and unreal and I can forget how boring life really is. It also makes me feel awfully clever and intellectual, because all the dreary people amongst whom I spend my life think it terribly highbrow and this gives me no end of a kick'."

They would be a healthier audience if only they would realise that ballet is the simplest and easiest of all forms of art to enjoy. It needs no knowledge of the technicalities of dancing, choreography or music to enjoy ballet as escapist entertainment. Incidentally, it is, next to strip-tease, the most sexual of all forms of theatrical entertainment. Its material is the human body. Every movement displays it, every costume is designed to show it off—which is perhaps why that hideous yowling which comes from parts of the house at the fall of the curtain often sounds uncomfortably like the yearning cries of the sex-starved.

I am not arguing that the ballet should be taken with desperate seriousness, that everybody should know the difference between a *pas de chat* and a *pas de cheval*, a *pirouette* and a *tour en l'air*, a *glissade* and a *jété*. I am merely urging that ballet fans should be made to realise that of all forms of art the ballet makes the least demands upon the intellect. I always suspect that a large proportion of the audience is not really applauding the ballet at all. It is applauding itself for being "artistic" enough to enjoy this simple, sensuous, colourful, tuneful and altogether enchanting form of entertainment. Otherwise it is difficult to understand why a ballet company is forced to take four or five times as many curtain calls as a company of actors in a straight play. Does a ballet audience really enjoy itself four or five times more than an audience in an ordinary theatre?

By moving to Covent Garden the Sadler's Wells company has probably saved ballet in England from becoming a cult. Long seasons at Covent Garden, which has room for far larger audiences than could be accommodated at the New Theatre or at Sadler's Wells, will ensure that the ordinary playgoer, for whom a visit to the ballet is simply a normal part of his theatre going, is not crowded out by the almost nightly attendance of those for whom ballet is neither art nor entertainment but an obsession. There is at last every hope that the ballet will now cease to be unhealthily isolated from the theatre as a whole.

This isolationism has been no fault of the Sadler's Wells company, which has continually striven to bridge the gap between "pure ballet" and other forms of stage production. Much of the strength of the company lies in the fact that besides being dancers with a high standard of technical excellence they are also a company of very good actors. There are, of course, other qualities that are highly developed in the company, such as the native gift for teamwork, and another essentially English quality which one critic has described as "a kind of spring-like freshness far removed from the hot-house exoticism of the Russian atmosphere"; but it is the company's ability to dramatise and characterise that gives it its individuality. Arnold Haskell has suggested that the English dancer's excellence in the acting of a positive dramatic role may also be a native quality due to a certain national diffidence which makes it easier to perform behind a mask. It is an instinct that has been highly developed in the company by Ninette de Valois, whose early experience at the Cambridge Festival Theatre and at the Abbey Theatre, working in collaboration with play producers, gave her a knowledge of acting and a sense of the theatre which is obvious in all her work. No choreographer is better at telling a story and creating characters. In her ballets the dancers are seldom types; they are individuals. In her masterpiece, *The Rake's Progress*, the corps de ballet are as carefully characterised as the small parts in a play by a skilful dramatist.

As a choreographer Ninette de Valois has influenced the whole art of ballet by making it more human. The Russian ballet was peopled with figures rather than characters. The fondness of the Russian choreographers for ballets about dolls and toys and fairy princesses and characters from fables and nursery books and the *Commedia del' Arte* was symbolic of the dreamland in which the ballet existed. Ninette de Valois' two finest characterisations, Satan in *Job* and Mister O'Reilly in *The Prospect Before Us*, belong to the larger world of the theatre rather than to the conventionalised world of the ballet. They are not figures; they are human beings. Their ancestors are not the characters from old ballets; they are in the direct line of descent from the creations of the English novelists and dramatists. Even when in a ballet such as *Checkmate* Ninette de Valois' subject is superficially an abstract one, she gives humanity to her symbols. The Black and Red Queens, the Knights, the old Red King, are individuals who feel intensely, so that the ballet is full of the excitement and tension of warring emotions.

Robert Helpmann, experienced in the theatre both as an actor and a producer, has followed Ninette de Valois' example in bringing the theatre and the ballet closer together. The groupings and movement he composed for Tyrone Guthrie's production of *Peer Gynt* provided the most excitingly successful example I have seen of this form of collaboration, which ought to be much more common in the theatre than it is. William Chappell does not exaggerate when he says that the theatre and the drama "desperately need the choreographer to revivify their almost inanimate bodies. . . . There is practically nothing from Shakespeare to Shaw, from melodrama to music-hall, from Congreve to cabaret, that a partnership in production between legitimate director and choreographer would not imbue with a fresh and more vital life".

In his first work, *Comus*, Helpmann made the experiment of introducing speech into ballet. Ashton had already used speech brilliantly in *Wedding Bouquet*, in the form of a satirical running commentary spoken by Constant Lambert from a stage box; but in *Comus* speech is used not as a commentary but as part of the leading role. The experiment has some justification on the grounds that *Comus* was written as a masque for speech and dancing, but it is performed in Helpmann's version as a ballet, not as a masque, and it is a negation of the whole essence of ballet when a climax, instead of being expressed in dance, is expressed in speech. In his second ballet, *Hamlet*, Helpmann proved to be the first choreographer to make a successful ballet from a Shakespeare play. Other choreographers who have attempted this have merely told the story of the play in ballet form. The results have been little more than a danced version of one of *Lamb's Tales from Shakespeare*. In *Hamlet* Helpmann has done something entirely different. He has told us what he feels about the play. In doing so he has stressed what has been missing from every production of the play I have ever seen —the foetid, decadent atmosphere of the court, that vicious little world foul with lechery and cynicism and treachery which filled young Hamlet with revulsion and despair. Shakespeare's *Hamlet* is full of horror, but there is little of it in the usual stage production with its trim little court as neat and pretty as the pictures of kings and queens and their courtiers in a child's story book. It has been claimed for Helpmann's ballet that it is literary criticism expressed in terms of the dance, that the choreographer has suggested Freudian explanations for Hamlet's actions by the identification of the Queen with Ophelia, by making the Gravedigger and Yorick one person in Hamlet's mind, and so on. There is no question that one's understanding of the play is increased by seeing the ballet, not because it is "literary criticism" but because the nightmarish impression of what flickers distortedly through Hamlet's dying brain makes one experience the events of the play afresh and with extraordinary intensity. The importance of this ballet is that it is the first to demand the minds as well as the emotions of its audience. It lifts ballet from its own purely sensuous little world into the wider world of the theatre.

The success of *Hamlet* both with the critics and the public was regarded with mixed feelings by some of the more thoughtful supporters of the Wells company who were beginning to feel that the choreographers were deriving their inspiration too much from literature, painting and the drama, that the purely sensuous appeal of the ballet was being underrated, that story and character were being given overmuch attention, that there was too much acting and not enough dancing. When Helpmann's *Miracle in the Gorbals* was produced several of the critics took up the cry of "not enough dancing" and the ballet was given less praise than I think it deserved.

It is full of dancing. The story is told with the minimum of mime, but without any long solos or *pas de deux*. When a ballet tells a story without holding up the action for an occasional aria, the majority of the audience usually feels that there is "not enough dancing". But there is another reason why *Miracle in the Gorbals* gives the impression of containing much less dancing than in fact it does. The characterisation is so vivid, the theme so dramatically handled, and the solidly built set so much more realistic than the usual ballet scene that the audience, absorbed in the story and its protagonists, are for long stretches hardly conscious that it is a ballet, not a play, they are watching. Yet it always *is* a ballet. The characterisation, although much fuller and more complete than anything hitherto attempted in ballet, is invariably expressed in terms of the dance. The purists may object that there is something badly wrong when an audience becomes more intent upon story and character than upon the steps and movements of the dancers; that in fact a ballet such as *Miracle in the Gorbals* is as much a misuse and debasement of its art as the sort of "programme music" which attempts a realistic imitation of everyday sounds and noises. I sympathise with this point of view, as I sympathise with those who ask nothing more from ballet than that it should continue to be the most perfect form of escapist entertainment, but I believe that in *Miracle in the Gorbals* Helpmann has given new vitality and importance to ballet by bridging the gap between drama, and ballet, and by doing so without the use of clumsy incongruous devices such as the interpolation of passages of declamation and scenes acted in dumbshow.

Having bridged the gap between drama and ballet, Helpmann in his next work, *Adam Zero*, crossed over the bridge and became a theatrical producer instead of a choreographer. *Adam Zero* hardly requires ballet dancers. With the exception of the part danced by June Brae, most of it could be performed by actors with some elementary knowledge of stylised movement, supported by a group of dancers in the early stages of their training. Judged simply as a theatrical production, it is old-fashioned and derivative. All the stale tricks of the German and American expressionists are dragged out again to deck out this platitudinous allegory of the birth, life and death of man presented as a series of unending cycles.

I have seldom seen anything in the theatre which invoked so many memories and comparisons. "That", I found myself thinking, "reminds me of Toller's *Masses and Men*: there's a scene just like this in Capek's *Adam the Creator*: surely Adam Zero can't be the same character as that Mr. Zero who was the hero of *The Adding Machine*: Kaiser used these tricks in *From Morn to Midnight*—and there goes another of his from *Gas*: isn't what's happening now very like what happened in Thornton Wilder's *The Skin of Your Teeth*: and this old 'anti-illusionist' stuff of showing the stage hands at work and exposing the lighting apparatus and the rest of the stage mechanism to the audience—we used to do that years and years ago at the Cambridge Festival Theatre after we had been on a trip to Germany."

I am not suggesting that the author and producer of *Adam Zero* have been guilty of deliberate plagiarism. It is unlikely that they have seen or read many of the expressionist plays of the 'twenties, and the author, Michael Benthall, has protested that he never even saw *The Skin of Your Teeth*; but the expressionist technique is so arid that anyone adopting it is inevitably forced to use much the same small repertoire of tricks, and they are tricks that once seen do not bear repetition. That was the chief reason why the expressionist drama so soon became sterile—that and the fact that it made so little use of the art of the actor, reducing him to a mere nameless symbol, a characterless puppet. In the same way *Adam Zero* denies the dancer the use of his art, and debases ballet to a mere tongue-tied imitation of a type of drama that the theatre invented and quickly discarded some twenty years ago.

To realise how crude and cumbrous is Helpmann's method in *Adam Zero* of stating the obvious, one has only to compare it with *Dante Sonata* in which Ashton says so much more and says it far more eloquently, using nothing but expressive, inventive movement and the simplest costumes and décor. All Ashton's work is purely choreographic. He is not much interested in story-telling or character. His primary interest is the dancer. While the originality of the Wells' other two choreographers lies mainly in their choice of themes and their experiments in enlarging the scope of ballet, Ashton's originality is in his genius for inventing steps and movements, especially for solos and *pas de deux*. Ballets such as *Les Rendezvous* and *Les Patineurs*—little more than a series of divertissements—are not generally regarded as being in any way particularly new or original, but choreographically they are far more genuinely original and inventive than much more strikingly and obviously unusual ballets such as *Hamlet* and *Job*.

In temperament his work is in marked contrast to that of de Valois and Helpmann. It has all the lyrical and romantic qualities that theirs lacks. He is at his best in evoking a mood rather than in developing a theme. In much of his work there is a note of nostalgic melancholy, and yet, paradoxically enough, he is the only English choreographer who has genuine gaiety as opposed to mere jollity. In spite of his wit and sophistication his work is less intellectual than that of the Wells' other choreographers and much more sensuous—so much so that at times it has been criticised as being too frankly sensual. In England we are curiously reluctant to admit and accept the fact that ballet is the most sexual of the arts, both in its origin and its appeal.

Ashton's greatest creation, *Dante Sonata*, achieves an intensity of emotion which hitherto had seemed to be beyond the scope of ballet. This work is usually described as being inspired by the sufferings of Poland. It may be so, but I had not heard this explanation when I first saw the ballet, and in spite of that it moved me as deeply as anything I have ever seen in a theatre. The theme is the clash of the forces of Good and Evil in the world, with neither side victorious in the end. It is a bitter work, created in a mood of passionate anger and despair. To me it will always symbolise not the agony of Poland but the impact of the outbreak of war on the mind of a creative artist. To the future historian of the ballet it may mark the beginning of a new development in ballet towards a more personal expression of intensely experienced emotions.

Ashton's first post-war ballet, *Symphonic Variations*, was produced at Covent Garden the week after *Adam Zero* and is so complete a contrast to Helpmann's ballet that it is difficult to believe that it was not composed as a protest against the "every picture tells a story" type of ballet of which *Adam Zero* is an extreme example. *Symphonic Variations* is an equally extreme example of "pure ballet". There is no story, no theme, no attempt to "interpret" the music, no characterisation, no drama. There are only six dancers. Setting and costumes could hardly be more simple. The choreography deliberately avoids any obviously startling effects. It is simply a continuous, intricate, unbroken pattern of movement. In spite of its completely abstract quality I found it much more deeply moving than any of the "human story" ballets. It is difficult to explain why, just as it is difficult to explain why one is moved emotionally by the lines of a beautiful building or by the formal pattern of a Bach fugue. Perhaps the explanation is that this is one of those rare ballets which heighten and intensify one's response to the mood and pattern of the music because the choreographer, besides reacting emotionally to music, has completely understood and appreciated its structure.

The choreographers at the Wells owe much more than is generally realised to the collaboration of Constant Lambert. It is rare, if not unique, for a ballet company to have as its musical director a musician of Lambert's standing. The work entails too much sheer drudgery to offer much attraction to a conductor of the first rank. Lambert, in his loyalty to the Wells' company, has sacrificed to it two careers: his career as a composer and his career as an orchestral conductor. At a time when the conductors of foreign ballet companies visiting London had the London Philharmonic in the pit, Lambert was patiently persevering with an orchestra which was no more than "the best that could be expected under the circumstances". His greatest contribution to the development of the Wells' company has been his unerring knowledge of what constitutes good ballet music. *Horoscope* is the only ballet he has composed himself, but his choice and arrangement of music for *Les Rendezvous, Les Patineurs, The Prospect Before Us* and *Promenade*, among others, show not only his unfailing understanding of the requirements of choreographer and dancer, but also his unfaltering taste. A part of his work which is seldom commented upon is his skill in rescoring for an orchestra much smaller than that for which the music was originally written. Anyone who has heard a concert performance of *Job*, will have realised how astonishingly little was lost in Lambert's brilliant rescoring for the Sadler's Wells orchestra. As a conductor of ballet he has a genius for satisfying the requirements of choreographers and dancers in the matter of tempi without doing violence to the composer's intentions, and he can nurse a dancer through a difficult solo with the utmost tact. The scrupulous care he takes over the performance of every work is particularly noticeable in a ballet such as *Giselle*. Most conductors spend little time or trouble over this pallid, thankless score, but Lambert manages to revitalise it and give it colour and charm and dramatic force.

A criticism often brought against the Sadler's Wells company is that it has discovered for itself only one solitary choreographer. With the exception of Robert Helpmann every new English choreographer of any importance has been discovered and developed by Marie Rambert, a woman who frankly acknowledges and accepts the fact that she has no creative ability of her own, but who has a remarkable gift for inspiring others to create. It was she who commissioned Ashton to produce his first ballet, and it was at the Ballet Club that he gained his early experience as a choreographer.

The Ballet Club was founded by Marie Rambert in 1931 to give Sunday evening performances of ballet at the Mercury Theatre, which had been built by her husband, Ashley Dukes. Most of the leading English dancers appeared there as guests stars at one time or another but the permanent company was drawn from the Rambert school. In those days the Ballet Club company seemed to hold much more promise for the future than Sadler's Wells. Almost every month it had something new to show us. A new ballet, or a new designer, or some young member of the company appearing triumphantly for the first time in an important role. There was an exciting air of creativeness about the place. Marie Rambert, with her passion for discovering new talent, fired her company with the idea that each and any of them might have creative gifts. Ashton was not the only choreographer she found among her dancers in those early days. Anthony Tudor was her next discovery. Soon there were Frank Staff, Andrée Howard and Walter Gore to be added to the list. She created designers, too, from among her dancers. William Chappell, for instance, was given his first opportunity to design when he was one of the Rambert dancers. While the Sadler's Wells company relied on established designers and well-known painters, Rambert, more adventurous in her search for talent, went farther afield and found Sophie Fedorovitch and Hugh Stevenson to share the designing with Chappell. In her choice of dancers Rambert showed the same flair for recognising undeveloped talent as she displayed in her choice of choreographers and designers. She has never been afraid of mistaking precocity for talent. When some of her swans turn out to be geese after all she wastes no time on regrets. She is too busy eagerly questing after still more new talent. For each of her new discoveries she excitedly predicts a glowing future. She makes no secret of her convictions, least of all to the dancers themselves; but her ebullient optimism is mingled with so many ferocious criticisms, exhortations and imprecations that there is little danger of her prodigies becoming complacent. At a time when Ninette de Valois seemed to be deliberately repressing any signs of individuality among her company, Rambert was encouraging her young dancers to develop character and personality. Or perhaps they developed it in sheer self-defence so as not to be overwhelmed by Rambert's own vivid, excitable, flamboyant personality. Whatever the reason, the dancing at the Ballet Club had a sparkle, an air of spontaneity and enjoyment which made the Sadler's Wells company seem ploddingly conscientious by comparison.

How was it then that Rambert with a company that included Frederick Ashton, Harold Turner, Walter Gore, William Chappell, Andrée Howard, Pearl Argyle, Diana Gould and Maude Lloyd allowed herself to be outstripped by the steady but by no means rapid progression of the Sadler's Wells company until eventually she had to surrender nearly all her best dancers as well as her chief choreographer to the other company? Rambert seemed to be every bit as well equipped as de Valois to create the first important English Ballet company. What she had to yield to de Valois as a creative artist was more than compensated for by her gift for inspiring others to create. As a teacher she was acknowledged to be the best in England, and she seemed to have a keener eye for new talent than de Valois. There was nothing to choose between the two women in taste, intelligence and integrity. Neither lacked anything of energy and enterprise. On the whole the advantage seemed with Rambert, especially as at the start the more interesting and colourful young dancers tended to rally round Rambert rather than de Valois, whose personality in those days seemed forbiddingly stern and repressive. But Rambert lacked one gift which eventually proved to be de Valois' strongest asset—a genius for long term planning. Rambert was, I think, taken a little by surprise by her own success. When it came she was not prepared for the next step. Ninette de Valois' progress was as carefully planned as the advance of a good general. Each objective was achieved in accordance with a timetable worked out long beforehand. Her first objective was to capture a suitable base for her operations, to install herself in a theatre where her company could become a permanency and where it would have room to expand. Had Rambert realised in time the necessity for finding a larger stage for her company, had she set about raising the financial backing, which I think she could have done without any difficulty, had she been as adventurous in her business policy as she was in her artistic policy, then perhaps the leading English ballet company of to-day would have been under a different director.

But it is unwise to sympathise with anyone for failing to achieve ambitions they may never have possessed. It may be that Rambert has had no desire to assume the responsibilities of a full scale company. I have never heard her speak with any bitterness of the loss of so much of her best talent to the Sadler's Wells company. She has accepted it as inevitable that dancers, choreographers and designers should seek larger opportunities. It may be that intimate "chamber ballet", which has been the Ballet Club's special contribution to choreography, is what she prefers. We owe to Rambert, and to the choreographers she has found and encouraged, exquisite miniatures such as Ashton's *Capriol Suite*, *Mephisto Waltz*, *Lady of Shalot* and *Foyer de Danse*; Andrée Howard's *Death and the Maiden* and her *Lady into Fox*, based on David Garnett's novel; Frank Staff's witty *Czernyana*, a satire on various fashions in choreography; Walter Gore's *Confessional*, an experiment in which the dancing is partly to music and partly to the rhythmic declamation of Browning's poetry; Anthony Tudor's *Jardin aux Lilas*, *Gala Performance* and *Dark Elegies*. The last of these is a perfect example of "chamber ballet". It is simply a suite of dances to Mahler's *Kindertotenlieder*. The note is one of infinite sadness, a mood which one would have thought to be beyond the scope of ballet. I very much doubt if the sadness and poignancy of *Dark Elegies* would be achieved in a longer ballet or in a larger theatre.

Anthony Tudor has been lost to America. Had he remained in England it is unlikely that he would have found his opportunities as a choreographer comparable to those he has been given in America. A full size ballet company such as Sadler's Wells cannot reasonably be expected to add more than three new works to its repertoire each year. Possessing its own choreographers of the calibre of Ashton, de Valois and Helpmann, it can hardly be blamed for not giving opportunities to others. Now that the Sadler's Wells Opera Ballet has been formed as a subsidiary company, there will be further opportunities for choreographers. But not enough. It is difficult to see how ballet in England can ever give reasonable opportunities to aspiring young choreographers. It is unlikely that for many years to come there will be a sufficient number of good dancers to provide the personnel for more than one first class company. A company working on the scale of Sadler's Wells must necessarily be cautious about entrusting a ballet to a young and untried choreographer. A ballet is not like a play, the merits of which can to a large extent be assessed from a script. The choreographer creates during rehearsals and can give no more than a very general outline of his intentions beforehand; and because a choreographer is at the same time the director and the creator of a ballet, he cannot, like an ordinary theatrical producer, be replaced during the early stages of rehearsal if he is not shaping satisfactorily. Success as a choreographer at the Ballet Club is no certain guarantee of an ability to produce a full scale work. The intimacy of the Ballet Club provides conditions which are far more favourable to the inexperienced choreographer than those in any ordinary theatre. A work of art for the theatre is a combination of two entirely separate processes, the process of creation and the process of projection. Creation is an instinct; projection is a matter of technique. Technique can only be developed by experience. At the Ballet Club the audience in even the back row of the theatre are so close to the stage that the problem of projection hardly arises. Another way in which the Ballet Club favours the apprentice choreographer is that the audience are satisfied with far shorter ballets than they would be in a normal theatre. It is largely a coterie audience, many of whom know one another, so the intervals are pleasantly sociable and nobody minds if the programme consists of four very brief ballets and three long intervals. The advantage to the inexperienced choreographer is that he is not called upon for a long and sustained effort, with the variety of invention which that necessarily entails.

It is fortunate for English ballet that even in the early days there was no real rivalry between the Rambert and de Valois companies. That the Sadler's Wells company has achieved so much in so comparatively short a time has been to a considerable extent due to the fact that it was able to make use of talent discovered and developed at the Ballet Club. Now that the prestige of the Sadler's Wells company ensures that its school will have the pick of the best young talent in the country, there is no longer the same need for the Ballet Club as a recruiting ground for the larger company, but it is even more necessary than before as a ballet workshop, as a place for experiment before a specialised audience, as a nursery for choreographers and designers, and, above all, as the home of *ballet intime* which Rambert has proved to be not just ballet on a reduced scale but a form of its own. The Rambert company also fulfils a great need by providing ballet in the smaller towns where the theatres are not large enough for a full size ballet company. During the war the company did valuable pioneer work playing one night stands in factory hostels and small towns where no first-class ballet had ever been seen before.

The Sadler's Wells company's provincial appearances will in the future be limited because of long seasons at Covent Garden and tours abroad. If the Rambert company is to retain its individuality it cannot be expected to take the place of the Sadler's Wells company in the larger provincial theatres. Obviously *ballet intime* is unsuited to a large theatre. To make up for the absence of the Sadler's Wells company, the provinces will have to rely mainly on the International Ballet.

This organisation, directed by Mona Inglesby, has yet to prove itself a properly balanced ballet company. At present it is no more than an assemblage of dancers supporting a solitary star. Recently the company has called in actors to their aid and begun to develop a policy which Mona Inglesby describes as "ballet with acting". Her contention is that "to a ballet company actors can bring just the necessary weight and strength required to give productions proper balance and power". Her first two experiments in this direction, *Twelfth Night* and *Everyman*, were little more than the plays in dumb-show incongruously dotted here and there with songs and speeches from the original texts. But in *Comus* Mona Inglesby found an entirely legitimate means for combining actors, singers and dancers. It was produced, not as in Helpmann's version as a ballet with a couple of interpolated speeches, but in its entirety as a masque with the ballet used as Milton directed it should be used.

There are exciting possibilities for the future in such marriages of the actor and the dancer, each respecting the other's art but making no attempt to imitate it. It is a union which should stir the imagination of the poets, and bring some of them back into the theatre again.

The Mercury already provides a theatre for poets, but the smallness of stage and auditorium tends to encourage an intimate, literary style. A masque on the scale of Mona Inglesby's production of *Comus*, designed to be played in huge theatres, demands bold, richly coloured, declamatory verse. It needs 'popular' poetry in the literal sense of that much debased word. The masque has never been fully developed as a form of theatrical entertainment. To suggest its revival in the modern theatre may sound suspiciously like artiness, but I have seen *Comus* played to an audience which packed out a huge theatre in Blackpool. Probably most of the audience had not the slightest idea of what they were going to see. *Comus* was being performed by a ballet company so they took it for granted they were going to see a ballet. Yet they listened to Milton's verse not just with respect but with enjoyment. *Comus* is the sort of entertainment one would have thought suitable only for a few special performances in the hall of an Oxford college or by one of the more esoteric Sunday societies. Something very odd is happening to English audiences. They are willing to listen to fine speech again. Mona Inglesby is performing a great service to the theatre by using the huge drawing power of the ballet to bring into the theatre audiences who would not otherwise come to listen to poetry, but who, having come, find they enjoy it.

The International Ballet is at its best in *Comus*, for with actors bearing part of the burden of the production the demands made on the ballet company are not beyond its very limited strength. More productions of this sort may provide a partial solution to the difficulties of attempting to run another full-scale ballet company in addition to Sadler's Wells while the number of first-rate dancers in England is still insufficient for more than one company.

The future development of English ballet is largely dependent on an increase in the supply of good dancers. Now that the Sadler's Wells company has become the National Ballet, with Covent Garden Opera House as its home and a government department giving it not only its blessing but also a financial guarantee, ballet dancing has achieved the status of an officially recognised profession, and parents will be more willing to consider it as a career for their children. The Sadler's Wells school now undertakes the general education of its younger pupils. There are scholarships which make it possible for promising children living in the provinces to come to Sadler's Wells instead of being dependent on local dancing teachers for their training. Thus English ballet dancers can now be trained from a very early age under conditions similar to those in the Imperial Ballet School, still maintained by the present régime in Russia under a different name but with its traditions unchanged.

Already the results of the long and rigorous training at the Sadler's Wells school can be observed in the very high standard of dancing among the younger members of the company. Particularly noticeable is the quality of some of the young male dancers. This is something entirely new in English ballet. Until very recently the male dancer in England began his training at far too late an age and consequently developed slowly. Parents who regarded ballet classes as a normal part of the education of their daughters were shocked if their sons showed any desire to learn ballet dancing. It was considered a sign of effeminacy. Consequently the male dancer was usually unable to begin his training until he was in his 'teens and at last able to wear down parental opposition. Gradually the ever-increasing popularity and understanding of ballet among all classes is beginning to have its effect in weakening this prejudice, and one of the most important features of the Sadler's Wells school is the number of young boys who are being trained to take their place in the company. But obviously it will be some years before these young dancers are ready for leading parts. Until then the development of English ballet will be severely handicapped by a lack of male dancers, due to the fact that the war deprived the ballet of all its male dancers except those physically unfit for service or under military age. The ballet dancer suffers far more than the actor from an enforced break in his career. An actor returning to the stage after an interval of several years can resume his profession with his talents unimpaired, sometimes even benefited by experiencing life away from the narrow confines of the theatre, and he can continue his career almost to the end of his days. But the ballet dancer rapidly deteriorates without constant practice and he returns unhappily aware that because the stage life of a ballet dancer is short there is no longer time for him to fulfil his ambitions. If the government had exempted even as few as half a dozen of our best male dancers English ballet would not now be arrested in its development while it waits for a new generation to grow up. Nor perhaps would the Sadler's Wells company have to endure so many scathing comparisons with the Soviet companies, made by visitors to Moscow and Leningrad who omitted to take into consideration the fact that during the war the Russians exempted all their male dancers from military service. In England the official attitude was that "the public wouldn't stand for the spectacle of obviously healthy young men skipping about in a ballet". Yet a number of obviously healthy young actors on the stage and films were exempted (and rightly) as key men, without causing public indignation. Presumably this differentiation between the actor and the dancer was because many people still think ballet dancing is "not a man's job" despite the fact that it demands infinitely higher standards of training, discipline and stamina than acting. If training to become an actor required anything like the amount of guts necessary to qualify as a dancer, the stage would be a considerably less crowded profession than it is. Whenever I have worked on productions including dancers as well as actors, the efficiency of the dancers during rehearsals, their quickness and their enthusiasm, their discipline and their capacity for hard work have made me ashamed for the straight actors in the cast who seem, by comparison, slow, fumbling, lackadaisical and ill-trained.

The English theatre has much to learn from the Sadler's Wells and Rambert companies about such matters as continuity of purpose, integrity, teamwork, respect for tradition combined with eagerness to experiment, and the maintenance of the highest possible standard of performance by means of constant practice and rehearsal. But the theatre will always be at a disadvantage compared with the ballet because acting has become, in London at least, only a part-time job. Filming and broadcasting absorb much of the actor's time, thoughts and energies. To-day in the theatre it is only the ballet dancer whose loyalty to his art is undivided and he practises it with a singleness of purpose now almost unknown among actors.

CHAPTER XI

BARRY JACKSON

One of the unhealthiest features of the English theatre is the subservience of the provinces to the standards and tastes of London. The provincial likes to think of himself as a sturdy, independent sort of fellow, with a mind and opinions of his own. He may be. I don't know. All that I do know is that as a playgoer he suffers from a bad inferiority complex. He is completely bedazzled by "the West End". He is convinced that in the theatre all good things come only from London. With humble gratefulness he accepts the worn-out, cast-off West End show after it has been run nearly to its death in London and is finally released to spend its dotage in the provinces. The "Full West End Cast", long ago bored to desperation with their parts, rattle through the play for the four or five hundredth time, bawling themselves hoarse in the faint hope of being heard in the farthest distances of some vast provincial auditorium. The provincial sees nothing wrong. "It's a London show." So there can't be anything wrong. The theatre is packed—just as it is also packed for the "prior-to-London" production, always provided that there are one or two big names in the cast. "So-and-so is in it, so it *must* be good", thinks the provincial. The theatre is sold out before the company arrives. Shows that have played to capacity in the provinces come to London and flop dismally. The players, misled by the uncritical enthusiasm of the bedazzled provincial audiences, are ingenuously surprised and disappointed, but the management is not unduly disturbed. Production expenses have probably been recovered on the provincial tour. A prior-to-London tour with big names in the cast has become a form of insurance against loss on a doubtful play.

Even provincial repertory theatres have to confine themselves almost entirely to plays that in the past have been approved by London audiences. Sometimes, to break the monotony, these repertories venture to revive a classic, but generally it has to be one recently revived in London. For instance, the West End revivals of *The Importance of Being Earnest*, *The Doctor's Dilemma* and *Ghosts* at once made these plays "safe for rep". In the eyes of the provinces they had become "West End plays".

The history of the Birmingham Repertory Theatre under the direction of Sir Barry Jackson provides a typical example of the provincial playgoer's lack of enterprise, judgment and taste. Birmingham is supposed to be a theatrically minded city. London companies on tour consider it a good date. Yet in twenty-one years Barry Jackson lost a hundred thousand pounds by persisting in running a repertory theatre as a place for fresh, creative work instead of as a pallid imitation of the London stage.

The population of Birmingham is over a million. The seating capacity of its Repertory Theatre is under five hundred. Three weeks has been the usual run of each production, so if only ten thousand of the million inhabitants of Birmingham had gone regularly to the Repertory once in every three weeks it would have been full at every performance.

Obviously there is something very badly wrong with a population of a million people out of which there were not even ten thousand who occasionally wanted to see plays by Shakespeare, Sheridan, Goldsmith, Chekov, Ibsen, Shaw, Synge, Granville Barker and Wilde. Not that Barry Jackson confined himself to the classics. He also gave his audience Barrie, Galsworthy, Pinero, Milne and Maugham. Admittedly he sometimes scared away all but the most faithful of his timid audience by experiments such as the first English production of Kaiser's expressionistic play, *Gas*, or by putting on *Six Characters in Search of an Author* when Pirandello was still popularly supposed to be an entirely incomprehensible dramatist. On the other hand, he discovered for Birmingham (and for London afterwards) new comedies such as *Bird in Hand* and *The Farmer's Wife*. He did not despise full-blooded melodrama, and included *The Corsican Brothers* and *Therèse Raquin* in his programmes. He put on musical burlesques such as *Ten Nights in a Bar Room*, and, as a Christmas entertainment for Birmingham, created *1066 and All That*—another of his productions which afterwards had a huge success in London. Undeterred by the smallness of his theatre he varied his programmes still further by the occasional production of small-scale operas including *The Boatswain's Mate*, *Cosi Fan Tutte*, *Don Giovanni* and *The Immortal Hour*. His greatest achievement was the first production on any stage of the whole of *Back to Methuselah*. Although people journeyed from all over England to see this, so few of the citizens of Birmingham were interested that there were empty seats at most performances.

These productions give some idea of the breadth and variety of Barry Jackson's tastes. He enjoys almost any kind of theatrical entertainment that is, of its kind, first-rate, but he refused to follow tamely on the heels of the West End managers. He was determined that his should be a theatre where new playwrights were given an opportunity. The standard of acting, production and design was far above anything to be seen elsewhere in the provinces, and considerably better than what the London theatres usually had to show. In his companies at Birmingham were players who rapidly became world-famous—Cedric Hardwicke, Gwen Ffrangcon-Davies, Leslie Banks, Peggy Ashcroft and Laurence Olivier. His producers—H. K. Ayliff and A. E. Filmer—were men with far more than local reputations. His chief designer, Paul Shelving, was one of the best designers in England. As to the theatre itself, it is central, it is comfortable, and the prices low.

Why then did Birmingham support the Repertory Theatre so poorly that twice Barry Jackson was driven in despair to announce the closing of the theatre and the transference of his theatrical activities elsewhere? The dull, timid, "wait-and-see-what-London-thinks" attitude of the provinces is only a part explanation. There was more than mere indifference in Birmingham's attitude towards the Repertory. There was also a certain amount of resentment, even hostility.

The reason for Birmingham's disapproval was, I think, the fact that here was a theatre which quite plainly was not being run primarily for profit. The implication was that it was being run to please the taste of the owner rather than the taste of the public. In a community where profit-making is the dominant motive the public is given an illusory sense of power. It is flattered and cajoled. Everybody is out to please the public, to give the public what it wants or what it is made to think it wants. It was exasperating for Birmingham to find that here in the middle of their city was a theatre which was not prepared to adopt a proper attitude of servility towards the public. Because the director of the theatre was a rich man, not wholly dependent on their half-crowns, they were not in a position to hector him into behaving as they thought fit. It was a challenge to their power and they resented it. The repertory was gibed at as a rich man's plaything. It was contemptuously referred to as Barry Jackson's "hobby". To run a theatre for any other reason than for profit seemed to the Midlander a frivolous occupation meriting contempt rather than admiration.

There were people in Birmingham who attributed a more sinister motive to Barry Jackson's activities. They suspected him of trying to educate the public. The Englishman has nothing against education but he thinks it should be kept in its place. He resents any attempt to mix it with his amusements. He knows what he wants, and he sees no reason why anyone should try to educate him up to wanting something else.

Birmingham was needlessly suspicious. Barry Jackson simply put on plays because there were a great many plays of every sort which he liked and wanted to see in his theatre, acted, produced and mounted in the way that he thought they ought to be done. As his taste in plays was anything but narrow he naturally, and not unreasonably, hoped that in a city the size of Birmingham there would be a minimum audience of at least a few thousand people to share his tastes. If not, he was prepared to pay heavily out of his own pocket for the pleasure of running a theatre to please himself. In fact, instead of being an altruist, a missionary, or an educationalist, Barry Jackson was, to the great benefit of the English theatre, a thoroughly selfish man who obstinately persisted in doing what he wanted, and not what the Birmingham public had wanted (and had been given) for the past ten or twenty years.

There is no need in this chapter to chronicle the history of the Repertory in any detail. That has already been done by Bache Matthews in *The History of the Birmingham Repertory Theatre*, which deals with the period from the opening until 1924, and by T. C. Kemp in *The Playhouse and the Man*, which continues the story up to 1943. But it may be useful to recapitulate the main facts.

In 1907 a group of amateur actors, which included John Drinkwater, started reading and acting plays at Barry Jackson's house at Moseley. Calling themselves The Pilgrim Players, with Barry Jackson as their producer, they gave performances of Shakespeare, Sheridan, Ibsen and Yeats in the surrounding district, acting in church halls and assembly rooms. Gradually the company became semi-professional and the name was changed to The Birmingham Repertory Company. In 1913 the company opened its own theatre in Station Street, Birmingham—the first theatre to be built in England for the purposes of repertory. Throughout the war of 1914–18 the theatre remained open. By the early 'twenties its reputation extended far beyond Birmingham, mainly as a result of the company's visits to London. But in Birmingham itself attendances remained so consistently poor that in 1924 Barry Jackson decided to close the theatre and transfer his activities to London.

The result of this announcement is described by Kemp in his book. "The bad news spread quickly and the city that had failed to support the theatre when open was alarmed at the prospect of its closing. It was a good thing to have an intelligent theatre in the place: it brought cultural credit: it was a fitting adjunct to the second city in the country: its disappearance from the civic scene must be prevented. The Birmingham Civic Society, a body with no direct official connections, but which had several sound civic achievements to its credit, immediately moved into action. A committee was formed on which the principal literary organisations and art societies were represented. The theatre was due to close on 9th February at the end of the run of *The Farmer's Wife.* That evening the Lord Mayor spoke from the stage giving details of a scheme by which an audience would be guaranteed if Barry Jackson would promise to reopen the theatre. Sir Barry's terms were that four thousand people should take tickets to attend the theatre once a fortnight for three months. Considering that Birmingham had over a million inhabitants and that the Midland area within easy reach had a couple of millions more, the conditions were not arduous; but it was not until July that the guarantee became sufficiently substantial to persuade Sir Barry to give Birmingham a second chance. The organising committee stuck valiantly to its job and rallied sufficient of the faithful to avert disaster. In September the theatre re-opened: but it had been a close call."

During the next ten years the theatre continued with its policy unchanged and the attitude of most of the citizens of Birmingham equally unchanged. Barry Jackson went on giving his audience Ibsen, Chekov, Shakespeare, Sheridan and Shaw, but he still gave them Lonsdale, Maugham, Coward, Barrie and Milne. Many plays were produced for the first time on any stage, including work by Bridie, Drinkwater, Eden Philpotts, Cicely Hamilton and Dorothy Massingham. Among the plays from other countries which Barry Jackson brought to England were Ghéon's *The Marvellous History of Saint Bernard*, Denis Johnston's *The Moon in the Yellow River*, and two plays by Elmer Rice, *Counsellor at Law* and *See Naples and Die*. Other notable productions of this period were Shaw's *Caesar and Cleopatra*, Pirandello's *Right You Are If You Think You Are*, Andreyev's *He Who Gets Slapped*, Molnar's *The Swan*, Capek's *The Macropulos Secret* and Klabund's *The Circle of Chalk*.

In 1934, the year of the theatre's coming-of-age, Birmingham was for the second time faced with the prospect of losing its Repertory Theatre. Ever since its opening, the story of the theatre had been, to quote Kemp again, "Barry Jackson versus Birmingham". He was exhausted and disillusioned by the long struggle. He announced that he could not continue it any longer. Once again the "cultural reputation" of Birmingham was at stake, and once again there were committees, meetings and leading articles in the local papers. This time Barry Jackson was adamant. There could be no question of his continuing to be solely responsible for the financial future of the theatre; but if funds could be raised to run the theatre on the same policy as before he was willing to be responsible for the general direction. An appeal for £20,000 was launched. The result was that about one-tenth of this sum was forthcoming. Meanwhile Barry Jackson and William Haywood, secretary of the Civic Society, agreed to be jointly responsible for a sum sufficient to guarantee the next season. Contributions continued to dribble in (the final total was only £3,000) and at the beginning of 1935 Barry Jackson transferred the whole of the shares, property and assets of the Birmingham Repertory Theatre to a local Trust on condition that the theatre's policy remained unchanged. In other words, Barry Jackson had given the theatre to the City. The Board of Trustees included representatives of the City of Birmingham, the University, the Rotary Club, the Repertory Playgoers' Society, and the Civic Society. Birmingham was thus the first city in England to have its own Civic Theatre.

The theatre restarted under the new régime with an unusually large number of serial ticket holders. Seemingly the hullabaloo over the threatened closing of the theatre had roused quite a number of people to become voucher-holders. In general outline the policy remained changed, but a fairly large proportion of recent West End successes found their way into the programme in the years that followed. On the other hand there were still new plays, and some interesting importations from America, such as Maxwell Anderson's *Winterset*. English and foreign classics remained on the programme, and just occasionally Birmingham was given something likely to startle and irritate it. But there were signs at last of a change in the Birmingham playgoers. When Auden and Isherwood's *The Ascent of F6* was put on it was expected to draw only a very limited audience. It packed the theatre and was revived the following season. But as an instance of the extent to which a policy of compromise was now influencing the programmes it is worth noting that the play which followed *The Ascent of F6* was a very trivial farce called *Our Ostriches* which had recently been running in London.

Under its new régime the Repertory was a less exciting and less important theatre than before. It lacked the adventurousness and the individuality which had made it so famous when it was run by a dictator instead of by a committee. On the other hand, now that it was Birmingham's "own" theatre, and no longer the property of a wealthy patron, there was not the same feeling of suspicion and distrust. Attendances were reasonably good, and up to the outbreak of war the Repertory continued without further crisis.

The war closed the theatre until 1941, when it was occupied for a year by Basil Langton's "Travelling Repertory Theatre". Then Barry Jackson took charge again on behalf of the Trust. Audiences were bigger than ever before, a large proportion of them part of the huge floating population that had come into the City on war work. With a view to making friends with this vast new potential audience a programme was chosen which consisted almost entirely of the lighter sort of play. It was only with a good deal of trepidation that a Shakespearian production was included. *The Taming of the Shrew* packed the theatre for four weeks. A few months later *As You Like It* played to equally good business. The third Shakespearian production was *The Winter's Tale*, generally considered to be one of the "unpopular" plays. Again the result was four weeks capacity business. Yet in the past some of Barry Jackson's bitterest experiences in Birmingham had been his failures with Shakespearian plays even as "safe" as *A Midsummer Night's Dream*.

An offshoot of the Birmingham Repertory Theatre was the Malvern Festival which Barry Jackson began in 1929. Obviously a festival presenting half a dozen plays in a season of only four weeks (it was less during the early years) can never be a paying proposition. Each year Barry Jackson stood the loss out of his own pocket. The Malvern Town Council contributed nothing, in spite of the fact that the town benefited to the extent of many thousands of pounds from the influx of visitors, as well as gaining immense publicity and prestige, not only in England but also on the continent and in America. It was only in the last year of the Festival, when Barry Jackson had withdrawn from it and its future seemed uncertain, that Malvern gave a guarantee against loss up to £1,000. Even then it was not a grant from the Town Council but a donation from two hundred and fifty of the townspeople who had banded themselves together as "The Keepers of the Festival".

Malvern made singularly little effort to contribute in other ways towards the success of the Festival. The attitude of the town was that of a grumpy old gentleman who having been persuaded against his will to go to a fancy dress ball, insists on going in his ordinary clothes and refuses to dance. Malvern obstinately refused to change either its habits or its appearance for the Festival. No festival ever had a less festive air.

At a summer festival the best part of the day should be in the evening after the show. Then is the time for a good talk over a leisurely meal and a bottle of wine. But Malvern refused to extend its licensing hours during the Festival, and no hotel at which I stayed would provide a meal after the show. I have dismal recollections of trying to prolong the evening in the Winter Gardens over a plate of sausage-and-mashed (if I were lucky) and a cup of aggressively English coffee, while a few couples shuffled round the dance floor in a despairing attempt to pretend that here was the very spirit of festival.

The first season at Malvern was a fortnight devoted to the plays of Bernard Shaw, including the first production of *The Apple Cart*. The rest of the programme consisted of *Back to Methuselah*, *Heartbreak House* and *Caesar and Cleopatra*. It had been intended that the second season should also be entirely Shavian, but a new play which had been expected did not materialise. Shaw was busy with the Collected Edition of his works. In order that the programme should not consist entirely of revivals, the first production of *The Barretts of Wimpole Street* was given at Malvern. In 1931 (when the Festival was extended to three weeks) and during the following two years, the programme was chosen to give a survey of five hundred years of English drama, ending with an entirely new play. Two of these were by Bridie (*The Switchback* and *The Sleeping Clergyman*); the other was Shaw's *Too True To Be Good*. From 1934 (when the Festival was extended to four weeks) until 1937 the programmes were a somewhat miscellaneous collection chosen according to no very obvious principle apart from the invariable inclusion of a Shaw play in acknowledgment of the fact that the Festival was dedicated to him. *The Simpleton of the Unexpected Isles*, *On The Rocks* and *The Millionairess* were given their first productions during these seasons.

After the 1937 season, Barry Jackson withdrew from the Festival. He was unable to agree with Roy Limbert, the lessee of the Malvern Theatre, on the future policy of the Festival.

The two seasons immediately before the war were presented by Limbert, whose policy was to depend entirely on new plays. On paper his first programme looked interesting. His authors were Bridie, Dunsany, C. K. Munro, Priestley and, of course, Shaw. But Bridie's *The Last Trump*, Dunsany's *Alexander*, Munro's *Coronation Time at Mrs. Beam's*, Priestley's *Music at Night* and Shaw's *Geneva* all seemed to be rather disappointing examples of the work of these authors. The solitary revival, *St. Joan*, was chiefly notable for an unfortunate piece of miscasting in the title role, which was played by Elisabeth Bergner. The following season, the last before the outbreak of war, consisted of Shaw's latest work, *In Good King Charles's Golden Days* and five new plays of little merit.

If the war had not intervened and the Festival had continued, it would obviously have been necessary to discover a new policy. It is unreasonable to expect people to give up a week of their holiday and travel from all over the country to take pot-luck with half a dozen new plays. Good new plays are too scarce for one management to find six each year, especially when the choice is limited by the plays all having to fit the same company of actors. Besides, any sensible playgoer realises that no good new play is going to be allowed to vanish into oblivion after a few performances at a summer festival. He knows that he will have plenty of opportunity later of seeing anything good that is discovered in a programme of half a dozen plays.

On the other hand, Barry Jackson's policy during the last four years that he directed the Festival was also unsatisfactory. During these seasons he presented the Birmingham Repertory Company in productions selected from their work during the past year, with the addition (except in 1934) of an entirely new Shaw play as the high-spot.

The practical advantages of such a scheme are obvious. The company and the producer are not subjected to the appalling strain of rehearsing six entirely new productions, all of which have to be given their first performance in the same week. But a festival requires more glitter and glamour and excitement than can be provided by any repertory company, however good. A festival must have an air of "something special". It needs big, exciting personalities.

It needs, too, more shape and design than can be discovered in a selection from a repertory company's work during a single year. There was a definite enough outline to the Festival programme of 1931–33, when each was a chronological survey of English play-writing, but these programmes had too specialised an appeal. Take, for example, the 1932 programme. It consisted of the anonymous *Conversion of St. Paul*, and *Gammer Gurton's Needle*, Heywood's *The Fair Maid of the West*, Dryden's *All For Love*, Sheridan Knowles' *The Love Chase*, Henry Arthur Jones' *The Dancing Girl* and Bridie's *The Sleeping Clergyman*. This is essentially a programme for the earnest student of the drama. Too many of these plays have little to recommend them to-day apart from their historical significance. Possibly the best policy at Malvern would have been to stick to Shaw. The Shavian repertoire is large, and first-rate performances of his plays are still comparatively rare. But it must be admitted that first-rate performances at Malvern were also rather rare. The system of using one company to perform six plays inevitably resulted in an unsatisfactory standard of production and acting. It was this that eventually forced Barry Jackson to use his Birmingham company at Malvern in plays they had already performed at the Repertory. The only satisfactory solution would have been the employment of several producers and a company so large that no member of it would have had to appear in more than three of the plays. Obviously this was financially impossible without a large subsidy. If in the future Malvern or any other town in England is to have a theatre festival it will have to contribute financially instead of relying on the generosity of a private patron to pay the losses while the town profits in prestige and extra business; and it will have to do more during out-of-theatre hours to welcome and entertain its visitors than Malvern ever attempted to do.

Birmingham and Malvern absorbed only a part of Barry Jackson's energies. Between 1922 and 1934 he produced forty-two plays in London. His policy as a London manager was simple. He disregarded all the theories of his fellow managers as to what the public wanted or didn't want and relied entirely on his own tastes and enthusiasms. For instance, at a time when the English public were supposed to have little use for opera even when it was very "grand", he put on an opera by a little-known composer with an unknown singer in the lead at a music hall opposite King's Cross Station and achieved a run of two hundred and sixteen performances. The opera was *The Immortal Hour* and the singer Gwen Ffrangcon-Davies. Although one of the firmest convictions of his fellow managers was that dialect plays were unpopular, he put on *The Farmer's Wife* at the Court Theatre and was rewarded with a run of one thousand three hundred and twenty-nine performances, the fourth longest run of a straight play in the history of the English stage—at a theatre which was supposed to be "off the map". Undeterred by warnings that the public would not stand for plays about literary figures, especially if they were Victorian, he grossed receipts of over £100,000 with a fifteen months' run of *The Barretts of Wimpole Street*. While on holiday in Savoy he saw a miracle play in the grounds of the Chateau de Menthon and made an English version of it called *The Marvellous History of Saint Bernard* which enchanted London until the general strike put an end to its run. He refreshed Shakespearian acting and production in England by putting on *Hamlet* in modern dress, which had a longer run than any production of the play for many years. He beat the so-called commercial managers at their own game with a year's run of a straightforward, good-humoured comedy, *Bird in Hand*. With a nine months' run of *The Apple Cart* he reduced to nonsense the managerial theory that Shaw was "uncommercial". He gave further proof of his versatility by scoring a smash hit with a new sort of musical, *1066 and All That*. For the minority playgoer he put on an example of German expressionistic drama, *The Adding Machine*, was responsible for the first public performance of *Six Characters in Search of an Author*, presented Edith Evans in *Rosmersholm*, and at the Court Theatre gave a series of performances of the whole of *Back to Methuselah* which took five consecutive evenings to play. During his twelve years in London he consistently ignored another principle of commercial management by never relying on ready-made stars. He made his own, including Cedric Hardwicke, and Gwen Ffrangcon-Davies. It was Barry Jackson who gave John Gielgud his first big chance when he cast him for Romeo, and he brought Laurence Olivier to London as Malcolm in the modern dress *Macbeth*, afterwards casting him for the lead in Tennyson's *Harold*. Edith Evans is another star whose development owes much to Barry Jackson who cast her brilliantly in several of his productions, and gave her the opportunity to make one of her biggest successes as Irela, the opera singer in *Evensong*.

Yet in spite of this record of achievement there are those within the theatre who still refer to Barry Jackson, with amiable contempt, as an amateur—the word that was so often used to describe Nigel Playfair too. The theatre has become so little an art and so much a business that anyone who is in theatre management because he wishes to impart and share his delight in his own enthusiasms rather than to amass huge profits is contemptuously regarded as unprofessional, an amateur. All the more so if he is a rich man who is so foolishly courageous that he backs his judgment with his private fortune instead of with money provided by other people. It was probably Barry Jackson's financial independence that irritated some of his fellow managers more than anything else. No wonder, since many of them were little more than the paid servants of their shareholders. They overlooked the fact that Barry Jackson would have needed to be a man of fabulous fortune to be able to put on forty-two plays in the West End as well as financing the Birmingham Repertory and the Malvern Festival had he not also been an excellent man of business. But his criterion of success was not, as it is with most managements of to-day, the size of the figure on his yearly balance sheet. Out of the profits on his successes he put on many plays on which he knew there was little or no hope of making a profit. They were plays in which he believed. When the ordinary manager says he believes in a play he means that he believes that it will make a lot of money. Barry Jackson believed in a play as a work of art. Often he was under no delusions that it was likely to appeal to a large audience, but he wanted to put it on the stage, he wanted it to be seen, and he hoped it would appeal to an audience of, say, fifty or sixty thousand people, enough to keep a play running for three months, but not enough for the play to be counted a box office success. Was this the behaviour of an amateur? According to present day standards of theatrical management it certainly was.

Barry Jackson's withdrawal from London management was an inestimable loss to the theatre. It was not forced upon him by financial failure. Two of his last productions, *Evensong* and *1066 And All That*, were among his biggest box office successes. It is unlikely that he was embittered by the comparatively short run of Maugham's *For Services Rendered*, as he could hardly have expected this harsh, relentless, tragic play to appeal to a large audience. Probably one of the reasons which finally decided him to leave the West End was the failure of *Too True To Be Good* after a run of only six weeks. "Failure" is a strange word to have to apply to a play which was drawing £1,000 a week into the box office when it had to be taken off. It is one of Shaw's least good plays, yet there were plenty of people in London who thought even one of Shaw's lesser works more worth seeing than many of the slick box office successes then running. But it was the cheaper seats that were packed. The stalls were sparsely filled. The thousand pounds a week which the "cheap" public were spending to see the play was six hundred pounds short of the weekly running expenses. This seemed to Barry Jackson final proof of the crazily unbusiness-like state of the finances of the West End theatre. It was not, of course, by any means his first experience of failure in London, but when previous productions of his had failed they had done so in a way that made it quite clear that the public were not interested in the play. *Too True To Be Good*, playing to £1,000 a week, was not, in his opinion, a failure. It thoroughly disheartened him that owing to the preposterously uneconomic cost of running a production in the West End he was compelled to take the play off when many people still wanted to see it.

There were of course other reasons besides the failure of *Too True To Be Good* which contributed to Barry Jackson's decision to withdraw to Birmingham and Malvern. I do not think he ever felt "settled" in the London theatre. Nobody who has built, owned and directed a theatre of his own can ever work altogether happily in someone else's theatre. He used to say that in London he felt as if he were always living in furnished apartments, with no roof of his own. Nor did he find these furnished apartments particularly good. They may have been clean, but they were certainly not comfortable. In his own theatre at Birmingham even the cheapest seat is a good one with a perfect view of the stage. It worried him that in the theatres he hired most of the cheaper seats were so uncomfortable, with such a peculiar view of the stage, that he used to marvel that anyone sat in them. During his years in London he worked in sixteen different theatres. He hated this haphazard, nomadic existence, wandering from theatre to theatre, working each time with a newly assembled company, achieving nothing permanent. The social life of the London theatre had no attractions for him. Whenever possible he avoided first night parties, lunches at the Ivy, suppers at the Savoy; which was perhaps one of the reasons why London theatre people never regarded Barry Jackson as one of themselves. Possibly they were right. He is a provincial, in the best sense of the word. His roots are in the Midlands. I think he is a happier man to-day than he ever was in London, now that he is back in his own theatre, directing his own company in his home town, with the nearby Shakespeare Memorial Theatre at Stratford-on-Avon as his other charge. Whether that is a tribute to him or a criticism of him I am not quite sure.

CHAPTER XII

THE SHAKESPEARE MEMORIAL THEATRE

THIS is a depressing chapter. It is a record of the failure to take advantage of a great opportunity.

In the spring of 1926 the Shakespeare Memorial Theatre at Stratford was burned to the ground. It was a peculiarly hideous and inconvenient building. Although there were some who for sentimental reasons regretted its end, most people shared the opinion of Bernard Shaw who sent a telegram which read: "Congratulations. You must be delighted".

Arrangements were immediately made for a local cinema to be converted into a temporary theatre and less than three weeks after the fire the leaders of the political parties—Stanley Baldwin, Lord Oxford and Asquith, and Ramsay MacDonald—together with Thomas Hardy, launched an appeal for the building and endowment of a new theatre. There was an immediate response from all over the world. Before the end of the year a large enough sum had been subscribed for the Governors to declare the plans for a new theatre open to competition.

This was the initial mistake. The wisest course would have been that adopted by the National Theatre Committee which appointed a sub-committee of technical experts to specify the requirements for a National Theatre and then select an architect to design a theatre according to those specifications. The Governors of the Shakespeare Memorial Theatre, when putting the design out for competition, did specify some of their requirements, but these were sketchy and inadequate, consisting of little more than a few measurements and an exhortation to competitors that they should design a building "simple, beautiful, convenient, a monument worthy of its purpose"; which is presumably the aim of any competent architect irrespective of whether he is designing a theatre, a town hall or a cricket pavilion.

No architect of standing will enter a competition unless the award is in the hands of the Royal Institute of British Architects. He very rightly demands that his work shall be judged by a jury of experts; but this means that those who are to employ the architect have no voice in his selection. It is no secret that the plans awarded first place by the assessors were not those that the Governors of the Shakespeare

Memorial Theatre preferred; but the decision of the R.I.B.A. in such a competition is final. Whether the R.I.B.A. or the Governors were right is not the point, although personally I think that the winning plans were easily the best of the six from which the final award was made. The point is that as a result of this disagreement Miss Elizabeth Scott, the architect, was immediately put in the unfortunate position of starting her work in an atmosphere of dissatisfaction and mistrust. Her work was made all the more difficult by the fact that during the planning and construction of the theatre the Governing Body was increased to such an extent that in the end there were over ninety governors, few of whom had the slightest practical experience or understanding of the theatre. This did not, however, deter many of them from voicing the strongest opinions on technical matters. On some points there were almost as many opinions as there were governors. As a result, almost every detail of the building in its final form was a weak compromise.

For instance, the technical committee which was headed by Norman Wilkinson and Barry Jackson and included the architect and engineers, decided after careful examination of other theatres both in England and the continent that a cyclorama was not desirable. The stage was designed accordingly. But at the last moment, in direct contravention of this decision, a cyclorama consisting of two hundred tons of steel and plaster was added to a stage which had never been designed for it. Similarly, the lighting equipment was designed for the remote control system, but at the last moment a standard switchboard was awkwardly crammed in.

The fundamental weakness in the design of the Memorial Theatre is the gulf between stage and auditorium. This would be a serious enough defect in any theatre, but it is doubly so in a theatre built for the plays of Shakespeare which were written for a platform stage with no proscenium arch and no barrier of any sort between actor and audience. One would have thought that the first aim of everybody concerned in the building of the Memorial Theatre would have been to minimise as far as possible the distance between actors and audience. Baliol Holloway has written of the difficulties with which an actor at Stratford has to contend. "The chief of these is due to the structure of the stage and auditorium. The acreage of blank walls between the proscenium arch and the ends of the circles, coupled with the immense distance between the lower edge of the stage proper and the front row of the stalls (which in an ordinary theatre would about correspond to the first row of the pit), completely destroys all contact between actors and audience. It is doubly hard on the actor that the audience does not realise this, and is aware only of the actor's comparative ineffectiveness."

It is true that at Stratford there is a forestage in front of the proscenium, but it is so badly related to the stage proper that it has every appearance of being an afterthought. It is impossible to combine satisfactorily a forestage and a conventional picture-frame stage. At Stratford when an actor moves forward on to the forestage he steps, quite literally, "out of the picture" framed in the proscenium arch. A producer attempting to use both forestage and picture-frame stage is faced with the insoluble problem of combining two totally different conventions of acting and production.

There are many other weaknesses in the design of the theatre. For instance, there is insufficient off-stage room for the sliding stages to roll completely out of sight. A section of each has been made flexible so that it slides up the side wall of the theatre. This makes it impossible to build a complete set on the sliding stages. The sections of the stage that are on lifts have proved still more impracticable. To be of any use for making changes of scenery these sections should sink to a depth of at least twenty feet. At Stratford they sink only eight feet. The whole of the back section of the stage is constructed to rise, but after it has risen only three feet, the heads of the actors standing on it are cut off from the view of the gallery. The proscenium arch should have had a minimum height of twenty-nine feet; its height is only twenty-one feet. It is an accepted principle of theatre design that access from the dressing-rooms to the stage should be up-stage. At Stratford it is down-stage. The doors leading on to the stage are inadequate for a theatre in which elaborately costumed crowds have frequently to make exits and entrances. The dressing-room doors are too narrow for an actress in Elizabethan costume to pass through without difficulty. Even the door handles seem to have been perversely designed to catch and tear any floating scarf or veil or piece of drapery. The star dressing-rooms are so awkwardly shaped and so narrow that it is difficult for the dresser to move to and fro without bumping into the actor as he sits at his dressing-table. The windows open directly over the heads of the gallery queue, so that in summer the actor is distracted by the chatter of the people in the queue if he has his windows open. The actual number of dressing-rooms is so small that it is seldom possible for anyone playing a leading part to have a room to himself. An actor playing an arduous part requires quiet and privacy before he goes on the stage, especially when he is playing a repertoire of parts and needs to refresh his memory by going over his lines. It is unfair on actors playing Othello and Iago that they should have to share the same room, that Hamlet and Laertes should have to dress together. There is no Green Room, a serious omission in a theatre where for weeks on end a company is in rehearsal and spends the greater part of the day as well as the evening in the theatre. There is no rehearsal room, and totally inadequate storage space.

It would be unfair to attribute the drawbacks of this singularly inconvenient building to its architect, engineers and technicians who were continually harassed and bewildered by conflicting opinions and instructions, and who worked from start to finish in an atmosphere of perpetual argument. The unhappy result is a theatre which may or may not fulfil the desire of its ninety-odd governors for a building "simple and beautiful", but which nobody can claim to be either "convenient" or "a monument worthy of its purpose". Most people who have worked at the Memorial Theatre in any capacity probably agreed with Herbert Farjeon's war-time article on Stratford in which he declared that "if the next bomb dropped by a Nazi raider on a public building in this country were to fall on the Shakespeare Memorial Theatre, the bones of the Bard might not lie uneasy in that unopened grave".

The new theatre was opened in 1932 with a singularly uninspired performance of *Henry IV Part I.* With the best will in the world the critics could not pretend that the performance was worthy of the occasion; but nobody wanted to be discouraging and it was easy to find excuses. During the whole of that season and the one that followed the critics treated Stratford very gently, always hoping for better things. But it was becoming increasingly difficult to pretend that all was well, especially when at the beginning of the 1934 season Bridges Adams suddenly resigned.

Bridges Adams had been director of the Stratford Memorial Theatre since 1919. It is extremely difficult to judge him as a producer. Such were the handicaps under which he worked during the whole of his time at Stratford that he was never able to present to the public a fully developed and polished production. Before the opening of the new Memorial Theatre the seasons at Stratford were comparatively short and were frequently run at a loss. Consequently salaries were of necessity low and the period of rehearsals had to be cut down to a minimum.

Bridges Adams' productions had unity and balance and a fine sense of the pictorial. At a time when most Shakespearian productions were still ponderously elaborate, he invariably moved rapidly from scene to scene. His settings, which he generally designed himself, were in the realistic tradition, but were never elaborate. He relied mainly on backcloths, curtains and rostrums, avoiding cluttering up his stage with any heavy piece of scenery which was difficult to move. Whether he was a good producer of actors it is impossible to say. Under his direction the acting was seldom more than competent and was sadly lacking in fire. But it is unreasonable to expect any producer to inspire an overworked and under-rehearsed cast to a spirited performance. He was criticised for being unenterprising in his choice of companies, but with the appallingly limited amount of rehearsal time at his disposal he was obliged to rely almost entirely on actors with previous Shakespearian experience.

During the six years when he was working on the makeshift stage of the cinema in Greenhill Street he must constantly have looked forward to the day when he would no longer be directing a little summer repertory theatre, but a theatre of international standing run on a scale befitting its importance. One sympathises with the bitterness of his disappointment when he found that the Governors showed a complete inability to adjust themselves to new conditions and were bent on running the theatre on the same scale as the old one.

At the annual meeting of the Governors of the theatre which took place a few days after his resignation Sir Archibald Flower said that he had had "a long and amusing chat with Mr. Bridges Adams about the imaginary newspaper interview in which it was stated that the resignation was a protest against the parochial policy of the Council of the theatre". The "imaginary interview" so airily dismissed in this speech was by George Bishop and had been published in the previous Sunday's *Observer*.

"Since the opening of the new Memorial Theatre", wrote George Bishop, "Bridges Adams has had one object in mind, to put the festival on a national, or even an international basis.

"Although there is a representative Board of Governors, the meetings are held at Stratford. The local Governors are able to attend, but only a small proportion of the others can spare a day for the journey. Mr. Cochran has just been made a Governor, and one cannot imagine a wiser decision, but he is one of the busiest men in England, and it will be difficult for him to take a very active share in the proceedings if the administration continues at Stratford.

"Bridges Adams' resignation was sent in on Sunday last, and it is interesting to notice that the Governors unanimously elected Mr. Cochran the following day. The director's statement about the necessity for 'the infusion of new blood' seems to have taken immediate effect.

"Bridges Adams had been agitating for an advisory committee that would meet in London. It appeared to be a reasonable proposition, and I gather that he has resigned because the idea has not been favourably received."

Replying to this article in his speech, Sir Archibald Flower pointed out that "this alleged parochial Council included Mr. Bernard Shaw, Sir Barry Jackson and Mrs. Alfred Lyttleton, and it had also included the late Norman Wilkinson whose loss they had deplored". Considering the size of the Council, these four names were hardly sufficient to convince anybody that it was either nationally representative or included a sufficient number of representatives of the theatre. What Sir Archibald Flower omitted to give in his speech was any reason for Bridges Adams' resignation.

As proof that there was not the slightest friction between the director and the Council, Bridges Adams was elected to the Governing Body. Before making this gesture, it would have been wiser if the Governors had discovered whether Bridges Adams was prepared to join in this disarming display of amiability. On hearing of his election Bridges Adams sent the following letter to Sir Archibald Flower:

"It was a considerable shock to me to read in to-night's evening papers that I had been elected a member of the Governing Body of the Stratford Memorial Theatre. My reasons for resigning were set forth with a moderation, which I am sure I shall never have cause to regret, in my second letter to you, of which I can find no mention in the press reports of the proceedings. Words fail me to express my appreciation of the honour which has been offered me and of the friendly feeling which inspired the offer. But it must surely be quite clear that, by accepting at this juncture, I should be condoning the very state of affairs which it is the dearest wish of my heart to see remedied, and I have no choice but to decline it."

One result of Bridges Adams' resignation was that the critics, although increasingly dissatisfied with the standard of performances at Stratford, held their fire. Obviously his final season was not the right time for violent criticism of Stratford; nor was the opening season of his successor, Iden Payne. It was by now generally realised that any director at Stratford was bound to be working under considerable difficulties and embarrassments. It was only fair that Iden Payne should be allowed some time to adjust himself to the peculiar difficulties of his post. But some of the critics, while refraining from any direct attack, had been sounding warning notes. *The Times*, although well-disposed toward Stratford, had pointed out that the policy of trusting rather to production than to acting was not working out well. "No method of staging", it warned, "can offset indifferent acting." Glancing through *The Times* criticisms one finds repeated references to languid acting, blurred characterisation, lack of sharpness of definition, and "the want of that extra half-ounce of energy on which depends distinction".

It was not until 1938 that the critics openly expressed their growing dissatisfaction. The attack was opened by W. A. Darlington with an article in the *Daily Telegraph* in which he frankly confessed himself dissatisfied and disturbed. "Stratford acting has never been very good since I've known it", he wrote. "Until recently there were excellent reasons why it could never become much better; but with the building of the new theatre and its steady financial success those reasons have ceased to exist. I felt, and I feel, that in these new circumstances Stratford ought to show us something not merely a little better but a very great deal better than anything it has shown us yet." Darlington then went on to state categorically exactly what he found wrong with Stratford acting.

"First, there are not enough really good actors in the company. Second, those who are there are overworked and cannot give their best. Third, no play is rehearsed long enough with the result that a great deal of mechanical hit or miss playing is allowed in every production." And the reason for this? "One thing is wrong and one thing only. The new theatre is being run—so far as the productions are concerned—on the same scale as the old one. The authorities who carried on heroically in the old days, running short seasons of plays often at a heavy loss, have not adjusted themselves to the new conditions in which the season lasts six months and plays to a steady profit."

Under the system then in force a repertoire of eight plays was given eight weeks' rehearsal. This meant that only six days' rehearsal was available for each play, and often as much as a week would elapse between the final rehearsal and the dress rehearsal. Nor was the dress rehearsal immediately followed by the performance. There were occasions when a fortnight elapsed between the dress rehearsal and the first performance. Leading actors and actresses could not be expected to risk their reputations playing leading Shakespearian roles under these conditions, so the company had to be recruited from the ranks of the young and inexperienced players and from among the older Shakespearian actors who already had many years experience of most of the parts which they were called upon to play.

In the following year the critics returned to the attack. *The Times* described the acting as "scarcely adequate". Ivor Brown, praising a performance by Jay Laurier, confessed that he began to wonder when that actor had left the stage "whether much remains at Stratford that is not just amateur theatricals after all". Darlington stated bluntly that "something is very wrong with Stratford acting and everybody whose judgment counts for anything in the theatre knows it". For years, he said, he had been engaged in friendly argument about the inadequate time allowed for rehearsals. "They assure me at Stratford that nothing can be done, but I don't believe it. If the same efficiency that has produced Stratford's seductive brand of beer were applied to the improvement of its drama, the two commodities might soon be comparable for quality. At the moment beer is best."

The problem of how to present plays properly at the Memorial Theatre in totally inadequate rehearsal time would never have arisen had the Governors carried out the policy outlined by Sir Archibald Flower when he was appealing for funds for building the new theatre:

"If a really fine stock company is to be available in the future, it must be kept continually in being. As the audiences at Stratford must be chiefly composed of visitors to the town, it is clear that the Festival season there can only run during six months—April to September. During the remainder of the year, the Festival company should be available to visit other places and other countries."

With a permanent company under long contracts there would have been no necessity to attempt eight entirely new productions each year. New productions could have been rehearsed at leisure while the company was touring, so that gradually a large and representative Shakespearian repertoire could have been built up. As Sir Archibald Flower definitely appealed for funds for the purpose of establishing a permanent company which would not limit its performances to Stratford, or even to England, it was hardly fair to the contributors that once the money was obtained, Stratford returned to its parochial policy of limiting its activities to a hastily rehearsed summer repertory season.

Financial difficulties could not be claimed as a reason for the Governors' failure to fulfil their promise. In 1936, for example, there was a surplus of nearly £10,000 on the year's working. In 1938 there was a profit of £8,500 of which £2,500 was made on the catering. That year there was at long last some signs of conscience stirring among the Governors. Sir Archibald Flower, when announcing the year's profits, cautiously hinted that "a grant of £1,000 might be made to subsidise a first-rate Shakespearian touring company in Britain". It was, to put it mildly, a little optimistic to imagine that a first-rate touring company could be financed for £1,000. How serious the Governors were in their intentions will never be known as the outbreak of war absolved them from making any further efforts and sent their consciences to sleep again.

In 1939 attendances at Stratford were naturally badly affected and the Festival performances showed a loss of over £4,000. Sir Archibald Flower now had every reason to congratulate himself on what had previously seemed an over-cautious financial policy. Pointing out that during prosperous times they had built up what he modestly described as "a good reserve fund", he stated that the

Governors were determined to carry on the Festival during the war although they had little hope that box office receipts would be sufficient to meet the costs. In 1940 receipts were under £12,000 as compared with £35,000 for the last Festival held before the war. The deficit on the Festival performances was £5,566, but income received from investments reduced the loss to only £404. In 1941 attendances at the Festival returned to pre-war figures and the surplus on the year amounted to £9,770. In 1942 the surplus was £7,981; in 1943 it was £9,232; in 1944, £22,945; in 1945, £21,936. The Report of the Council for 1945 showed that the theatre's investments totalled £206,860.

During the early years of the war the critics made every allowance for the difficulties under which Stratford was working. Weaknesses in the company had to be excused because of the shortage of actors. But when in 1943 Milton Rosmer, who had succeeded Iden Payne as director, resigned after a single season as a protest against conditions at Stratford, another storm blew up.

Milton Rosmer stated his reasons for resigning in a letter to the *Daily Telegraph*:

"My reasons are that I find the conditions, largely, I confess, imposed by the war, will not allow me to prepare and put on productions of the standard that I believe fitting to a Shakespeare Memorial Festival, which should represent the best England has to offer, and, if I may add, even up to my own standard.

"Personally I think it high time that some public protest should be made against the inadequacy of the Festivals.

"My own refusal of the Council's offer to return as Director for 1944 is in the nature of a personal protest, and I should be grateful if you would call attention to it."

Lord Iliffe, President of the Trustees of the Memorial Theatre, replying to Milton Rosmer's letter, admitted that he had already come to the conclusion that it would be good policy to "loosen our purse strings just a little". He went on to say that he thought "by spending more in salaries and in certain other directions we might be able to attract talent which would otherwise be denied to us".

Mr. Darlington, seeing in this some sign that the Governors of the Memorial Theatre were perhaps at last being shaken out of their complacency, renewed his mission to better conditions at Stratford and weighed in with the following letter:

"Lord Iliffe's letter on Stratford's theatrical future shows that he is already acting on views which he mentioned to me some time ago and it fills me with hope.

"Stratford acting has always been mediocre in my twenty years experience of it; and it seemed that the local authorities, disliking the development of their theatre from a wayside shrine to a temple of world-wide repute, desired no improvement.

"When I or my fellow critics demanded a higher standard, they would seek us out and explain the enormous difficulty of getting the best actors to come to Stratford. There is a difficulty, of course; but the authorities have always seemed to me to accept it as a protection rather than react to it as a challenge.

"'Visiting stars? Only over my dead body', a Stratford worthy once said to me. Well, I admit that visiting stars might be tiresome, but the proper alternative is not mediocrity but resident stars.

"The Stratford acting standards should be high enough for the best of our actors to feel honoured at an invitation to join the company for a season. It has never been so yet; but under this new leadership it might well become so."

That Milton Rosmer's gesture in resigning had not been altogether in vain was proved by an innovation made in 1944 when Robert Atkins succeeded him as director. Seemingly the Governors had at last begun to realise that it is impossible to produce a Shakespeare play in six days, so there was a brief preliminary tour of the opening plays of the Festival to give the company more time to rehearse the rest of the programme. But the tour was not nearly long enough, and it was not possible to produce and act the plays in touring theatres as they would eventually be done at Stratford.

The company was as undistinguished as ever, but under Atkins' direction there was at least much more pace and gusto than during Iden Payne's régime when the plays more often seemed to be soberly recited than acted.

After Atkins had been two seasons at Stratford the Governors decided to abandon the policy of having a producer-director. Instead, Sir Barry Jackson was appointed as director of the Festival with a free hand to choose his own producers. His first innovation was to engage a separate producer for each play. This, he declared, would "deal a death-blow at the stereotyped, that unhappy issue of the solitary producer who is drained and overburdened by eight plays on one pair of shoulders. One nurse is not enough for quintuplets". While eight plays are certainly too much for one producer, eight producers are equally certainly too much for one company. Apart from the fact that it is a severe strain on a company to be continually adapting themselves to the methods and personalities of a host of different producers, it is impossible under these conditions for a company to develop any style of its own. I am not advocating a return to the single producer-director. Much of the lack of vitality in the acting at Stratford was due to the fact that the producer was exhausted by overwork. But I think it is essential that there should be a producer-in-chief, with not more than two other producers to relieve him of part of the burden of production. It would be the responsibility of the producer-in-chief, relieved by the director of all matters concerning administration and policy, to establish a definite standard of Shakespearian acting at Stratford. If the company were a permanent one, in being the whole year round, trained and directed by a producer of experience and prestige, then a standard and tradition of acting would begin to emerge which might be comparable to that of the Benson company. At present there is not even a tradition of good speech at Stratford. Here if anywhere one has the right to demand to hear verse finely spoken. There has not been a company at Stratford in recent years capable of speaking verse rapidly without gabbling, or rhetorically without ranting.

Another innovation by Sir Barry was his decision to open with only three productions, adding one new play every third week until the entire repertoire was presented, a plan which ensured something approaching adequate rehearsal time for each play. This was an innovation more popular with the actors than the audiences. Visitors to Stratford during the early part of the season resented not being able to see a different play every night. Few people have the time to spend a whole week in Stratford in order to see three plays. Sir Barry suggested a way out of this difficulty without returning to the old system of putting on an entire new repertoire in a single week when he hinted in an interview that some of the plays produced in his first season at Stratford would probably form the nucleus of the following season's repertoire. So we may have seen the end of what he described as "the old policy of play a season, finish and begin again".

Sir Barry was perhaps premature in announcing during the same interview that "Stratford has ceased to be parochial or even national; it is increasingly international. By the standard set every incentive will be given to the world to make its pilgrimage to the shrine of the Playwright of All Time". Unfortunately his choice of company hardly justified this jubilant statement. He started his plan for building a new tradition of acting at Stratford by making a rule to engage no actor who had been a member of the company in the past. The result was a youthful, enthusiastic and talented company, but lacking in weight and authority and personality. Sir Barry had repeated an old mistake made year after year at Stratford. He had engaged only one leading man and one leading woman. It is impossible for a Shakespearian company to do justice to a repertoire of eight plays without at least four leading men and two leading women.

Why is it that Stratford seems so reluctant to employ our leading actors and actresses? At a Governors' Meeting, Captain Cunningham Reid protested that the salaries offered at Stratford were too low to attract stars. Barry Jackson replied that he "would rather have enthusiasm and keenness than all the stars with their airs and graces which simply drive the management to distraction". He added that in any case it was impossible to engage stars because they would not leave London.

Captain Cunningham Reid's statement can hardly be accepted as a complete explanation; the Old Vic has no difficulty in engaging leading players at salaries considerably lower than the highest figure now paid at Stratford. Nor can one believe that reluctance to leave London is the real reason; most stars spend many months away from London on tour in the provinces. The old objection of lack of adequate rehearsal time has now been overcome and the fact that in 1946 the total amount spent on salaries was increased by sixty-six per cent is sufficient proof that the Governors are now prepared to pay their actors more lavishly. If only Sir Barry can be persuaded that not all stars drive the management to distraction, and that enthusiasm and keenness are by no means the monopoly of young and unknown players, then perhaps at last we may see the great Shakespearian roles greatly played at Stratford. It is Stratford's plain duty to give us the best Shakespearian acting in England and no amount of careful production and conscientious teamwork will compensate for the absence from Stratford of proved Shakespearian players such as John Gielgud, Edith Evans, Laurence Olivier, Ralph Richardson, Fay Compton, Godfrey Tearle, Sybil Thorndike, Lewis Casson, Peggy Ashcroft, Ernest Milton, Flora Robson, Jean Forbes Robertson, Donald Wolfit, Eric Portman, Sonia Dresdel, Michael Redgrave, John Clements and Miles Malleson.

It may be objected that the engagement of stars means sacrificing all hopes of a permanent company and abandoning the policy of teamwork in which Sir Barry puts so much faith. But there is no reason why the maintenance of a permanent company should not be combined with the engagement of guest stars, a few on long contracts, others for a few months, some for only a small number of special performances. Ballet companies and opera companies make frequent changes in the leading roles; I see no reason why a Shakespearian company should not do the same. As for teamwork, I doubt if Shakespeare ever gave it much thought. He was a journeyman playwright who mostly wrote for companies in which the shares were held by the leading actors. It was his job to provide his employers with star parts. The great scenes in Shakespeare have much more in common with the arias and duets of grand opera than with the naturalistic scenes in modern plays which often largely depend on exact and detailed teamwork. Incidentally, it is a mistaken idea that teamwork is best achieved by a youthful and enthusiastic company. It is largely a matter of technique. As a producer I have generally found the stars in a company much better at teamwork than the eager young players in the small parts. There is no reason why a leading actor should not be able to take his place as a guest in an already existing production at Stratford. It is not unusual in the West End theatre during a long run for one star to take over from another without damage to the production. On the contrary, the change usually has the effect of refreshing and invigorating the other performances. The teamwork of the rest of the company is tested by the extent to which they are able to adapt themselves to a new performance by making the necessary small adjustments in tempo and timing.

If leading actors are to be persuaded to appear at Stratford, increased rehearsal time, increased salaries and increased confidence on the part of the management in their ability to handle stars are not in themselves sufficient. Two more reforms will be required. One is the reconstruction of the forestage and proscenium arch so that the actor no longer has to struggle against the handicap of being isolated from his audience. The other is the drastic reorganisation of the Governing Body. One of the reasons why the prestige of Stratford is so low among the theatrical profession is because there is a feeling that it is run mainly by amateurs and local busybodies. There are far too many members of the Governing Body who have no qualifications beyond the fact that they are influential residents of Stratford. The Memorial Theatre is no longer a local concern. It is a national institution built and endowed by money contributed not only from all over England but from all over the world. The report of the Council published in 1946 prints a list of eighty-five governors. Of these only eight have, or have had, an active interest in the professional theatre. The Board of Governors should be reduced to not more than a dozen. Local representation should be limited to one fourth of the total number of governors. The rest should consist of distinguished representatives of the theatre, art, music and literature. The Executive Committee, at present the real government of the theatre, should be abolished. The Governors, meeting at frequent intervals, should assume the active government of the theatre, and the Director should be given greater authority so that he can make decisions concerning the general management of the theatre which in the past have had to be referred to the Executive Committee.

The old complacency has gone from Stratford. At the annual

meeting of the Governors in 1946 Colonel Fordham Flower, the new Chairman of the Council, warned the Governors that there was a tremendous task ahead and an enormous distance to be covered before they reached their goal. He said that since he returned to Stratford he had been acutely conscious of the need to infuse fresh blood into the Governing Body. He announced that an Extraordinary General Meeting would be called to approve "drastic amendments, particularly with regard to the qualifications for governorship and the election of Council", and added that it would be extremely difficult for him, or anyone else, to continue as Chairman unless these amendments were passed.

Colonel Fordham Flower's plans to reform Stratford will have only limited success unless he can count upon the co-operation of the theatrical profession. Stratford is very much the concern of the profession as a whole. Visitors to England judge our Shakespearian acting and production from what they see at Stratford and, not unnaturally, they take it for granted that at the Memorial Theatre they are seeing Shakespeare's plays done as well as the English theatre can do them. They are surprised and disappointed to find the standard of Shakespearian acting is apparently far below that to be seen in our productions of modern realistic plays. It is essential for the prestige of English acting that our leading players should appear with the Stratford company. Sir Barry Jackson's irritable dismissal of stars as tiresome and unimportant must be forgiven as having been provoked by the exasperations of a stormy Governors' Meeting, and forgotten. Future Stratford companies must combine both promise and achievement.

At the end of each Stratford season the company must come to London. As the standard of the productions at Stratford improves only a small proportion of those who will want to see them will be able to spend a week at Stratford on Avon. London has every right to demand to see the Stratford company. It can no longer be regarded as existing merely for the entertainment of tourists to Stratford. It is endowed as our national Shakespearian company and the provision of a summer festival at Stratford is only part of its duties. The prospect of a London season will have a healthy effect on the standard of production and acting at Stratford. However conscientious the actors may be, playing to uncritical audiences consisting largely of holiday makers and school children is not conducive to self-criticism. In London the company will have to stand comparison with the best acting and production in the West End theatre. There is every hope that in time the Stratford company will not only equal but surpass anything to be seen in the London theatre. But, as Colonel Fordham Flower made plain in his first speech as Chairman of the Council, "there is a very long row to hoe before that is achieved. There will be many disappointments, and if we happen to achieve any interim success, may it never be said again about the Governors of the Stratford on Avon Theatre that the tinkle of silver and the rustle of notes in the box office deafened their ears to the criticism and comments of their many well-wishers".

CHAPTER XIII

THE REPERTORY THEATRES

NOWADAYS one of the disadvantages of being "a West End producer" is that most of one's time is spent in the provinces. Because of the shortage of theatres, productions destined eventually for the West End have to be produced first in the provinces and toured for months until a suitable theatre at last becomes vacant. A producer, besides having to be with a show during its opening weeks, has to pay it frequent visits to keep it in shape; so if he has two or three productions waiting for London theatres he sees very little of the West End. Continually scurrying about England from one provincial town to another has at least given me the chance to see a great deal of the work of the repertories. During the last three years I have seen something of the work of over forty repertory companies of all sorts and sizes, and I have been, quite literally, appalled by what I have seen.

It is difficult to estimate the number of these companies with any accuracy. The *Stage* has done its best to list every repertory company in the kingdom. In the summer before the outbreak of war there were seventy-five companies on the list. By the summer of 1946 the total was 220. This figure includes many companies which are only seasonal. During the holiday months even the smallest seaside town usually has a hastily assembled repertory company playing in the pier theatre or in the local assembly hall, or even in a schoolroom temporarily fitted up as a theatre. Many of the provincial and suburban theatres divide up the year between visiting companies, pantomime, and a long season of weekly repertory. The same repertory company may appear for seasons in three or four theatres during the course of the year, sometimes changing its name in each town to give an air of "belonging" where it is playing, thus artificially swelling the Stage's total. But there are at least a hundred permanent repertory companies in England and Scotland. The number of these which achieve an adequate standard of acting and production does not reach double figures. This may seem a sweeping statement to make after admitting to seeing less than half the total number, but I have seen enough to be convinced beyond all doubt that no company of actors can do justice to a play in a week's rehearsal. The number of repertories which give longer than this to rehearsing each production is less than a dozen.

As far back as 1923 St. John Ervine began a campaign against "the pernicious system of weekly repertory". In his Shute Lectures at Liverpool, in his book *The Organised Theatre* and in innumerable articles in the *Observer*, he advocated a system which would combine the virtues of both the repertory and touring systems by linking the repertories into groups, so that each company would only have to stage a new production every three or four weeks. He suggested, for instance, combining Bath, Cheltenham and Gloucester in one group; Bristol, Cardiff and Swansea in another; York, Leeds and Bradford in a third. His maximum was a four town circuit such as Aberdeen, Dundee, Edinburgh and Newcastle upon Tyne. He did not advocate the circuit system for towns large enough to support a repertory theatre playing a production for three or four weeks. Since Ervine's retirement from the *Observer* his campaign has been continued with equal persistence by Ivor Brown with the support of other dramatic critics who have been shocked into protest by some of the repertory performances they have seen.

Meanwhile the repertories, apparently deaf to criticism and suggestions, continue to churn out a play a week without making any effort to extend their rehearsal time by co-operating with their neighbours, or by seriously attempting to extend their runs to a fortnight, or by experimenting with a genuine repertoire system. There are, of course, practical difficulties in the adoption of the circuit system, such as the varying sizes of stage and auditorium in the different theatres, but neither this nor any of the other difficulties are insuperable. After talking to many repertory managers and producers I have come to the conclusion that the real reason why they are uninterested in any such scheme is because their standards are so low that they see no need for more rehearsal time. Unfortunately their complacency is encouraged by their audiences. Most repertoires are very profitable businesses. Audiences in all but the largest towns appear to be perfectly satisfied with the performances they are given. Nor do they get tired of seeing the same players week after week. On the contrary, one of the chief attractions of repertory from the audience's point of view is that they like going to see their favourite actor every week. They do not ask that he should be very different in each part that he plays. They are content with the sketchiest attempt at characterisation. In fact, the more the actor is himself, the more easily recognisable under any disguise, the better the audience is pleased.

When Wilson Barrett ran two admirable repertory companies in Edinburgh and Glasgow, interchanging them week by week so that each company played the same play for a fortnight and had a reasonable time to rehearse, his audiences protested against this "chopping and changing". They disliked having to wait a week between each appearance of their favourite. When Barrett abandoned the system and instituted seasons of weekly repertory in each town there was an immediate increase in business despite the inevitable deterioration in the performances.

So why should St. John Ervine, or Ivor Brown, or myself, or anybody else pester the repertory managers to change their policy when audiences are well content with things as they are? Because "weekly rep" is having a deplorable effect on the standard of English acting and production. It is literally impossible to rehearse a play properly in a week, especially when only a small part of the day can be devoted to rehearsals. An actor playing long seasons in repertory cannot go on for month after month rehearsing morning and afternoon, playing in the evenings, learning his lines when he can snatch a few minutes to himself. So the usual routine in a repertory theatre is to rehearse in the mornings only, with the company given one day off to learn their lines. The average time spent on the rehearsal of a play by a weekly repertory company, excluding the dress rehearsal, is fifteen hours. The average time spent on a West End production up to the dress rehearsal is at least eighty hours.

What is the effect of this system on the repertory actor? He has time to do no more than learn his positions and his lines (if he is playing a succession of long parts he can hardly do more than commit to memory a paraphrase of them) and rely on a collection of superficial tricks and mannerisms to get him through the part. "An actor", pointed out St. John Ervine in one of his articles on repertory theatres, "does not only repeat words, he interprets character. He cannot learn words by heart and develop his understanding of a part in a week. It is common nowadays to hear people referring to a player as 'a repertory actor'. By this they mean that he has spent so long in places where the programme is changed weekly that he has acquired tricks which will enable him to get through a part even when he scarcely knows it."

London managers and producers are more and more inclined to fight shy of the repertory actor. They know from experience that he may give an excellent reading and make rapid progress during the first days of rehearsal but it is likely that after a week he will be able to do no more with the part. By the first night what promised to be an excellent performance seems by comparison with the rest of the cast slick, superficial and shoddy. A producer can do little to help. The repertory actor, unused to detailed production, is apt to get rattled when called upon for more delicate variations of tone, tempo and characterisation than he has been accustomed to attempt. After the first week or two of the run his performance may go to pieces completely because in repertory he has had no chance of learning the technique of "holding" a performance.

I have the greatest admiration for the skill with which repertory directors manage to get a play on the stage with only a week's rehearsal; but they are not producers. If they were, they would not tolerate the conditions under which they work. They would be ceaselessly agitating for the re-organisation of the repertory system. The reason they do not do so is that they have no idea of what real production entails. Given another week in which to rehearse, most of them would not know what to do with it. Occasionally a producer from the weekly repertories is given a chance in London. The result is almost invariably the same. During the first days of rehearsal he maps out the production rapidly and efficiently. Then he stops work. He has no idea what to do next. The cast are left to go through their scenes without being given any more real rehearsal. In fact most repertory producers are not producers at all; they are stage managers. Most of them have had no experience of the theatre outside weekly repertory, in which they generally started as actors. They have never been in a fully rehearsed production. Most of them think that a West End producer who needs to spend three or four weeks on a production is just inefficient. What chance has a young repertory actor to learn his job under the direction of men who know nothing of the finer points of acting and have no time to correct obvious faults and mannerisms?

Admittedly some experience of weekly repertory is useful to an actor. It teaches him to learn his lines rapidly, to waste no time at rehearsals and to be resourceful in an emergency. It accustoms him to the ordeal of first nights. Above all, it teaches him versatility. As a member of a company playing a different play every week, he is inevitably often miscast, and there is no better training for an actor than having to cope with a part at variance with his personality and physique. It is only by experimenting over a wide range of parts that an actor can discover both the extent of his limitations and the type of work for which he is best suited. But having learned all he can in weekly repertory, he must get out of it. Otherwise his faults become ingrained, technique means to him nothing more than a series of short cuts, he loses the ability to study a part as opposed to merely learning it, and, because he always has to discard a part long before he has finished with it, he knows nothing of how to develop it to maturity during performance.

Most young actors in weekly repertory are fully conscious of the fact that after a certain time they remain on at their peril. The few repertories which run their productions for more than a week, such as Liverpool, Glasgow, Dundee, Birmingham and Sheffield, are inundated with applications to join their companies. Beginners from the dramatic schools are increasingly reluctant to join the weekly repertories, knowing that they will get no proper production; so they hang on in Town, sometimes getting a part at one of the small private theatres, picking up a living from occasional broadcasts and small parts in films, learning little about their job.

Fortunately there are, here and there, at long last, some signs of the beginning of the group system. The Arts Council has given a lead with its West Riding Theatre consisting of three interchangeable repertory companies based at Halifax, Huddersfield and Wakefield. The Council has also installed an Old Vic company at the Theatre Royal, Bristol, playing each production for three weeks at Bristol and then visiting the ordinary touring theatre at either Bath or Weston-super-Mare for the fourth week. During their absence the Bristol theatre is occupied by one of the Company of Four productions from the Lyric Theatre, Hammersmith.

So far the only sign among the existing weekly repertories of a desire to collaborate with their neighbours has been shown by the Amersham Repertory which has joined with the newly formed repertory at Guildford to exchange productions weekly.

Repertory managements who are opposed to interchange of companies might at least consider whether it is possible to run each of their productions in their own town for a fortnight instead of a week. The invariable reply to any such suggestion is that "it would mean doubling our audience and there isn't a big enough public in the town for that". This is probably true of the smaller towns, but if Birmingham, as well as maintaining a touring theatre, can now also support two repertories, one running each production for at least a fortnight, the other for a minimum of three weeks, then surely there are many other towns in the country where the repertory (often the only theatre in the town) could run its plays for more than a week.

Dundee has tried the experiment with complete success. Productions are put on for a minimum run of a fortnight and if they prove specially popular the run is extended to three or four weeks. The success of this policy refutes the argument that a repertory theatre depends mainly on its regular audience who acquire the habit of going to the theatre each week, usually on the same night. The Dundee theatre is an example of what can be done if the director really believes that it is vital to have proper time for rehearsal. When A. R. Whatmore went to Dundee he was not a repertory producer. He had a number of West End productions to his credit and had also played many parts in the London theatre. He was not prepared to put up with the scamped rehearsals of weekly rep. It was not just that he thought it might be worth while taking the risk of extending runs to a fortnight or longer. To him it was essential.

The importance of a theatre such as the Dundee Repertory is far more than local. Besides providing an ideal training ground for young actors, it is also a theatre where experienced West End players can take a refresher course. The organisation of the Dundee company is flexible. There are no long contracts, so Whatmore is able to make constant changes in the company to ensure more exact casting than is usual in repertory. First-rate actors who feel stale and out of practice after a long West End run are very ready to go up to Dundee for a few weeks to get back into training by playing three or four parts in quick succession, though they would not be willing to join a weekly repertory and adapt themselves to the "get-the-play-on-somehow-in-the-time" method. It would have a healthy effect on both the repertories and the West End theatre if there could be more coming and going between the two. West End actors often have long periods between engagements. Many of them would prefer to spend this time acting in a repertory theatre (provided it was not a weekly one) instead of hanging about London with nothing to do. Another way in which the repertories which run plays for more than a week are important to the theatre as a whole is that they give opportunities to new authors. The weekly repertories are no help to a new author. Every new script needs alterations and adjustments during rehearsals. Obviously there is not time for this during the hurlyburly of a weekly production. Nor have the producers of the weekly reps the necessary experience of collaborating with an author during rehearsals.

The Dundee Repertory is a Scottish theatre only insofar as it happens to be situated in Scotland. In its choice of plays and company it has nothing to differentiate it from any English repertory theatre. The only genuinely Scottish theatre is the Glasgow Citizen's Theatre, founded by James Bridie in 1943 with a capital of £1,500 and a guarantee from the Arts Council of £1,000 which never had to be drawn upon. Its declared policy was to present plays "of artistic or didactic merit which would not otherwise be seen in Glasgow, of a quality sufficient for Scottish dramatists (if any) to write up to". So that there should be adequate time for rehearsal no play was to run for less than three weeks. It began in a small theatre belonging to the Scottish Academy of Music, but in 1945 moved to the Princess's Theatre, a seventy-year-old house on the south side of the river which had been previously devoted to melodrama and pantomime. The Citizen's Theatre owed its foundation to Bridie's belief that Scotland is a good laboratory for decentralisation experiments "because it has never been thoroughly centralised either in spirit or in fact and it has never had a theatre of its own. It is a country abounding in natural drama. It dramatises its domestic and political events from the smallest to the greatest. It has a tradition of racy, pithy, expressive speech. Better still, when it applies itself seriously to a venture, it is in the habit of making a kirk or a mill of it and not allowing it to dissipate in hot air". But so far the output of plays by new Scottish dramatists has been disappointing. Most of the good Scottish plays presented by the Citizen's Theatre have been by old hands such as Joe Corrie, John Brandane, Robins Millar, Gordon Bottomley and Bridie himself, who were all discovered years ago by the Scottish National Players. Nor have the Glasgow audiences shown any particular enthusiasm for Scottish plays. I asked Bridie the reason for this. He replied that "it isn't entirely that the Scot wants to see only English toffs on the stage behaving in an English fashion, though this element is present. The truth is that we have never had a Theatre, at least not for 400 years. The Theatre is a very traditional organism and we have always associated showmanship with London. Our ear has become attuned to the London accent on the stage and to the London idiom in playwriting. It is that association I am trying to break down". It is somewhat ironical that an Irish play is a safer box office proposition than a play by a Scottish author in spite of the kiltartan accents of the company. The explanation is that an Irish play draws a Scottish-Irish audience that does not come to any of the other plays. More than half of the plays produced at the Citizen's Theatre to date are by Scottish and Irish authors. Among the plays of other nations have been Gogol's *The Government Inspector*, Richard Hughes' *A Comedy of Good and Evil*, Massinger's *A New Way to Pay Old Debts*, Molnar's *Liliom*, Obey's *Noah*, Afinogenev's *Distant Point*, Goldsmith's *The Good-Natured Man*, Priestley's *Johnson over Jordan*, Maugham's *The Breadwinner* and Ustinov's *The House of Regrets*.

The oldest existing repertory theatre is the Liverpool Playhouse, which even in its earliest days never ran a production for less than two weeks. Founded in 1911, with Basil Dean as its first producer, it was the third repertory theatre to be started in this country. Its two forerunners were the Gaiety Theatre, Manchester, now a cinema, and the shortlived Glasgow Repertory Theatre. Most repertory theatres owe their existence to the enthusiasm of an individual, often someone not previously connected with the town; but the Playhouse genuinely "belongs" to Liverpool. Instead of being the property of one person it is owned by some 1,500 shareholders.

In its early days the Playhouse found it difficult to make ends meet and was often on the verge of closing down. Its prosperity dates from the appointment of William Armstrong as producer and director in 1922. Armstrong is one of the most enchanting personalities of the English theatre. He is a Scotsman with those curiously conflicting characteristics so typical of the Scot. He is impulsive, sentimental and generous, but at the same time he is shrewd, cautious and business-like. Grace Wyndham Goldie, in her book on the Liverpool Repertory Theatre, attributes William Armstrong's success mainly to the atmosphere he created in the theatre and to his skill in selecting material. "His informality, his sense of humour, his wit, his appreciation of youth and his almost overtender regard for the feelings of his company and of his staff made him immensely popular. He is anything rather than a martinet. His discipline, except on the rarest of occasions, is negative rather than positive. Displeased, he becomes gloomy, depressed and withdrawn and a pall descends upon the theatre. But this rarely lasts long. For though he enjoys emotions, indulges moods, these are reserved for minor affairs and unimportant moments. When things are critical he is at his best. At dress rehearsals, when everybody is at their most temperamental, when everything seems difficult, when it looks as though a miracle is needed if the play is to be ready next day, he is at his calmest, soothing anybody who is ruffled; insinuating criticisms so that they do not sting; reassuring the nervous with praise; treating every crisis with humour."

As a producer his chief characteristics are his zest and his sense of humour. His rehearsals are lively and entertaining. He handles his actors with a loose rein, encouraging and helping them to build up their own conception of the part, only restraining them when their conception is out of key with the author's ideas or the other performances in the play. Not all actors like this method of production. Some of them prefer to have their thinking done for them by the producer, to be given more definite instructions, to be drilled rather than produced. The justification of Armstrong's method is the long list of former members of the Liverpool Playhouse who are now leading players on the London stage. It includes Robert Donat, Diana Wynyard, Rex Harrison, Michael Redgrave, Hugh Williams, Mary Hinton, Muriel Aked, Wyndham Goldie, Catherine Lacey, Marjorie Fielding, Herbert Lomas, Ena Burill, Robert Speaight, Judy Campbell, Robert Flemyng and Cecil Parker.

The Liverpool Playhouse has not so fine a list of plays to its credit as the Birmingham Repertory, nor has it anything like that theatre's record of enterprise and experiment. But for many years the Birmingham Repertory was a subsidised theatre, financed by Barry

Jackson, while Liverpool has always been self supporting. So it has never been able to risk advancing far ahead of its public. The policy of the Playhouse, according to its directors, "is first and foremost to produce plays which are worth producing and acting and which would not be seen in Liverpool but for its repertory theatre. It caters for no definite class of audience and is not run for any one type of playgoer". Looking through past programmes of the Playhouse one finds that in practice the choice of plays has been much more limited than this expression of policy leads one to expect. The programme for the last season before the war consisted of: *Street Scene, Time and the Conways, The Boy David, The Barretts of Wimpole Street, Bonnet Over the Windmill, The Princess and Mr. Parker* (a Christmas play for children), *The Haxtons, Eve Had No Father, I Killed the Count, I Have Been Here Before, The Late Christopher Bean, Arms and the Man, Reunion in Vienna, Believe It or Not*, and *Mrs. Lipscombe's Birthday*. This programme hardly justifies the directors' claim that the Playhouse caters for "no definite class of audience". There is nothing here for the more adventurous type of playgoer, and not a single classic. Although there are five new plays on the list, they are all light comedies. In fact this is a programme catering for a very definite class of audience, an audience which liked Dodie Smith's *Bonnet Over the Windmill* best of the season's plays and kept it running far longer than any other production. The Playhouse directors can hardly be blamed for thinking this was not an audience likely to support a more varied and ambitious programme. But there was another audience in Liverpool which had given up going to the Playhouse because so little effort was made to cater for their tastes. When T. S. Eliot's *Murder in the Cathedral* was performed in Liverpool, not by the Playhouse but by amateurs, St. John Ervine wrote in the *Observer* that this was a grave reflection on the Playhouse policy. In his article he pleaded for a more catholic policy, picking on certain recent West End successes produced at Liverpool as a sign that "the bitch goddess, success" was receiving more adoration in Liverpool than she deserved. "No one who reads my articles regularly", he went on, "will accuse me of having any respect for those dull dogs who will not be content with anything but continual performances of the gloomier works of Strindberg and Gorki; but they will, I hope, remember also that I have pleaded time and again for a catholic theatre, one in which there shall be variety of work performed, and not one in which only a single sort of play is ever seen. . . . I assert without serious fear of contradiction that those who go to the Playhouse see better plays better acted and produced all the year round than are seen by those who go regularly to London theatres. It would disappoint me bitterly if 'the bitch goddess' were to bring the Playhouse down to the level of a West End theatre."

The Playhouse could not plead financial difficulties as an excuse for always playing for safety. From 1922 until the outbreak of war every season showed a profit. The policy was to select the best plays provided by the London theatre and re-present them in Liverpool. On an average only fifteen full-length plays were produced each year, so the Playhouse was able to be genuinely selective, taking from the London theatre only what seemed particularly suitable for the Repertory's own audience. A weekly repertory, producing between forty and fifty plays a year, cannot pretend to be selective. It has to produce the plays it can get. Many plays the ordinary repertory might like to produce are ruled out for practical reasons such as the size of the cast, the number of scenes, expensive costumes, or the fact that the repertory rights are not available. Out of the plays that are left it can hardly hope to find forty or fifty a year and at the same time preserve much sign of individual taste.

There was one direction in which the Playhouse showed a certain amount of courage. It chose its plays from the London theatre without being unduly influenced by the length of the West End run. Some of the biggest successes at the Playhouse were plays of quality which were comparative failures in London, such as Robert Sherwood's *The Road to Rome*, Sherriff's *Badger's Green*, Dorothy Massingham's *The Lake*, and *You Can't Take It With You* by Kaufmann and Hart. This is a good example of how a repertory theatre can score over the touring theatre. Touring managements naturally will not risk a play in the provinces unless it has had considerable success in London.

At the Playhouse audiences were not given mere reproductions of the London shows. Because a play never ran for less than two weeks, and often for four, it was possible for Armstrong to do his own fresh and individual production of every play. Thus there was creative element in the work of the Playhouse entirely lacking in the work of the ordinary weekly repertory company. Playhouse audiences generally got a much better performance of a West End success than they would have been given by a touring company.

The Playhouse has to its credit a fair number of first productions of importance including St. John Ervine's *The Ship* and his *Anthony and Anna*, Monkhouse's *Paul Felice*, Keith Winter's early work, three plays by Priestley, the first English performances of Susan Glaspell's *The Inheritors* and *Alison's House*, and two of the best plays for children ever written—A. A. Milne's *Toad of Toad Hall* and Vera Beringer's *What Happened to George*. More effort might have been made to discover plays typical of the north of England.

At one time when Herbert Lomas and James Harcourt were in the company, a number of one-act plays were presented which mirrored the robustness and common sense of provincial life at its best, but when these two actors left the company Lancashire plays became more and more infrequent, possibly because in personnel the company had become very similar to that of any West End theatre, and were not capable of portraying Lancashire characters with sufficient reality to satisfy the local audience. The only local playwright of real promise discovered by Liverpool has been Philip Johnson. Some of his one-act plays have a local setting, but in his longer plays he set himself to imitate the conventional West End theatre. One of these, *Lover's Leap*, had a London run but it was a play almost indistinguishable from other cut-to-pattern light comedies.

The season of 1939–40 was the last at the Playhouse under Armstrong's direction. Before the next season was due to begin Liverpool was being heavily raided and the Playhouse was closed. Armstrong came to London and in a series of productions for various managements proved that after eighteen years in repertory his skill and his standards were as high as those of any producer in the West End. But he was not happy in the West End theatre which he always referred to as The Jungle. Although one of the most sought after producers in London, after four years he returned to the provinces to work with Barry Jackson as assistant director of the Birmingham Repertory. "I have left The Jungle", he wrote to me, "because it was getting me down. My heart has always been in repertory and the theatre with a definite policy. I have had some unhappy experiences producing plays with stars who shall be nameless. On the other hand I have got the greatest pleasure from producing *Old Acquaintance* with Edith Evans, *The Circle* with John Gielgud, *A Man about the House* with Flora Robson, and *Pink String and Sealing Wax*. One of my happiest experiences was producing *The Rest is Silence* for George Black, one of the kindest and most sympathetic managers I ever met. In spite of the arduous work at Liverpool, made more difficult by constant illness, it was the greatest and happiest experience of my life. I love working with young people, and moulding them into potential stars. There is a lovely spirit of adventure and excitement in repertory which one never gets elsewhere."

In the autumn of 1942 it was decided to re-open the Playhouse, but Armstrong did not feel he could resume the directorship of the theatre. He believed the job needed a younger and fitter man. It was difficult in the middle of a war to find a suitable successor, so the Old Vic was invited to take over the theatre.

At first there was no permanent company. The various Old Vic companies on tour visited the theatre in turn. The plays were *Othello*, *Jacob's Ladder* by Laurence Housman, *The Merry Wives of Windsor*, *Six Characters in Search of an Author*, *Androcles and the Lion*, *The Beggar Prince* (a play for children), *Abraham Lincoln*, *The Merchant of Venice*, Vanbrugh's *The City Wives' Confederacy*, and an adaptation of Charlotte Brontë's *Shirley*. In the spring of 1943 there was an exchange of companies between the Liverpool Playhouse and the Cambridge Arts Theatre. I took a company from Cambridge up to Liverpool in a repertory consisting of *Uncle Vanya*, *The Gay Lord Quex*, and *Frolic Wind*. We were gloomily received on our arrival at the Playhouse. Business had not been good during the Vic season and there was a general feeling that A Great Mistake was being made in departing from the old Playhouse policy in the choice of plays. *Six Characters in Search of an Author* had been A Disaster. It had only been possible to run it for a week. We were told that the old supporters of the Playhouse, people who had come regularly to every show for twenty years, "wouldn't stand for these highbrow plays". It was tentatively suggested that perhaps it was not too late to substitute a production of *George and Margaret* for one of the plays on our programme. That, it was thought, might do something to get the old supporters back.

The general opinion was that we were about to strike the death blow of the Playhouse by putting on *Uncle Vanya* for a fortnight. In the old days the play had been produced for a few special matinées and "nobody had liked it". We certainly did not pack the Playhouse with *Uncle Vanya* but business was by no means bad and we did not lose money on the fortnight's run. The audience was mainly a very youthful one, most of them in uniform. These young people stayed away from *The Gay Lord Quex* because they suspected Pinero of being a dusty old dramatist. Their place was taken by the pre-war Playhouse audience who had stayed away from *Uncle Vanya* but found *The Gay Lord Quex* very much to their taste. The third play in our repertoire, *Frolic Wind*, attracted both types of audience. The "regulars" came chiefly because photographs of the play showed a dinner party scene which looked "quite West End". I am afraid many of them were deeply shocked by the play.

Financially that season of 1942–43 was the least successful in the history of the Playhouse. The old audience, apart from disapproving of many of the plays, disliked the policy of constant change of companies. As one of them said to me, "You never have time to get *used* to the actors". Next season the Old Vic wisely decided to install a permanent company at Liverpool. John Moody was the producer. The choice of programme was uncompromising. Eight of the fifteen plays were classics, and the remaining seven hardly provided much light relief. They included Obey's *Noah*, Jean-Jacques Bernard's *The Sulky Fire*, and Peter Ustinov's *The House of Regrets*. The only play in the whole season really to the taste of the old Playhouse audience was *Scandal at Barchester*, adapted from Trollope's *The Last Chronicle of Barset*. Business was far below pre-war standards. A fortnight was the longest run that most of the plays were able to achieve.

The season of 1944–45 brought a sudden change of fortune. Peter Glenville was appointed to direct the season. He chose a company headed by Mary Ellis, which was far stronger than the previous season's company, and, as far as was possible in war-time, equal to the Old Playhouse companies. *John Gabriel Borkman* opened the season, with the leading parts played by Mary Ellis, Nancy Price and Frederick Valk. It was a risky play to open with, but so well acted and produced that it drew larger audiences than any of the previous season's plays. The rest of the programme might have been chosen in response to St. John Ervine's plea that the Playhouse should be "a catholic theatre, not one in which only a single sort of play is ever seen". The plays were *Lisa* (an adaptation from Turgeniev by Peter Glenville), *The Second Mrs. Tanqueray*, the first English performance of Coward's *Point Valaine*, a brilliant production by Tyrone Guthrie of *He Who Gets Slapped* (re-entitled *Uneasy Laughter*), *The School for Scandal*, *Anna Christine*, *Hamlet*, a modern dress production by Tyrone Guthrie of *The Alchemist*, and *His Excellency the Governor*. The result of this policy of a well varied programme, extremely well acted and produced, was that the average run of each play increased from a fortnight to six weeks. The "regulars" consisted no longer of the elderly inhabitants of the suburbs of Liverpool but were mainly a young Service audience, many of whom were seeing plays for the first time.

The Vic gave its last season at Liverpool in 1945–46 with Eric Capon as producer. The company was not nearly as strong as that of the previous year and although the policy of a well varied programme was continued, the mixture was not quite as skilful as before. The classics were *The Knight of the Burning Pestle*, *As You Like It*, and Farquhar's *The Recruiting Officer*. The nineteenth century was represented by Harold Scott's adaptation of Wilkie Collins' *The Moonstone*, the father of all modern thrillers. There were two new plays, Ustinov's *Tragedy of Good Intentions*, a play about the Crusades, and *No Birds Sing*, a comedy by Jenny Laird and John Fernald. The other plays were *Pygmalion*, *Eden End*, *Mr. Bolfry* and O'Casey's *Purple Dust*.

Now the Directors of the Playhouse have resumed control, with a company of their own and John Fernald as their producer. Many of the older supporters of the Playhouse were frankly relieved when the Vic handed back the theatre. They hoped that once more it would be their likes and dislikes which would dictate the Playhouse policy. The Vic had catered for a Liverpool audience instead of the very limited class of playgoer represented by the "Playhouse audience". In fact the Vic simply followed the policy which the Directors of the Playhouse themselves formulated in the early days of the theatre when they stated that they were determined to "cater for no definite class of audience or for any one type of playgoer". If in the future the Directors carry out their own policy more courageously than they have done in the past, then the Playhouse will not revert to being a theatre for a cautious, elderly audience but will continue to attract the young, eager and enterprising playgoers who formed so large a part of the audience during the Vic's tenancy.

This chapter, which started as an account of the work of the repertory theatres, has ended by becoming mainly an account of the Liverpool Playhouse. The other important repertory theatres—the Birmingham Repertory, the Cambridge Festival Theatre and the Oxford Playhouse under J. B. Fagan's régime—are dealt with in other chapters. There is little of interest to be said about the rest. Looking through the lists of plays produced by the various repertories during the course of a year, it is difficult to find any signs of individual taste or policy. Each theatre puts on the same succession of West End successes, old and new, varied by an occasional "safe classic". (The safest of all, judging from the number of times it appears on the lists, is *Ghosts*, presumably because it is still regarded as rather a shocking play.) Here and there one finds a repertory which sometimes struggles out of the rut of weekly performances to run an occasional production for a fortnight; some employ a company at least twenty strong, which ensures that no one actor is overworked even if he is inevitably under-rehearsed; some make frequent changes in their companies in an attempt to keep performances fresh; others believe it is good box office to retain the same actors as long as possible (I know of at least two actors who remained in the same town for twenty years without a break); some take immense trouble over their settings; others bother to do little more than provide some sort of box for the actors to perform in with the necessary number of doors and windows; a few employ two producers, an arrangement that every weekly repertory ought to adopt; some, not content with producing a play a week, play it twice nightly.

But all these are minor differences which do little to alter the general standard of mediocrity imposed by the inexorable time-limit to rehearsals in "weekly rep". I have seen performances by weekly repertory companies which were amazingly good considering the time in which they were rehearsed, but these performances made one all the more resentful of a system which denies the actors the time to finish their work to the best of their abilities. The argument that "the audience are satisfied, so why worry" is not good enough. By no means all the audience are satisfied. Many are well aware of the deficiences of the performances, but they continue to go to the local repertory theatre because often it is the only theatre in the town where it is possible to see a straight play, and they prefer to see a poor performance of a play rather than no play at all. Others after "trying the Rep" once or twice, decide they prefer the more efficient entertainment provided by the cinemas and the local music-hall. The repertory manager forgets these people when he talks about his satisfied audience. Nor does he seem to draw any conclusions from the fact that in the average provincial town the proportion of cinema-goers to theatre-goers is about forty to one. If repertory performances were better it would surely be possible to induce some of the huge number of cinema-goers to vary their weekly or bi-weekly visits to the cinema with an occasional visit to the repertory. If only three per cent of the filmgoers in a town could be persuaded to become theatre-goers as well, it would be enough to double the audience of a repertory theatre and make it possible, in fact, essential, for each production to run for a fortnight instead of a week.

Fortnightly runs are in every way preferable to the circuit system as a means of achieving adequate rehearsal time. The circuit system is merely a modified form of the touring system. It is difficult for a town to take any proprietory interest or local pride in two or three companies making visits to the town every two or three weeks. There is a third system, as yet untried in the provinces: the repertoire system. The advantage of this system is that successful and important productions need not be scrapped after a week or a fortnight but can be maintained in the repertoire and performed once or twice a week over a period of many months, or even years, until their popularity is finally exhausted. On the other hand, an unsuccessful production can be scrapped after a very few performances instead of being run at a heavy financial loss while another production is being got ready. Such a system would allow a repertory company to be more adventurous in its choice of plays. Repertory audiences are apt to be cautious and conservative, but their tastes are generally much more catholic than they themselves realise. When they can be induced to go to a play that is not cut to a standardised pattern they usually enjoy it, but the experience of most repertory companies is that it takes some days for word to get round that "it's quite a good show at the Rep this week after all", so by the time interest has been aroused the play has come to the end of its regulation number of performances. Under the repertoire system such productions could be gradually nursed into popularity by allowing several days to elapse between each performance so that there is plenty of time for the play to be talked about. From the actor's point of view the repertoire system is ideal. Playing two or three parts a week ensures a much more alert and lively performance than can be expected from a nightly repetition of the same part; alternating heavy leading roles with less exacting parts conserves his energies; the days which elapse between repetitions of a role give him time to reflect on his performance and revise it at leisure. From the management's point of view there are obvious practical difficulties. Two or three changes of programme in the course of a week entail increased expenditure on stage staff, additional storage space, and a large stock of scenery, furniture and properties. Instead of merely painting more or less the same set of flats a different colour every Sunday, the repertory theatre would have to keep five or six productions in being at once. Furniture, properties and costumes, instead of being hired for a week or a fortnight, would have to be bought; otherwise the normal hire charges would be multiplied five or six times.

In the long run the repertoire system would, I believe, prove far more economical than the present method of running every play for the same number of consecutive performances irrespective of whether it is a smash hit, a moderate success, or a complete failure. Both the Birmingham Repertory and the Glasgow Citizen's Theatre are at present contemplating adopting the repertoire system, but owing to the large capital outlay required it is unlikely that many repertory theatres will be able to follow their lead unless they are encouraged to do so by some scheme of local or state subsidy. In 1942 the Council of the British Drama League appointed a committee to draw up such a scheme which was "respectfully offered for the consideration of His Majesty's Government" with the support and approval of British Actors Equity and a list of signatories including, among others, the Archbishop of Canterbury, Lord Esher, Sir Edwin Lutyens, James Bridie, T. S. Eliot, Dr. Julian Huxley, Desmond MacCarthy, Professor Gilbert Murray, J. B. Priestley, Dr. Malcolm Sargent, Bernard Shaw, and Dr. Edith Summerskill. The Memorandum claims that "the Theatre deserves support from the community on the same lines as those on which assistance is already granted to the arts of Literature (through the

Public Libraries), Painting (through the Public Art Galleries), and Music (with Municipal Orchestras, etc.)". It is suggested that such financial assistance as may be necessary can be most fairly secured by a combination of Local and State subsidy, fifty per cent of the necessary funds guaranteed by the Government and fifty per cent raised from Rates or from voluntary subscriptions, or by a combination of both, but it is emphasised that any State-supported scheme should aim at ultimate self-support. The Civic Theatre, as envisaged in this scheme, would not limit its activities to its own city but would also serve the surrounding district. The company attached to each Civic Theatre would be a large one, large enough to undertake the performance of any Shakespearian play for example, but whenever a play was being performed at the Civic Theatre which did not require the full company, then a "neighbourhood group" would be available to visit the surrounding towns and even the larger villages, taking plays to outlying places usually entirely deprived of any form of professional theatre.

The Memorandum recommends that the repertoire should consist of classical plays, new and original plays, contemporary plays and translations. "Contemporary plays should only include those of recognised merit which have already had their run elsewhere or have been neglected by the Commercial Theatre. This provision is intended to prevent the production of an excessive number of ephemeral works, and to secure a fair field for Touring Managements." It is emphasised that under the heading "New and original plays" every opportunity should be given to local playwrights of promise in order to encourage the growth of a genuine "regional drama". When Mr. Ernest Bevin addressed the Inaugural Meeting of the newly formed Provincial Theatre Council he expressed the hope that the theatre would undergo great changes. "In this mechanical age", he said, "we look to the theatrical world to preserve the characteristics of our people—not merely national characteristics but (and that is what most appeals to me) local characteristics. In the British people there exist great divergencies of character which are endangered by the current tendency towards uniformity, and I look forward, at the end of this great struggle, to the living theatre not merely coming into its own as a means of livelihood, but to its becoming one of our great national institutions to convey to the peoples of the world the real character of the ordinary British people." If a few provincial theatres could become centres of creative work and break away from the drab uniformity which they impose upon themselves by a system which gives them no time to do more than reproduce smudged copies of cut-to-pattern London successes, then at last Mr. Bevin's hopes may be realised.

Many Corporations are now planning Civic Centres which will include a theatre. There is every possibility that in a few years most of the big cities will have a Municipal Theatre as well as a Municipal Library and a Municipal Art Gallery. Already the General Purpose Committee of the Council of the Association of Municipal Corporations has recommended that the Minister of Health should be requested to introduce legislation to enable local authorities to provide and to manage Municipal Theatres. In towns which decide to build and manage their own theatre an existing repertory theatre run for profit by private enterprise need not necessarily be affected. The programme policy of a Civic Theatre will still leave room for a theatre presenting the type of play upon which the average repertory mainly depends, so long as there is an audience satisfied with the perfunctory performances of a weekly repertory company. But there are also repertories which are not primarily concerned with the making of profits. These should eventually become the nucleus of the Civic Theatre companies if in the meantime they can achieve a sufficiently high standard. This will only be possible if they train their actors properly and give adequate time to the rehearsal of their productions, which means either extending their runs to a fortnight or arranging an interchange with neighbouring companies.

During the war hundreds of thousands of men and women in the Services and the factories saw plays for the first time in their lives as a result of the work of E.N.S.A., C.E.M.A. and of the various Service Welfare organisations which arranged visits to ordinary theatres for members of the Forces. A large proportion of these new, young playgoers have returned to towns where there is either no theatre or only a music-hall, or, at best, a weekly repertory company. The audiences which recently were packing huge theatres in France and Germany to see the Old Vic Company in *Peer Gynt*, The Sadler's Wells Ballet, Donald Wolfit in his Shakespearian repertoire, Roger Livesey and Ursula Jeans in *The School for Scandal*, Ann Casson in *St. Joan*, and many other West End stars in their current successes are not going to be content with the provincial theatre as they now find it. If most of this huge new playgoing public is not to be lost to the cinema again, the provincial theatre must seize its opportunity and do everything in its power, both through private enterprise and municipal effort, to meet this new demand.

CHAPTER XIV

MANY OTHERS

THERE is not much more room in the book, so this will have to be an omnibus chapter into which a dozen managements left out of the previous chapters are crammed unceremoniously together.

The most obvious omission so far has been the Sadler's Wells Opera. It deserves a chapter to itself, but I am not the person to write it. As a producer of plays I am inevitably more interested in the acting and production of opera than in the singing. To write about the Sadler's Wells company with the emphasis on the acting would be unfair. Most of the acting is distressingly bad. But nobody can be blamed for that. So little opera is given in England that opera singing is not a full-time profession in this country. Singers have to make their money on the concert platform. Opera is a sideline. There is no incentive to train as an opera singer and no school in England where it is possible to do so. Consequently English opera is performed mainly by people who all too obviously look what they are, oratorio singers in fancy dress.

The Sadler's Wells company has for years gallantly been attempting the impossible. It has been striving to present good performances of opera at popular prices in a theatre far too small to make such an achievement financially possible without a large subsidy. Opera properly presented requires an orchestra of at least seventy-five players, highly paid singers, elaborate scenery and costumes, and expensive rehearsals. An opera singer's training is long and costly, he is seldom equal to important roles until he is in his thirties and may decline rapidly as he approaches fifty, so in his prime he rightly demands a high salary, a salary much higher than that earned by most star actors when one takes into consideration the fact that a singer cannot undertake heavy parts more than two or three times a week. Lilian Baylis started her opera company at the Vic by giving performances every other Thursday, with an orchestra of only eighteen players, and an unpaid chorus of amateurs who had their own work to do during the day so could only rehearse in the evenings. There is nothing in the whole history of the theatre to match the dogged persistence with which, in the face of appalling financial difficulties, from these occasional scratch performances there gradually developed an organisation providing London with its only regular performances of opera.

It is useless to pretend that these performances have, except on rare occasions, come anywhere near to the standard maintained in the opera houses of other great capitals, or even in the smaller municipal opera houses on the continent, but considering the difficulties it is astonishing that the performances are as good as they are. The producers have often achieved miracles in spite of being handicapped by wretchedly inadequate time for rehearsal, far too little money to spend on scenery and costumes, singers untrained in the art of opera acting, and a stage and auditorium which could hardly be more ill-fitted for opera. The standard of production has steadily risen in recent years. The policy of importing producers from the ballet and the straight theatre has resulted in far more attention being paid to acting, grouping, movement and décor. At last there are signs that English opera singers are beginning to realise that part of their job is to act as well as to sing, that opera is drama set to music. Perhaps they could hardly be blamed for not realising this fact in the days when they had to sing either a language they did not understand or the doggerel of the old translations, but now Sadler's Wells has versions of most of the standard operas in good, lively English which is both actable and singable. This has been due mainly to the persistence of Professor Dent—one of the Governors of Sadler's Wells and himself a brilliant translator of Mozart—in persuading others too to undertake the laborious, thankless and highly specialised task of retranslation. But the retranslation of existing operas is not enough. When it becomes an accepted fact that in opera the author is as important as the composer, then at last writers of repute may be induced to turn their attention to opera. It is encouraging to find so famous a musician as Dent bluntly declaring that "if we are to prevent opera from dying of some horrible disease, names for which I hardly dare to suggest, we must look not to the musicians to save it but to the poets".

I have excused myself from writing at length about the Sadler's Wells opera because I feel I am not the right person to do it. For the same reason I can only write very briefly about the Open Air Theatre. I detest seeing plays out-of-doors. On the hottest summer night I prefer sweltering in a stuffy theatre to watching a play in the comparative coolness of the wide open spaces of Regent's Park, though perhaps I might enjoy playgoing in an open air theatre which seated only three or four hundred people, where all the audience were reasonably close to the stage and there was no need for microphones. In the Regent's Park theatre, which seats four thousand, the actors are not only frequently inaudible but also, from the more distant seats, almost invisible. But the success of the Open Air Theatre founded by Sidney Carroll in 1933, with Robert Atkins as his producer, proves that there are plenty of people who do not share my prejudice. Robert Atkins' own modest argument in favour of open air performances is that "apart from providing theatrical interest and employment during months that are usually practically 'dead', they help to create larger audiences for the ordinary indoor winter theatre. The non-theatregoer is often tempted to visit an open air show and may be tempted afterwards to become a regular theatregoer. To my knowledge many thousands of people have seen Shakespeare for the first time through the open air theatre movement, and they have liked what they have seen, although without scenery and artificial lighting, and, in recent years, under bad weather conditions".

The fact that many thousands of people have seen Shakespeare for the first time in the open air is perhaps not altogether unconnected with the fact that in London it is often very difficult to see it indoors. The playgoer whose appetite for Shakespeare is not satisfied by an occasional star production generally has to go farther afield than the West End in search of more. And not only for Shakespeare. For those willing to venture only a short distance outside the confines of the West End, the Westminster Theatre has over a period of fifteen years presented a series of plays of a sort only rarely seen in the neighbourhood of Shaftesbury Avenue. Herbert Farjeon was hardly exaggerating when he declared that "the Westminster Theatre has probably housed during the present decade a higher percentage of interesting plays than any other theatre north of the Thames". It was built in 1931 by Anmer Hall; or rather, he converted into a theatre a building which had been a cinema and previous to that one of those proprietary chapels which were such a feature of eighteenth century London. This one was called Charlotte Chapel and London flocked there to hear the preaching of Dr. Dodd who was hanged at Tyburn for forging the signature of the Earl of Chesterfield. Now the building has been reclaimed for religion and Dr. Buchman presides in place of the unfortunate Dr. Dodd.

When Anmer Hall opened the Westminster he was not a professional man of the theatre although from time to time he had presented in London distinguished plays such as *A Month in the Country* and *The Kingdom of God*, and had given four seasons at the Cambridge Festival Theatre. His taste in plays was not that of the majority of playgoers, so he built the Westminster in order to have a small theatre in which he could put on the plays of his own choice.

It is difficult to understand how a man with so genuine and disinterested an enthusiasm for the theatre could in the end have surrendered the Westminster to the Oxford Group at a time when there was a desperate shortage of theatres. But perhaps the explanation is that Anmer Hall, in spite of his distinguished record in the theatre, has always remained at heart an amateur. Perhaps the theatre was, after all, no more to him than a hobby. He built a theatre to indulge his taste for good plays just as he built one of the few "real" tennis courts in the country because tennis was another of his enthusiasms.

His opening play was Bridie's *The Anatomist*, with Henry Ainley and the then almost unknown Flora Robson in the leading parts. This was Tyrone Guthrie's first production in London. Notable productions during the first four years were *Six Characters in Search of an Author*, *Tobias and the Angel*, *Jonah and the Whale*, *The Lake* by Dorothy Massingham, and *The Lady from Alfaqueque* by Serafin and Joaquim Quintero. When there was a part in one of the plays that Anmer Hall thought he would like to play himself he appeared on the stage under the name of Waldo Wright. In the autumn of 1934 the theatre was let to Baxter Somerville for a season of fortnightly repertory. The ten plays he presented included *The Moon in the Yellow River*, *Children in Uniform*, *King Lear*, Masefield's *The Faithful* and Sidney Howard's *Alien Corn*. In the following year the Dublin Gate Theatre company appeared at the Westminster in a season which included *Hamlet*, *Yahoo*, Lord Longford's play about Dean Swift, and Denis Johnston's *The Old Lady Says "No"*. The most memorable of Anmer Hall's presentations in 1936 was Granville Barker's *Waste* rehearsed by the author. In 1937 the outstanding production was O'Neill's *Mourning Becomes Electra* played by Beatrix Lehmann and Robert Harris, directed by Michael Macowan who had become Anmer Hall's resident producer. In 1938 the London Mask Theatre was established at the Westminster by J. B. Priestley and Ronald Jeans because they believed that "there should be in London a permanent theatre with a policy, character and company of its own, where intelligent playgoers can always be sure of finding a first-class play at very much lower prices than is charged by the West End theatre". Macowan stayed on to produce for them. His first production for the new management was a highly successful modern dress version of *Troilus and Cressida*. Subsequent productions were *Dangerous Corner*, *Marco Millions*, *Major Barbara*, *Desire Under the Elms*, *Abraham Lincoln*, and two more plays by Priestley, *Music at Night* and *Cornelius*. During the war the theatre was let to a variety of managements including Donald Wolfit, Robert Atkins, the Mercury Theatre and the Arts Theatre, Cambridge. In 1944 Robert Donat became lessee. He achieved a long run with his first presentation, *An Ideal Husband.* This was followed by Bridie's *It Depends What You Mean*, a revival of *Yellow Sands* and Walter Greenwood's *The Cure for Love.* In 1946 Anmer Hall returned to the Westminster to present *Golden Eagle*, a play about Mary, Queen of Scots by Clifford Bax. It was not a success and the theatre was again let, first for a production of *The Sacred Flame*, then to Henry Sherek for Ronald Millar's play *Frieda.* The final production at the Westminster before it was lost to the theatrical profession was *A Message for Margaret* by James Parish in which Flora Robson gave one of the finest performances of her career on the stage where she had made her first London success in the play which opened the theatre.

It was at the Westminster that the Group Theatre began. It was founded in 1932 by some young actors and actresses playing there. The Group never seemed able to define their policy very clearly. There was much talk of "bringing about a directness and freshness of playing and presentation" and we were promised "an attempt to include the spectators in the action of the play". Rupert Doone, the director of the Group, writes: "Our concern at that time was mostly with the masque, or, in modern terms, the revue aspect of the theatre. What we sought to present was not portraiture but a cartoon. The first play written for us was by W. H. Auden. I had asked him to write me a ballet on the theme of Orpheus in the Underworld. Auden, no doubt considering there was enough hell on earth, wrote a political masque". This was *The Dance of Death.* Like most of the Group productions it was performed without scenery on a completely bare stage, with costumes and masks by Robert Medley and music by Herbert Murrill. Later Auden collaborated with Isherwood in writing three more plays for the Group, *The Dog Beneath the Skin*, *The Ascent of F6*, and *On the Frontier*. Stephen Spender contributed *Trial of a Judge* and Louis McNiece, besides translating *The Agamemnon* of Aeschylus for the Group, also wrote *Out of the Picture*. The enterprise of the Group in persuading poets to write their plays had on the whole disappointing results. None of the authors showed any real sense of the theatre or an ability to write dramatic poetry. The general pattern of all the plays was the same, consisting of long passages of verse, most of which did little to advance the action of the play, alternating with moments of violent melodrama. There is much fine poetry in all the plays written for the Group, but most of it is poetry of the sort which reads better than it speaks. Generally I found the productions by Rupert Doone more interesting than the plays. Not only was scenery dispensed with but often props as well, so that the producer and his actors had to rely on expressive grouping, movement and gesture to a much greater extent than in any ordinary production. This method was not just an arty stunt. The Group believed that if there was a theatre in which the actors were trained to make their effects without the aid of scenery and props, playwrights would find there a new freedom to move about in the course of a play from place to place, unconfined by canvas walls. Years afterwards when the American production of *Our Town* was brought to London, West End theatregoers saw for the first time the same kind of production and acting that had been practised by the Group. Most of the critics attacked it as a stunt production, but few seemed to realise that the play could not have been performed realistically because of the constant movement to and fro, from house to house, from room to room, from street to street. It would have been impossible to produce it in even the most elaborately equipped theatre without continual breaks in the action of the play as the scene changed.

The Group Theatre did not survive the war, but the policy of providing a stage for the poets is being continued at the Mercury Theatre by Martin Browne who has been directing a repertoire of plays by poets which has included Ronald Duncan's *This Way to the Tomb*, Anne Ridler's *The Shadow Factory*, and Norman Nicholson's *The Old Man of the Mountains*. The Mercury was opened in 1931 as the Ballet Club, and licensed as a public theatre in 1933. As the theatre has usually been able to depend on the Ballet Club to provide the rent, Ashley Dukes, its director, has been in the enviable position of being able to put on plays merely when he has something he particularly wants to present. As a result the Mercury has a slightly dilettanti air. So has Ashley Dukes. A connoisseur of food, wine and poetry, a writer of charming prose and elegant plays, an enchanting conversationalist, he seems to belong to a more leisured and highly civilised age than the present. But his disarming air of being an amiable, cultured dabbler in the arts conceals a shrewd sense of business, and he has deservedly made considerably more money out of his theatrical ventures than many of the so-called business men of the theatre. For instance, he transferred T. S. Eliot's *Murder in the Cathedral* from Canterbury Cathedral to the Mercury and then to the West End, running it for many months to packed houses and afterwards touring it in the provinces with equal success. The average run of a play at the Mercury is from six to ten weeks, but some have continued for two or three hundred performances. Among the most interesting productions, besides those already mentioned, have been Henri Becque's *Parisienne*, Machiavelli's *Mandragola*, Humbert Wolfe's *Reverie of a Policeman*, W. J. Turner's version of Molière's *Amphitryon* under the title of *Jupiter Translated*, Kataev's *Squaring the Circle*, Lenormand's *In Theatre Street* and Archibald Macleish's *Panic*.

A neighbour of the Mercury at Notting Hill is the Lindsey Theatre which had no clearly defined policy and little success until in 1946 it was reconstituted as the New Lindsey Theatre with the aim of producing "vital plays under the direction of Frederick Piffard and Peter Cotes". One of the first productions of the new management, *Pick Up Girl*, was vital enough to get itself transferred to the Prince of Wales Theatre. It is to be hoped that the New Lindsey Theatre will have a longer life than most of the club theatres. Usually the more confident the manifesto of a new club theatre the briefer its life. For instance, there was the Neighbourhood Theatre which opened in 1940 in Harrington Road. A bombastic announcement warned us that the Neighbourhood Theatre "would inaugurate *a new style of theatre* for this country . . . a theatre with a policy—the production of plays of high artistic quality from an international repertory, along the lines of definite artistic method, with the ideal aim of forming a permanent company . . . the basic method will be that of Stanislavsky. . . . It will be a fearless theatre". The Neighbourhood justified its existence by producing *Thunder Rock* and then closed after two more productions of no importance whatsoever. In the same year that the Neighbourhood opened and closed, the Threshold was started in Chepstow Villas at Notting Hill Gate with a translation by Peter Ustinov of Jean Serment's *Fishing for Shadows* followed, somewhat surprisingly, by a revival of *The Scarlet Pimpernel.* Later the theatre was renamed the Gateway and continues to be run under no clearly discernible policy. On the other hand, the Torch Theatre in Knightsbridge, opened by Gerik Schelderup with Romain Rolland's *The Game of Love and Death*, firmly announced itself as "a theatre with a policy". The policy was to be "plays of high artistic merit, whether new or established classics, which had not been seen in London before, and occasionally an interesting revival". One seemed to have heard all that before. The management survived for only five productions of which the most interesting was Ibsen's *When We Dead Awaken.* The theatre was then taken over by Gerald Cooper who ran it until 1940. It was he who discovered *Jeannie* for the West End, but the most memorable of the productions under his régime was Pirandello's *Henry IV*. In 1945 the Torch was reopened by the London Theatre Group which survived for only a brief time. Its most notable productions were Joyce's *Exiles* and Ibsen's *Rosmersholm.*

The oldest of the still existing theatre clubs is the Arts, opened in 1927. The president was Bronson Albery and there was an impressive list of vice-presidents including Madge Kendal, Johnstone Forbes Robertson, Martin Harvey, Arnold Bennett, Barry Jackson, and Sybil Thorndike. The first production in the Club's theatre was *Picnic*, a revue by Herbert Farjeon. This was followed by Kate O'Brien's *The Bridge*, Galsworthy's *Joy*, Strindberg's *Creditors*, Bourdet's *La Prisonnière*, *First Class Passengers Only* by Osbert and Sacheverell Sitwell, George Moore's *The Makings of an Immortal*, *Ghosts* (with Mrs. Patrick Campbell), a recital by Yvette Guilbert, Strindberg's *Easter* and Tolstoy's *The Fruits of Enlightenment*. Gradually the Arts Theatre Club put on fewer and fewer productions of its own, contenting itself with letting out the theatre to anyone who had a show to put on, irrespective of whether the play fitted into any sort of policy. Looking through a typical year's work during the 'thirties, one finds an extraordinary hotch-potch of shows ranging from Hasenclever's *Ehen Werden in Himmel Geschlossen* presented by J. T. Grein's Cosmopolitan Theatre to *And So To Bed* acted by a Jewish Girls' Club. Only three productions were under the direct management of the Arts Theatre Club. The rest were given by a diverse collection of managements and societies including the Play Society, the Pivot Club, the New Shop Window, the Monkey Club, the Blue Circle Dramatic Society, the Toc H Drama League, the Anglo-Norse Players, and the Bank of England Dramatic Society. In addition to the plays there were various recitals including one by La Meri, describing herself as "the most eclectic dancer in the world".

It was not until 1942 when it was taken over by Alec Clunes that the Arts at last became a theatre with a permanent management and a more or less permanent company. Clunes' first dozen productions, all but two of them revivals, showed no clearly defined policy and no markedly individual taste in plays. The most interesting and important of these twelve productions was Peter Ustinov's first play, *The House of Regrets*. A definite policy was initiated with a Festival of English Comedy which ran for many months. To run a repertoire changing almost nightly in a theatre as small and as cramped for stage space as the Arts was a remarkable feat of organisation. The plays were *The Constant Couple*, *The Rivals*, *The Magistrate*, *The Watched Pot* and *Misalliance*. Then came another long succession of plays chosen apparently at random. They included *Anna Christie* and *The Critic*, old West End successes such as *The Breadwinner* and *Bird in Hand*, and a couple of plays by Shaw. The only new play was Peter Powell's *The Two Children*, the winner of a play competition held by Alec Clunes. Most of the plays submitted were of very poor quality. Then a return to the repertoire system with a Festival of English Drama, consisting of *Getting Married*, *The Thunderbolt*, *The School for Scandal*, *The Constant Couple* and *Hamlet*. This was followed by an International Season of new plays. The most interesting of these was *Exercise Bowler* presented in partnership with the Reunion Theatre and written by T. Atkinson, a name that concealed no less than five authors, the chief of whom was William Templeton, one of the two authors put under contract by Alec Clunes on a yearly salary. This method of attempting to increase the supply of good new plays is one that ought to be adopted by all the established managements. Before the actor-managers were elbowed out of the theatre by the business men it was very usual to spend a considerable sum every year commissioning plays. Nowadays managements continually bewail the shortage of good new plays, but make not the slightest effort to encourage promising young authors to turn their attention to the theatre.

A theatre club with a character entirely different from all the others is the Players' Theatre, which opened at 43 King Street, Covent Garden on the third floor of a building which from 1844 to 1880 had been Evans's Music-and-Supper-Rooms. The Players' was founded by Peter Ridgeway who had been running a tiny studio theatre, first in Greek Street and later in Great Ormond Street. His early productions included Beatrice Mayor's *Little Earthquake* and *Heaven and Charing Cross* by Aubrey Danvers Walker, afterwards transferred to a West End theatre. On Friday nights there was an informal cabaret, in which the performers included Arthur Askey, Cyril Fletcher and Alec Clunes. These performances were so successful that towards the end of 1937 Ridgeway decided to revive, under the title of *Late Joys*, the Song-and-Supper-Room entertainment which had started nearly a hundred years before four floors below. The producer was Harold Scott who with Elsa Lanchester and Charles Laughton had run the Cave of Harmony, a Victorian cabaret in Seven Dials. Performances began at 11.30 p.m. and later extra shows were given on Tuesdays and Fridays at 1.30 a.m. At first the performances burlesqued the Victorians, but gradually there was less guying and more honest reproduction. The characteristics of the performances were charm, humour and gusto combined with good singing. Meanwhile plays were still given during the early part of the evening. The most memorable was a revival of *Charles and Mary* in which Peter Ridgeway made his last appearance. He died at the end of 1938, and Leonard Sachs who had helped Ridgeway to found the Players', took over the direction of the Club.

In 1940 the Players' moved to Albemarle Street and in 1946 to Hungerford Arches. Those who have affectionate memories of the crowded little room in King Street which was the Players' first home may perhaps regret the move to more spacious premises, but the ever-increasing membership of the Players' made larger premises essential. Ten years ago few people would have predicted the long and prosperous life of the Players'. Guying the Victorians seemed hardly likely to be more than a passing fashion. But the vitality of the Players' depends on more than this. It is the only theatre in London where the audience is part of the show. They lustily bellow the choruses, indulge in jovial repartee with the chairman, and at the end of the evening feel that the success of the show is as much due to themselves as to the actors. It is not unusual for the same people to go two or three times a week to shout the same jokes at the chairman and indulge in the same backchat with the performers. It is the happiest audience in London, but when I am there I must confess to being one of the least happy members of it. The atmosphere is too uproariously hearty for me. I always become miserably self-conscious when I find I am supposed to take part in community singing. So perhaps it is mere envy of those more vocal than myself which makes me feel that I would enjoy the style and wit of the performance more if the audience were a little less ostentatiously pleased with their own part in it.

Now that the Players' has roomier premises the intention is to use the *Joys* to subsidise at least four productions of straight plays each year, preferably by British dramatists. The first of these was *The Cave and the Garden*, a thoroughly original and interesting play by Ormerod Greenwood, exceptionally well produced and staged. But it drew poor houses. Evidently most of the members of the Players' are not prepared to be mere silent spectators.

A small theatre which no longer exists but deserves to be remembered is the Children's Theatre, founded by Joan Luxton and Agnes Lowson and opened in the autumn of 1927 at 81 Endell Street. With a seating capacity of only 115, it was the smallest theatre that has ever been licensed for public performances. The prices ranged from 5*s*. 9*d*. to 6*d*. and children were admitted at half price to all seats. The hour of performance was 5.45 daily, which fitted in nicely between teatime and bedtime for the audience, and between matinée and evening performances at other theatres for the company. The policy of the theatre was "to produce an entertainment colourful, tuneful and humorous, that would appeal to children's imagination, without striving to be consciously educational or highbrow". Most of the company consisted of actors who were working in the West End theatres, so they were able to play at the Children's Theatre for a very small nominal salary. Among them were Basil Radford, Ann Casson, Esmond Knight, Terence de Marney, Charles Hickman, Leslie Mitchell, Mackenzie Ward, Norman Shelley and Geoffrey Wincott. The opening programme consisted of sea shanties, folk songs, dances, mimes, and a two-act play called *The Dutch Doll*. The most popular items with the audience were *Matilda* from Hilaire Belloc's *Cautionary Tales, When Father Laid the Carpet on the Stairs*, and *The Lady and the Swine*. The theatre was too small and the prices too low for the venture to be a financial success. The anonymous backer behind the scheme hoped that someone with greater financial resources would take up the work on a larger scale, but his hopes were not realised. He was unable to go on backing the venture alone, so the theatre had to close in February 1931. To-day the financial difficulties of running such a theatre are eased by a grant from the Arts Council and exemption from entertainments tax. The Old Vic now has a Young Vic, and in 1944 the Glyndebourne management opened its Children's Theatre at Toynbee Hall backed by a six weeks' contract from the L.C.C. Education Committee. The play chosen for the first production was Alec Guinness's adaptation of *Great Expectations*, produced by Anthony Quayle. Afterwards the company toured for six months, giving 200 performances to total audiences of 80,000 children.

Now that some provision is being made for school children to see plays it is more than ever important that when they leave school in their 'teens, they should be able to continue their playgoing in the ordinary theatre at prices they can afford. This is easier for them in the provinces than in London. It used to be possible at the Vic to get a seat in the gallery for 3*d*. and a stall for 2*s*., but apart from Lilian Baylis, the only manager in London to make any real effort to cater for young audiences with little money to spend was Robert Newton who in 1933 leased the Grand Theatre, Fulham and re-named it the Shilling Theatre. His policy was to run twice nightly, except on Monday evenings, with a sixpenny gallery and every other seat in the house at 1*s*. The plays were mostly new plays. One of the most interesting was *Night's Candles*, an adaptation by Grant Yates of de Musset's *Lorenzaccio*. The scheme was based on the theory that a theatre that sells its whole house at 1s. a seat can be a self-supporting concern if it is a big enough theatre. The Grand seated 1,000 which meant an approximate capacity of £40. Twelve performances a week gave a capacity of £480. The rent was only £20. As established West End players were willing to act for a top salary of £15 the salary list was never more than £100 a week. The theatre staff cost £40 a week; rates were £5; printing and advertising £30; royalties £20; lighting £10; production expenses £25; totalling £240. The position of the theatre made it dependent on a local audience which was not large enough to support a play for more than a week. But with a weekly change of programme it was found impossible to maintain a high enough standard of production, so the project had to be abandoned.

Farther up the river from Fulham, at Barnes, Philip Ridgeway had in 1925 converted a cramped little cinema into a theatre and appointed as his producer Theodore Komisarjevsky, only recently arrived in England after being director of productions for both the Soviet Opera House and the Moscow Grand State Theatre of Opera and Ballet. On the tiny stage at Barnes he produced *Ivanov*, *Uncle Vanya*, *The Three Sisters*, *The Cherry Orchard*, Andreyev's *Katerina* and Gogol's *The Government Inspector*. These productions had an enormous influence on the whole art of producing in the English theatre. At that time most producers were trying to emulate the glittering efficiency of Basil Dean's productions which had set a new standard of realistic exactitude with their photographically accurate settings, their meticulously detailed stage business, their elaborately naturalistic acting and carefully directed teamwork. In Komisarjevsky's productions there was little factual realism. In his settings, which he designed himself, he was more concerned with mood than with detail, which he reduced to a minimum. His lighting, soft, rich and mellow, was romantic rather than realistic, and with the skill of a painter he made dramatic use of highlights, shadows and half-tones to give emphasis to his beautifully composed groupings and ensembles. I have seen nothing more lovely in the theatre than the stage pictures Komisarjevsky created on that cramped little stage at Barnes. His productions were as satisfying to the ear as they were to the eye. His use of subtle variations of tempo, modulation of tone and delicately timed pauses was far in advance of anything in the English theatre of that time when producers were just beginning to attempt to enliven the leisurely, measured tempo of English acting by borrowing something of the snip-snap speed of American production. But the final test of a producer is his ability to get the best out of his actors, and at Barnes everybody seemed to act better than they had ever acted before, sometimes better than they ever acted again. The same was happening at the St. Martin's Theatre where Basil Dean was directing the Reandean company, but the methods of the two producers were very different. Dean moulded his actors painstakingly and exactly to his own conception of each part while Komisarjevsky's method was to wait and see what the actor would bring to the part. He was very ready to accept the actor's conception of the part even if it was different from his own, provided it fitted within the framework of the play. If an actor was not prepared to use his brains and imagination Komisarjevsky quickly lost interest in him. He achieved his results quietly and unobtrusively with the minimum of fuss and talk. John Gielgud, who was a member of the company at Barnes, has described in *Early Stages* how Komisarjevsky would "let the actors find their own way, watch, keep silent, then place the phrasing of a scene in a series of pauses, the timing of which he would rehearse minutely. Very occasionally he would make some short but intensely illuminating comment, which was immensely significant and easy to remember".

If Komisarjevsky's group of actors at Barnes could have been put on a permanent basis I think they would have developed under his direction into a company comparable to the greatest on the continent. With him at Barnes, in addition to John Gielgud, were Charles Laughton, Claude Rains, Ion Swinley, Jean Forbes Robertson, Jeanne de Casalis, and Martita Hunt. But actors could not be expected to play indefinitely for the tiny salaries which were all that could be paid at Barnes, and at the end of 1926 the company was disbanded and the theatre reverted to being a cinema. Afterwards Komisarjevsky did many fine productions elsewhere, but he was never able to settle down happily in the commercial theatre. He believed too intensely in his own creed, that "an actor who is an artist must be prepared to fight against the taste of the greater public and to realise that his job is nothing but self-sacrifice. The Theatre as an art is inconceivable unless it is served by self-sacrificing artists, and run on a small non-mercantile scale by people who understand the nature of the Theatre, and make it exist on but a limited patronage".

At the other end of London there was another suburban theatre which had a great influence on the West End stage. This was the Everyman at Hampstead, a drill hall converted into a theatre by Norman Macdermott, a Liverpool business man, who opened it in 1920. Although he had little practical knowledge of the theatre he had a first-rate taste in plays and great courage and pertinacity. As a producer he was badly handicapped by his lack of professional knowledge, but he understood the plays he produced, played no tricks with them, cast well and showed a good pictorial sense in his grouping, settings and lighting. If he lacked originality, imagination and technical skill, at least he never got in the way of the play, which was always allowed to speak for itself.

Opening with a somewhat arty production of Benavente's *Bonds of Interest*, the first season included Masefield's *The Tragedy of Nan*, Galsworthy's *The Foundations* and *The Little Man*, Zangwill's *The Melting Pot*, Arnold Bennett's *The Honeymoon* and an excellent children's play, *Through the Crack*. During the first season the company was mainly a permanent one, headed by Nicholas Hannen, Muriel Pratt, Brember Wills and Lawrence Hanray. But, again, it became impossible to hold a permanent company of first-class actors at the small salaries the Everyman was able to pay, so subsequently a fresh cast was engaged for each production and everybody was paid a flat rate of £5 a week. There was much fine acting to be seen at the Everyman in those days. For instance, Leslie Banks and Jean Cadell in O'Neill's *Diff'rent*, Isabel Jeans in *The Country Wife*, Claude Rains in *The Doctor's Dilemma*, Mrs. Patrick Campbell in *Hedda Gabler*, Athene Seyler and Frank Cellier in *The Mask and the Face*, and Lilian Braithwaite and Noel Coward in *The Vortex*. These last two plays were among several which, after they had been produced at the Everyman, had long runs in the West End. Others were *Outward Bound* and *At Mrs. Beam's*. In 1925 Malcolm Morley took over the direction of the Everyman from Macdermott. His most notable productions were Strindberg's *The Father*, Bernard's *Invitation to a Voyage* and a series of Ibsen's plays including *The Master Builder*, *The Wild Duck*, *Ghosts* and *Little Eyolf*. Morley was not so fortunate as Macdermott in finding good new plays, and perhaps this was the reason why eventually he had to close down. A theatre as small as the Everyman, if it is not a club theatre to some extent subsidised by the subscriptions of its members, needs an occasional transfer to the West End to provide a further source of income.

The place of the Everyman has been taken by the Embassy Theatre built in 1927. The success of the Lyric at Hammersmith had encouraged the idea that it was possible for a suburban theatre to run a production for many months, so the original plan at the Embassy was to put on each play for an unlimited time. But there was nobody of Playfair's calibre to direct the Embassy and it quickly became a try-out theatre on the lines of the Q Theatre, running productions for a fortnight. Soon it was being let to touring companies for a week at a time and after that it was available for any amateur company that cared to rent it. In 1930 it was taken over by Alec Rea and A. R. Whatmore. Their policy was fortnightly, but they were not a try-out management. Their programmes included Goldoni's *The Liar*, Maugham's *Home and Beauty*, Karel Capek's *The Macropulos Secret*, *Romeo and Juliet*, and Monkhouse's *Mary Broome*. Among the new plays produced by this management at the Embassy were Mary Webb's *Precious Bane* (with Robert Donat), Mordaunt Shairp's *The Crime at Blossoms*, Rodney Ackland's *Strange Orchestra*, and *Britannia of Billingsgate* by Sewell Stokes and Christine Jope-Slade, all of which afterwards went to the West End. But business was poor and in February 1932 Rea terminated his tenancy. Ronald Adam who had been Rea's business manager decided to carry on. His first plays were revivals. Then he opened his autumn season with Hans Clumberg's *Miracle at Verdun*. This was the first of a long list of plays given at the Embassy under Ronald Adam's direction which afterwards went to other theatres. During his seven years' tenancy he provided the West End managers with no less than twenty-eight plays. These included *Ten Minute Alibi*, *The Cathedral*, *All God's Chillun* (with Flora Robson and Paul Robeson), *The Tudor Wench* (with Beatrix Lehmann), *Sixteen*, *The Road to Rome*, *The Dominant Sex*, *Distinguished Gathering*, and a revue, *Let's Go Gay*.

Adam's management of the Embassy ended at the outbreak of war and the theatre remained closed until 1945 when it was re-opened by Anthony Hawtrey. His policy also is to use the Embassy for trying out plays likely to prove suitable to the West End. So far his most notable discovery has been Joan Temple's *No Room at the Inn*, a play which even after its great success at the Embassy was rejected again and again by West End theatre owners. Eventually, after wandering the provinces for months, the play found lodging in the Winter Garden Theatre. It was expected to survive for only a week or two in this theatre which seemed far too large for the play, but the theatre-going public once again refused to live up to its reputation for wanting only escapist entertainment and kept it running for many months.

The latest venture in the suburban theatre has been the rejuvenation of the Lyric Theatre, Hammersmith, reopened in 1945 by the Company of Four, consisting of Tennent Plays Limited, Glyndebourne Opera, the Arts Theatre, Cambridge and Tyrone Guthrie, working in association with the Arts Council. So far the results have hardly justified so impressive a muster of managements. Production, acting and staging have generally been excellent but the Four have not yet discovered any particularly good new work, perhaps because they seem to have a predilection for a rather pretentious type of play stuffed with platitudinous philosophising. The most interesting feature of the scheme is the arrangement whereby each play, either before or after running for four weeks at the Lyric, visits Cambridge, Bristol, Brighton and Cardiff. This is the first time an experimental theatre in London has worked in close collaboration with a circuit of theatres in the provinces.

The Hammersmith scheme, now gathering strength and showing signs of being able to stand firmly on its own legs, was for many months supported by a subsidy from the Arts Council. Or rather, it was subsidised from the profits on *Lady Windermere's Fan*. Tennent Plays Limited, the non-profit-making branch of H. M. Tennent Limited, debarred from using the proceeds of their production of *Lady Windermere's Fan* except for another non-profit-making venture, was able to use them to keep the Company of Four at Hammersmith when otherwise they would have been starved out through lack of money in the box office. One thinks rather wistfully of how different this chapter would have been if some of the managements mentioned in it had been exempted from entertainments tax and given a small guarantee such as is now provided by the Arts Council. Komisarjevsky might have been able to hold together his company and eventually settle them in a larger theatre, the Everyman would perhaps not now be a cinema, the Shilling Theatre might be a flourishing People's Theatre and from the little theatre in Endell Street there might have developed a chain of Children's Theatres throughout the country. Now that help is forthcoming for enterprises such as these it is ironical that there is little hope at present of any new ventures of the kind being started until it is possible, if not to build new theatres, then at least to convert some existing building into a theatre.

CHAPTER XV

TWENTY-FIVE YEARS LATER

THE week of the Victory Celebrations, 1946. One year after the end of the war, a convenient moment to survey the theatre as it is and speculate on what it may become.

There are forty theatres advertising in *The Times* this week, exactly the same number as were advertising in the Entertainments Column one year after the war of 1914–18. Many of the theatres in that old list are absent from to-day's column. The Alhambra, the Empire, Daly's and the Pavilion are cinemas. The Lyceum is a dance hall. The Gaiety and the Royalty stand derelict. The Court, the Little, the Kingsway, the Queens, the Shaftesbury and the Old Vic are war casualties. Drury Lane, just released from war service, has not yet re-opened as a theatre. Taking the place of some of the names that have vanished from the list are the Duchess, the Mercury, the Palladium, the Phoenix, the Piccadilly, the Westminster, Sadler's Wells, the Whitehall and the Fortune, all built since 1919.

Although the names of many of the theatres in the Entertainments Column are different, what they are offering is much the same as in 1919. The only marked difference is that twenty-seven years ago melodrama was still popular. *The Great Day* by Louis N. Parker and George Sims was at Drury Lane, and at the Savoy there was *Tiger Rose*, billed as "A Drama of the Great North West". Musical shows to-day occupy exactly the same number of theatres as in 1919, but there is nothing among the fifteen musicals in the present list to compare with *The Maid of the Mountains*, *Chu Chin Chow* and *The Lilac Domino*, though *Sweetest and Lowest* can stand comparison with *Bran Pie* and *Buzz Buzz*, the intimate revues of 1919. The popularity of farce seems no more variable than the popularity of musical shows judging from the fact that there are two on both lists. Light comedies and thrillers totalled nine in 1919 as against five in 1946. Shakespeare appears three times in the old list. His plays were to be seen at the Court, the Scala and the Old Vic; but during this week of Victory Celebrations, when London is packed with visitors from the Dominions and the Colonies, the only Shakespeare is *As You Like It* at the Open Air Theatre, and the only Shaw is *Man and Superman* at the King's Theatre, Hammersmith. Otherwise there is not a single play by any of the great English dramatists to be seen in the London theatre, a fact which is sufficient reply to those who argue that we do not need a National Theatre.

The best that the London theatre had to offer a year after the war of 1914–18 was Henry Ainley in Tolstoy's *The Living Corpse*, *Le Bourgeois Gentilhomme* performed by a company of French players, the Gilbert and Sullivan operas, Drinkwater's *Abraham Lincoln*, plays by Maugham, Sutro and Arnold Bennett, a Beecham season at Covent Garden, and three Shakespearian productions. How does this compare with what the London theatre now offers a year after another war? Opera and ballet occupy three theatres; Shakespeare has been turned out-of-doors; there is a glossy revival of *Lady Windermere's Fan*, and two good historical plays, *The First Gentleman* and *The King Maker*; in *The Winslow Boy* and *The Guinea Pig* big themes are cautiously handled so as not to obtrude at the expense of laughter and sentiment; *Frieda* treats a contemporary theme more boldly if less efficiently; there is an adaptation of *The Brothers Karamazov* at the Lyric, Hammersmith, and a season of plays by poets at the Mercury. The two best plays in London, *Red Roses For Me* and *No Room at the Inn*, have only just succeeded in fighting their way into the West End after first being produced at the Embassy in Hampstead, and then touring for months while they were denied a London theatre.

It is in the provinces that the theatre has changed most. The first page of the *Stage* this week lists 106 touring theatres. In 1919 the number was 255. Of the 106 touring theatres still remaining (excluding music-halls) sixty-seven are given over to twice nightly revues. The main attraction of these shows is indicated by titles like *Giggles and Girls*, *Up Girls and Atom*, *All Girls Together* and *Naughty Girls of 1946*. There remain only thirty-nine touring theatres in England and Scotland to house straight plays, musical comedies, opera and ballet. Musical comedies occupy sixteen of these this week. The present poverty of the musical comedy stage is reflected in the number of revivals. *Mercenary Mary*, *No, No, Nanette*, *The Quaker Girl*, *The Belle of New York*, *Florodora* and *The Waltz Dream* are still plodding round the provinces. There are two opera companies on tour, and one ballet company. No Shakespeare, no plays by any of the great English dramatists. The only play of importance in the whole list is Rodney Ackland's adaptation of *Crime and Punishment* with John Gielgud and Edith Evans.

In 1919 touring revues occupied eighty-four theatres, leaving 171 for other forms of theatrical entertainment. Musical comedies were playing at eighteen theatres. There were five opera companies on tour; Shakespeare was provided by Henry Baynton, and there were two Shakespearian plays in Martin Harvey's repertoire; the Compton Comedy Company was giving the old English comedies, and the Irish Players were on a provincial tour. The only other straight plays of any particular quality were *Abraham Lincoln*, *Dear Brutus*, *Hindle Wakes* and *The Land of Promise*. Melodrama still flourished in the provinces judging from the number of titles like *The Curse of the Black Pearl*, *The Custody of the Child*, *The Unmarried Mother*, *Forbidden Love*, *Disgraced*, *Soiled*, *The Heart of a Thief*, *The Mill Girl's Wedding*, *The Tainted Woman*, *The Woman Who Lied*. The rest of the plays were the light comedy successes of the London theatre during the war; farces with oh-so-naughty titles like *Bedroom Wedding* and *Dora Stays the Night*; historical romances such as *A Royal Divorce* and the plays in Fred Terry's repertoire; and of course, *The Passing of the Third Floor Back*, *Daddy Long Legs*, *Eliza Comes to Stay*, *Nothing But the Truth*, *Charley's Aunt*, *Peg o' My Heart*, and *The Private Secretary*. There were fifteen repertory companies playing seasons in the smaller provincial towns, but they had little in common with the repertory companies of to-day. Most of them were descendants of the old fit-ups, playing melodramas and crude farces, often changing their bill nightly. Liverpool and Birmingham were the only towns with their own repertory theatres.

Financially the theatre in 1946 is even more unhealthy than it was in 1919. At that time the boom in theatrical business had been going on for five years; during the last war it only started towards the end, when London was at last free from the threat of raids, flying bombs and rockets. The constant fluctuation in business caused by these attacks from the air kept the speculators out of the theatre during most of the war. Then theatrical history began to repeat itself. Theatres were sold and resold at prices so inflated that none of the established managements would buy. Because of the sums paid for the theatres that came upon the market, their rents were forced up to a hopelessly uneconomic figure. For instance, a theatre which before the war had difficulty in getting a tenant at a rent of £50 a week, plus a percentage which brought the rent up to £250 if the theatre played to its capacity business of £2,000 a week, a few months ago demanded, and got, a minimum rental of £600 a week plus a percentage over a certain figure.

To make matters worse, the theatre is mainly controlled by a small group of managements. At present there are only sixteen straight plays to be seen in the centre of London, if one excludes two farces from the list. One management is responsible for eight of these sixteen plays. Obviously it is undesirable that the taste of a single management should govern the choice of half the straight plays running in London, however good the taste of that management may be, and however well it presents its shows, especially when this management is in partnership with a firm which controls nearly all the important touring theatres in the provinces. If a straight actor or a producer does not happen to be popular with this management, it means that his chance of employment in London is halved. The effect on an author is equally serious. If his play is turned down by this management there remain only a very few theatres in which he can hope to get his play produced. A healthy theatre is one in which there is the maximum amount of variety. That can only be achieved when there is a large number of managements choosing plays according to their own individual tastes.

A still more serious form of monopoly, because it is likely to prove more lasting, is that exercised by landlords controlling groups of theatres. To give one instance, eight of the most important theatres in the West End are owned by a landlord who is also a director of other firms owning three more West End theatres, as well as being on the board of the management controlling nearly all the important touring theatres. Apart from the fact that monopoly has the inevitable effect of keeping theatre rents at an artificially high level, a landlord has considerable say as to what plays shall be presented in his theatres, so variety of choice is still further limited.

That theatrical fare is not even more monotonous than it is at present is largely due to the work of the Arts Council and the small outlying theatres. Plays at present produced in London in association with the Arts Council are *Lady Windermere's Fan*, *The King Maker*, *Red Roses For Me*, *Frieda*, *As You Like It* at the Open Air Theatre, *The Brothers Karamazov*, the season of plays by poets at the Mercury, the ballet and opera seasons at Covent Garden and Sadler's Wells, the festival of new plays at the Arts Theatre Club, the productions at the Embassy Theatre, and the season by the Travelling Repertory Theatre at the King's, Hammersmith which has included *Romeo and Juliet*, *St. Joan*, *Electra*, *Man and Superman*, and two new plays, *In Time to Come* by Howard Koch and *The Wise Have Not Spoken* by Paul Vincent Carroll.

The Arts Council, originally called The Council for the Encouragement of Music and the Arts, and financed by the Treasury, was founded in 1940 with the declared purpose of "maintaining the highest possible standard in the Arts". The State had already begun to give some encouragement to the drama before the war; at least it had ceased to discourage the production of fine plays by heavily taxing the takings irrespective of whether the play was running at a profit or a loss. Remission of tax was granted for plays which could be classed as "educational", a vague word which was often somewhat oddly interpreted.

When one recalls the hullabaloo in Parliament and the press before the war over a suggestion that a small grant should be made to finance the opera season at Covent Garden, it is remarkable how little opposition there was to C.E.M.A. being provided with some of the tax-payers' money to finance plays, opera and ballet, as well as concerts and exhibitions of pictures. Perhaps this was due more to the prestige and tactical skill of Lord Keynes, to whom C.E.M.A. owed its existence, rather than to a change of attitude towards the arts on the part of the public and its members of parliament. For many years Keynes had believed that the State should give practical help to the arts, but he was patient and far-seeing, and it was one of his guiding beliefs that it is worse than useless to urge a reform until the moment is ripe for its adoption. So he quietly waited his opportunity. It came during the first winter of the war. A large part of the population had been redistributed to work in localities far from their homes. The cinemas were too few and too small to provide enough entertainment for the swollen population of these districts during the long black-out evenings. It was realised that their morale would soon begin to suffer. Lord de la Warr, President of the Board of Education, approached the Pilgrim Trust for a grant to provide concerts in villages and small towns crammed with transferred workers and evacuees. Keynes saw that here was his opportunity. Through his influence the Treasury agreed to double the grant of £25,000 made by the Pilgrim Trust. Three months later the Treasury doubled its own grant.

Thus, unobtrusively, without any special legislation, with the minimum of fuss and discussion, the State began to subsidise the arts. The Board of Education lent some of its staff to set up a small organisation called The Council for the Encouragement of Music and the Arts, with Lord Keynes as Chairman. As the activities of C.E.M.A. rapidly developed, the Treasury continued to increase its grant and the Pilgrim Trust was relieved of further financial responsibility. It was taken for granted that C.E.M.A. was a temporary war-time organisation—by everybody except Keynes. He believed that if C.E.M.A. could be run efficiently and economically it would supply a need which would not pass with the ending of the war. In spite of the heavy burden of his work at the Treasury and his failing health, he continued to give a great deal of time and thought to the development of C.E.M.A. Even during the conferences at Washington he kept in touch and found time to make detailed suggestions and lay plans for the future. His belief that C.E.M.A.

could be the means of establishing State aid to the arts on a permanent basis was justified when five and a half years after its foundation C.E.M.A. was given permanent status as The Arts Council of Great Britain.

C.E.M.A.'s first theatrical venture was a tour of Martin Browne's Pilgrim Players. The Market Theatre, directed by Vivienne Bennett, was the next company with which it co-operated. Then it took the Old Vic and Sadler's Wells companies into its care, and it was under C.E.M.A.'s auspices that Donald Wolfit gave his lunch-time Shakespeare shows at the Strand Theatre during the worst period of the blitz. In 1942 touring companies were sent to some of the hostels for factory workers. By 1945 sixty-nine hostels were being regularly visited by C.E.M.A. companies. There was no attempt to play down to the audiences in the choice of plays. Among the biggest successes were *Twelfth Night* with Wendy Hiller as Viola, *Hedda Gabler* with Sonia Dresdel in the lead, and *They Came to a City* played by the West End company. Other plays were *She Stoops to Conquer*, *Lady Precious Stream*, *Sheppey*, *Arms and the Man*, *A Doll's House*, *The Importance of Being Earnest*, *Doctor Knock*, *A Bill of Divorcement*, *Milestones*, *Candida*, *The Brontës*, *I Have Been Here Before*, *You Never Can Tell*, *The Shoemaker's Holiday*, *Outward Bound*, *The Village Wooing* and *The Man of Destiny*. In addition to the plays there were performances by the Rambert Ballet and the Ballets Jooss.

I am surprised how few people know that all the large factory hostels had well-equipped theatres, seating on an average an audience of 600, though books and articles on the Russian theatre published in this country have given wide publicity to similar "workers' theatres" in the U.S.S.R. But the C.E.M.A. companies were not sent only to the factories. They went also to small out-of-the-way towns and to larger provincial towns which for many years had seen nothing at their theatre except twice nightly musical shows.

In 1942 C.E.M.A. bought the Theatre Royal, Bristol, one of the oldest theatres in the country, which was in danger of being pulled down as the citizens of Bristol could not be roused to make any real effort to preserve it. Thus the Theatre Royal, Bristol became virtually the first State theatre in England. At present it is occupied by an Old Vic company. Later C.E.M.A. acquired the Arts Theatre, Salisbury, which was originally a cinema and had been converted into a Garrison Theatre during the war. A new production is put on once a month which runs for ten days at the Arts Theatre and then plays in public halls in Southampton, Winchester, Chippenham and other surrounding towns, none of which has a proper theatre. A company working on a similar plan has now been installed at

Coventry with its headquarters at the theatre of the Coventry Technical College.

In London the Arts Council operates mainly in collaboration with the Old Vic, the Sadler's Wells Opera and Ballet companies, and with Tennent Plays Limited, the management which under the auspices of the Arts Council has presented *Macbeth*, *Love for Love*, *A Month in the Country*, *They Came to a City*, *Lady Windermere's Fan*, *Crime and Punishment*, and the repertoire seasons at the Haymarket.

State aid to the drama is at present limited to "properly constituted non-profit-making organisations and bodies functioning under charitable trusts". The most substantial assistance is that given in the form of remission of entertainments tax. The authority to remit tax is not exercised by the Arts Council but by H.M. Customs and Excise. A company need not necessarily be associated with the Arts Council to obtain this concession. Donald Wolfit's company, for instance, now operates independently of the Arts Council but is exempt from tax. Financial assistance from the Arts Council is provided in several ways; it may take the form of a grant, or a guarantee against loss up to an agreed figure, or a returnable loan. In addition, the Arts Council has a number of companies under its direct management, for which it assumes entire financial responsibility.

The fact that only non-profit-making companies can qualify for assistance, whether in the form of a guarantee or remission of entertainments tax, limits the effectiveness of State aid to the theatre. Up to now this stipulation has been accepted by commercial managements which have collaborated with the Arts Council because E.P.T. has made it impossible for them to amass large profits; so a convenient method of extending their activities and gaining prestige without much danger of incurring losses was to form a subsidiary non-profit-making company for "prestige productions", and thus obtain a subsidy in the form of exemption from tax. When E.P.T. is abolished or substantially reduced, these managements may not be so ready to produce plays under conditions which deny them a profit. There is a strong case to be made for the classics, at least, being exempt from tax irrespective of whether or not the management is prepared to forgo all profits.

Another argument against the non-profit-making clause is that a West End management which presents a play in association with the Arts Council can outbid other managements when casting and looking for a theatre. As there is no point in budgeting to make profits, the forty per cent of the takings which would normally go in entertainments tax are apt to be spent on filling the cast with more "names" than any taxed production could carry, and on making certtain of a theatre by paying a rent higher than could be afforded by a management presenting a play under commercial conditions. A better method than the present one might be to make no remittance of entertainment tax and use the money thus saved to give limited guarantees to worth-while productions, irrespective of whether the management is a "properly constituted non-profit-making organisation".

In addition to the assistance given to companies by means of loans, grants and guarantees, the Arts Council has also made various ventures into management on its own account, thus stepping from State aid to State control. When a government department becomes a direct employer of actors, there is a danger that it may develop a form of monopoly even more dangerous to the independence of the actor than that now exercised by the largest of the London managements.

The greatest service that the State can give to the drama is by doing everything within its power to encourage the building of more theatres. At a time when there has been a phenomenal increase in the demand for good drama the theatre is unable to meet it because of the lack of buildings. The increased demand for books from the new reading public has to some extent been catered for by over 200 new publishers which have set up in business since the outbreak of war. In the theatre there are fewer managements and fewer theatres than there were in 1939.

The Arts Council's first concern should be with those towns which have no theatre or whose only theatre is occupied year in and year out by twice nightly revues. The Civic Theatre scheme outlined in the previous chapter offers a possible solution to the present famine conditions in the provinces. The possibility of the Government and the municipalities becoming builders and owners of theatres has already become sufficiently real to alarm the theatrical industry. A recent article in *The Theatre Industry Journal* argues that "as there are not enough suitable straight plays appealing to the public to keep the theatre open for fifty-two weeks in the year, or even forty weeks, putting up more buildings is not going to increase the supply; in fact, it will have the opposite effect". This is nonsense. The reason why the touring theatre finds it so difficult to obtain "enough suitable straight plays appealing to the public" is because on an average only fifteen theatres in London are devoted to the production of straight plays, and as some of these run a year, two years, or even longer, the number of good new plays produced in London in the course of a year is pitifully small, certainly totally inadequate to supply a sufficient amount of good entertainment to even the thirty-nine once nightly touring theatres which are all that now remain compared with 171 after the war of 1914–18. Owing to the hopelessly inadequate number of theatres, many authors who have an urge to write for the stage realise that the odds against their plays ever being produced are so heavy that they confine themselves to other forms of writing instead. Municipal theatres capable of giving new plays a good production would do more than anything else to encourage dramatic authorship and eventually enlarge the choice of plays for the commercial theatre both in London and the provinces.

Any scheme for a number of subsidised theatres is immediately greeted with angry, frightened shrieks of "unfair competition" from the theatrical industry; but a subsidised theatre, relieved of the burden of entertainments tax and the necessity for showing large profits, can take far greater risks than it is reasonable to expect a profit-making organisation to undertake, and by producing the works of dramatists which seem "risky propositions" to the commercial manager, the subsidised theatre will increase the number of plays which the commercial managers require to keep their theatres open. Shaw is now the biggest box office draw in the English theatre, and the commercial managements have profited by his popularity. But it is a popularity which was slowly and expensively built up through productions subsidised by private patrons of the drama such as Sir Barry Jackson, and the members of the Stage Society.

It is sheer bad business on the part of the commercial managements to oppose the enlargement of the theatre by State-aided enterprise. More opportunities for theatre-going will inevitably result in an increase in the habit of theatre-going, especially among those people who so far, mainly through lack of opportunity, have shown little or no interest in the living theatre. The colossal size of the cinema-going public is largely due to the fact that there are so many cinemas in every town that "going to the pictures" has become an easily acquired habit. The theatre-going habit is much more likely to be acquired in a town where there are two or three theatres than where there is only a single theatre and therefore no choice of play. If a playgoer only occasionally finds something at the local theatre to appeal to his taste, say once in six weeks, he does not acquire the habit of theatre-going and as a result is apt to lose interest in the theatre altogether. But if there are several theatres in the town, providing a varied choice of entertainment, he is much more likely to get into the habit of going every week to the theatre, choosing the one that has something he thinks will be to his taste.

When the B.B.C. founded a subsidised symphony orchestra there was that familiar howl of "unfair competition" from the concert promoters, but it is now recognised that the huge new public for symphony concerts has been largely due to the work of the B.B.C. in popularising orchestral concerts. In the same way a National Theatre in London and municipal theatres in the provinces will create new audiences which will not confine their theatre-going solely to subsidised theatres. Anything that is likely to increase interest in the theatre benefits the theatre as a whole. On the continent a flourishing commercial theatre has always existed side by side with theatres financed by the State and municipalities. From the point of view of the theatre-goer it is preposterous that a great art should be the monopoly of organisations whose main aim is the amassing of large profits.

A deplorable example of the opposition of theatre proprietors to any attempt on the part of a municipality to augment the inadequate amount of entertainment in their city was the objection raised to the project of the Manchester City Corporation to install a company of actors in the small theatre in the Central Library. A leading article in the *Manchester Guardian* dealt with this opposition from the point of view of the theatre-goer. "Manchester is the last city, surely, where the voice of the theatre proprietor should be heard in pained protest against competition. Those of its citizens who can remember the glories of the Manchester stage are already few, and ageing. Most of the time now we have one theatre left for 'the legitimate' and in some weeks not even that. A fully fledged municipal theatre, employing professional companies and entering into direct and downright competition with trade interests, may soon become a necessity if the drama is not to die on our hands. The actors will be found supporting it, and the managements, which at present offer them (and their authors) no opportunity to be seen or heard in this great English-listening centre, will have no case to make against it which was not derelict and dead a generation ago. How much less a case there is behind the opposition to the present over-mild project of the city corporation to employ the tiny theatre in the Central Library so as to get full value out of the educational and cultural activities for which it was designed. They propose to employ real actors in order to cultivate more effectively the public taste for drama (in other words, the inclination to theatre-going), on which the commercial theatre itself depends for its profits. And they are to be told that they must only employ amateurs on the presumption that the job will be less efficiently done. Clearly the theatre managements do not know on which side their bread is buttered; we must rely on the corporation to insist that it is the public's bread, too."

Present conditions in the theatre date from the war of 1914–18 when the control of the theatres passed out of the hands of the actor-managers and producing-managers into the hands of men of business, who had no feeling of responsibility towards the theatre either as an art or a profession, and were more interested in a quick return on their money than in long-term planning. It is difficult to imagine one of the actor-managers selling his theatre as a cinema, but to-day the theatrical profession can only look on helplessly while negotiations proceed for more theatres to be sold for conversion into cinemas, and the Westminster Theatre is disposed of to the Oxford Group for its amateur theatricals.

The ever-increasing shortage of theatres makes it difficult to end this book on a hopeful note. In the old days dwindling audiences were generally the reason for periodic outbreaks of speculation about "What's wrong with the theatre". To-day, when audiences are larger and more enterprising than they have ever been before, there are not the buildings in which to accommodate them. There is little hope of any alteration in this state of affairs in the immediate future, and by the time it is possible to build more theatres most of the new audience built up during the war by C.E.M.A. and E.N.S.A. will have drifted away from the theatre again because of the lack of sufficient opportunities for playgoing. It is unlikely that apart from the National Theatre any new theatres will be built in London during this century. At least two of the badly damaged theatres are to be rebuilt as blocks of offices. As property in the centre of London becomes more and more valuable it is likely that unless the Government takes action to prevent it many existing theatres will be sold at huge prices to be pulled down and rebuilt as hotels or business premises. As London theatres grow fewer rents will soar and prices of seats will have to be substantially increased to pay these rents. Theatre-going in the West End will become so expensive that except for the very rich it will be confined mainly to "a night out" for the celebration of some special occasion. The non-commercial theatre which between the two wars saved the London theatre from stagnation by providing a constant flow of new plays and new players, will not be able to operate on anything like the scale it did after the last war. This time there are no longer any out-of-the-way empty theatres to be found. Immensely increased costs make it almost impossible for a Sunday society to put on any but the simplest productions without incurring crippling losses. The output of new plays will be reduced to a mere trickle unless great provincial cities such as Manchester, Oxford, Edinburgh, Leeds and Newcastle can build theatres which will become centres of creative work, housing companies fine enough to equal the prestige achieved in the musical world by provincial orchestras such as the Hallé and the Liverpool Philharmonic.

During the years which must elapse before municipal theatres can be built in the provinces a great responsibility rests on the repertory theatres. It is imperative that they should re-organise themselves so as to be able to work under conditions which make it possible to create new playwrights and properly trained actors. If there are to be no more than a dozen theatres in London and only three or four repertories in the provinces capable of giving adequate productions of new plays, there is a real danger that the race of English dramatists may soon become almost extinct.

INDEX OF PLAYS, THEATRES AND COMPANIES

A

Abbey Theatre, Dublin, 92, 149
Abraham Lincoln, 35, 135, 201, 211, 225
Adam the Creator, 58
Adding Machine, The, 45, 74, 76, 91, 151, 171
Adults Only, 83
After All, 74
Agamemnon, 212
Alchemist, The, 202
Alice in Thunderland, 101
Alien Corn, 211
Alison's House, 68, 199
All Change Here, 101
All For Love, 67, 170
All God's Chillun, 222
Amersham Repertory Company, 194
Amphytrion, 76, 213
Anatol, 111
Anatomist, The, 211
Androcles and the Lion, 18, 201
And So To Bed, 28, 215
Anna Christie, 202, 215
Anthony and Anna, 199
Applecart, The, 14, 169, 171
Aristocrats, 100
Arms and the Man, 198, 229
Arts Council, 133, 194, 195, 207, 218, 222, 223, 227–234
Arts Theatre, Cambridge, 201, 211, 222
Arts Theatre Club, 14, 214–216, 227
Arts Theatre, Salisbury, 229
As You Desire Me, 50
As You Like It, 35, 58, 66, 168, 202, 224, 226, 227
Ascent of F 6, 167, 212
Asmodee, 97, 120
At Mrs. Beam's, 74, 221
At the Gates of the Kingdom, 75
Awake and Sing, 75

B

Back to Methuselah, 91, 163, 169, 171
Ballet Club, 154–158
Ballet Rambert, 154–158
Barnes Theatre, 11, 218–219
Bartholomew Fair, 76
Barretts of Wimpole Street, The, 14, 169, 171, 198
Bastos the Bold, 68
Beaten Track, The, 26
Beaux' Stratagem, The, 36, 39, 97
Beggar Prince, The, 201
Beggar on Horseback, 70
Beggar's Opera, The, 33, 35, 36, 37
Believe It Or Not, 198
Bells Are Ringing, The, 98
Bernice, 43
Bill of Divorcement, A, 98, 229
Bird in Hand, 163, 171, 215
Birds, The, 58
Birmingham Repertory Theatre, 12, 19, 22, 35, 55, 56, 163–168, 197, 205
Bluestone Quarry, 75
Boatswain's Mate, The, 153
Bonds of Interest, The, 220
Bradford Civic Playhouse, 91, 98
Bright Island, The, 76
British Drama League, 87, 88, 205
Britannia of Billingsgate, 221
Brothers Karamazov, The, 45, 225, 227

C

Caesar and Cleopatra, 29, 58, 166, 169
Camargo Society, 82–83
Cambridge Festival Theatre, 13, 14, 26, 47, 49, 53–71, 102, 106, 108, 109, 114, 139, 141, 149, 210
Candida, 23, 229
Captain Brassbound's Conversion, 23
Carthaginian, The, 58
Cathedral, The, 222
Cave and the Garden, The, 217
Cave of Harmony, The, 216
C.E.M.A., (See Arts Council)
Cenci, The, 91
Cherry Orchard, The, 23–26, 128, 134, 219
Chicago, 110
Children's Carnival, The, 81
Children's Hour, The, 114, 115
Children in Uniform, 211
Children's Tragedy, The, 74, 76
Circle of Chalk, The, 166
City Wives' Confederacy, The, 201
Confederacy, The, 26
Conquering Hero, The, 81
Constant Couple, The, 215
Conversion of St. Paul, The, 170
Coriolanus, 95, 131
Cornelius, 211
Coronation Time at Mrs. Beam's, 169
Corsican Brothers, The, 163
Counsellor-at-Law, 166
Country Wife, The, 221
Covent Garden Opera House, 142, 148, 152, 158, 159, 225, 227, 228
Coventry Technical College Theatre, 230
Creditors, 215
Crime and Punishment, 225, 230
Critic, The, 36, 40, 215
Cure for Love, The, 212

D

Dance of Death, The, 43, 212
Dandy Dick, 23, 28, 67
Dangerous Corner, 222
Danton, 91
Dark Lady of the Sonnets, The, 23
Dark River, The, 83
David, 75
Death Takes a Holiday, 28
Deirdre, 26
Deirdre of the Sorrows, 23, 67
Derby Day, 40
Desire Under the Elms, 48, 211
Devil's Disciple, The, 58, 132
Devil's in the News, The, 75

INDEX

Dictator, The, 74
Diff'rent, 221
Discovery, The, 79
Distant Point, 100, 117, 196
Dr. Knock, 45, 58, 70, 229
Doctor's Dilemma, The, 162, 221
Don Juan, 79, 97
Douaumont, 48, 74
Double Dealer, The, 76
Dreamy Kid, The, 58
Duchess of Malfi, The, 76
Dublin Gate Theatre, 211
Duenna, The, 36
Dundee Repertory Theatre, 194–195
Dybbuk, The, 91

E

Easter, 26, 215
Eater of Dreams, The, 48
Ecole de Cocottes, 81
Eden End, 202
Edward II, 76
Ehen Werden in Himmel Geschlossen, 215
Electra, 227
Elizabeth, La Femme Sans Homme, 117
Embassy Theatre, 221–222, 225, 227
Emperor Jones, The, 12, 58, 70
End of the Trail, The, 43
Erdgeist, 45
Epicene, 97
Everyman, 91, 158
Everyman Theatre, 11, 13, 121, 220–221, 223
Exercise Bowler, 215
Exiles, 75, 214

F

Fair Maid of the West, The, 76, 170
Faithful, The, 73, 211
Faithful Shepherdess, The, 76
Family Reunion, 97
Fanny's First Play, 28
Fantastics, The, 26
Farmer's Wife, The, 163, 166, 171
Fashion, 48
Father, The, 91, 221
Fear, 74
Fellowship of Players, The, 80
First and the Last, The, 23
First Class Passengers Only, 215
First Gentleman, The, 115, 225
Fishing for Shadows, 214
Florodora, 225
For Services Rendered, 173
Foundations, The, 220
Frieda, 212, 225, 226
Frolic Wind, 201
From Morn to Midnight, 43–45, 47, 49, 52, 58, 73, 95, 151
Frozen Glory, 117
Fruits of Enlightenment, The, 215
Full Moon, 26

G

Gala Performance, 156
Game of Love and Death, The, 214
Gammer Gurton's Needle, 170
Gay Lord Quex, The, 201
Gas, 152, 163
Gate Theatre, 11, 15, 42–52, 105–124
Geneva, 169
Gentleman Dancing Master, The, 76
Gentleman's Agreement, 83
George and Margaret, 14, 80, 201
George Barnwell: or The London Merchant, 39
George Dandin, 43
Getting Married, 23, 215
Ghosts, 162, 203, 215, 221
Glasgow Citizen's Theatre, 195–196, 205
Glasgow Repertory Theatre, 196
Glyndebourne Opera Company, 218, 222
Golden Eagle, 212
Good Friday, 91
Good Natured Man, The, 132, 196
Government Inspector, The, 219
Grand Theatre, Fulham, 218
Great Adventure, The, 28
Great Expectations, 218
Great God Brown, The, 74
Great Romancer, The, 115
Green and Pleasant Land, 100
Group Theatre, 212–213
Guildford Repertory, 194
Guilty Souls, 79

H

Hail Nero, 28
Hairy Ape, The, 47, 58, 97
Hamlet, 12, 135, 171, 202, 211, 215
Happy and Glorious, 48
Harold, 172
Harvest of the North, 100
Haxtons, The, 193
He Who Gets Slapped, 26, 166, 202
Heart Was Not Burned, The, 119
Heartbreak House, 20, 58, 169
Heaven and Charing Cross, 216
Hedda Gabler, 229
Heir, The, 48
Henry IV, 178, 214
Henry V, 131
Henry VIII, 12, 63, 66
Hindle Wakes, 18
Hinkemann, 45, 50
Hippolytus, 93
His Excellency the Governor, 202
His Widow's Husband, 23
Hoppla, 47
House Into Which We Were Born, The, 43
House of Regrets, The, 196, 202, 215

I

I Hate Men, 50
I Have Been Here Before, 18, 198, 229
Identity Unknown, 82
If, 35
If Four Walls Told, 80
Immortal Hour, The, 163, 171
Importance of Being Ernest, The, 18, 20, 40, 162, 229
In a Glass Darkly, 68
In Good King Charles's Golden Days, 169
In Time to Come, 227
Infernal Machine, The, 74
In Theatre Street, 213
Inheritors, The, 58, 199
Insect Play, The, 70
Intermezzo, 74
International Ballet, The, 158–159
Intoxication, 26
Intruder, The, 120
Invitation to a Voyage, 97, 115, 119, 221
Iphigenia in Tauris, 26, 67
Irish Players, The, 12, 226
Italian Straw Hat, The, 98
Ivanov, 74, 76, 219
It Depends What You Mean, 212

J

Jacob's Ladder, 135, 201
Jealous Wife, The, 26
Jeannie, 14, 214
Jersey Lily, The, 121
John Ferguson, 34
John Gabriel Borkman, 23

Johnson Over Jordan, 44, 196
Jonah and the Whale, 211
Journey's End, 14, 74
Joy, 215
Juno and the Paycock, 12, 98
Jupiter Translated, 213

K

Karl and Anna, 82, 111
Katerina, 219
King John, 134
King Lear, 133, 211
King Maker, The, 225, 227
Kingdom of God, The, 98, 133, 210
King's Theatre, Hammersmith, 225
Kirkstall Miracle Play, The, 91
Knight of the Burning Pestle, The, 58, 68, 91, 202

L

La Marquise d'Arcis, 82
La Serva Padrona, 35, 36
Lady from Alfaqurque, The, 211
Lady from the Sea, The, 23
Lady into Fox, 156
Lady of Shalot, The, 155
Lady of the Camélias, The, 50
Lady Precious Stream, 229
Lady Windermere's Fan, 222, 225, 227, 230
Lady with the Lamp, The, 14
Lake, The, 198, 211
Land of Heart's Desire, The, 23
Last Hour, The, 58
Last Trump, The, 169
Late Christopher Bean, The, 198
Late Joys, The, 216
Le Cocu Magnifique, 76
Leeds Arts Theatre, 90
Leeds Civic Theatre, 13, 89–92
Les Parents Terribles, 121
Les Patineurs, 152, 154
Les Ratés, 82
Les Rendezvous, 152, 154
Let Sleeping Dogs Lie, 50
Liliom, 196
Lindsey Theatre, 214
Lion Tamer, The, 48
Lionel and Clarissa, 36
Lisa, 202
Little Earthquake, 216
Little Eyolf, 221
Little Man, The, 220
Liverpool Playhouse, 55, 135, 196–203
Living Corpse, The, 225
London International Theatre, The, 83
London Mask Theatre, The, 211
London Theatre Group, The, 214
Lorenzaccio, 218
Lord Adrian, 115, 119
Lord of Burleigh, The, 82
L'Otage, 81
Lot's Wife, 83
Lower Depths, The, 45
Love Chase, The, 170
Love for Love, 14, 68, 76, 230
Love in a Village, 36, 39
Love on the Dole, 14
Lover's Leap, 200
Lysistrata, 112

M

Macbeth, 63, 134, 172, 230
Machine Wreckers, The, 74, 76
Macropulos Secret, The, 166, 221
Madame Pepita, 23, 58
Maddermarket Theatre, The, 64, 92–97
Madras House, The, 12
Magistrate, The, 215
Maid's Tragedy, The, 78
Make Believe, 33
Making of an Immortal, The, 215
Malvern Festival, 168–171
Man about the House, A, 200
Man of Destiny, The 229
Man Who Ate the Popomack, The, 47, 58
Man with a Flower in his Mouth, The, 23
Man with a Load of Mischief, The, 14
Many Waters, 80
Marco Millions, 68, 211
Marlborough Goes to War, 26
Marriage, 26, 67
Marriage à la Mode, 36, 40, 58, 76
Marriage of Blood, The, 75
Marriage of Hamlet, The, 50
Marvellous History of St. Bernard, The, 91, 160, 171
Mask and the Face, The, 26, 67, 221
Masque of Kings, The, 118
Masses and Man, 74, 76, 151
Maya, 45, 47, 49, 52
Measure for Measure, 128, 130
Melting Pot, The, 220
Mental Athletes, The, 74
Merchant of Venice, The, 64, 134, 135, 201
Mercury Theatre, 154, 159, 211, 213–214, 225, 227
Merry Wives of Windsor, The, 135, 201
Message for Margaret, A, 212
Midsummer Night's Dream, A, 212
Milestones, 229
Millionairess, The, 169
Miracle at Verdun, 221
Miracle in America, 107, 108
Miracle in the Gorbals, 150–151
Mirandolina, 20
Misalliance, 215
Mob, The, 18
Monna Vanna, 19, 45
Moon in the Yellow River, 166, 211
Moonstone, The, 202
Mourning Becomes Electra, 211
Much Ado About Nothing, 12, 93
Murder in the Cathedral, 97, 198, 213
My Heart's in the Highlands, 97

N

Napoleon, 75
Napoleon of Notting Hill, The, 81
National 6, 111
Neighbourhood Theatre, 214
Newcastle People's Theatre, 97
Nichevo, 108
Night Arrival, 83
Night's Candles, 218
No Birds Sing, 202
No Longer Mourn, 112
No More Music, 83
No More Peace, 113
No Room at the Inn, 222, 225
No Trifling With Love, 20
Noah, 196, 202
Northampton Repertory Company, 56

O

Oedipus Rex, 23, 91
Of Mice and Men, 120, 121
Old Bachelor, The, 40
Old Lady Says No, The, 211
Old Man of the Mountains, The, 98, 213
Old Vic, The, 12, 14, 22, 125-138, 186, 194, 201–203, 207, 224, 229, 230
On the Frontier, 212
On the Rocks, 169
One More River, 49

Open Air Theatre, The, 209–210, 224, 227
Oresteian Trilogy, The, 59, 61, 139, 140
Orphée, 47
Oscar Wilde, 114, 115, 121, 123
Othello, 135, 201
Our Town, 213
Out of Sight, 115
Out of the Picture, 212
Outward Bound, 14, 221, 229
Oxford Playhouse, 14, 19–29

P

Panic, 213
Parisienne, 213
Parnell, 113, 115, 123
Passion Flower, The, 58
Paul Among the Jews, 72
Paul Felice, 199
Peer Gynt, 49, 91, 149, 207
People's Palace, The, 102
Peter's Parade, 48, 50
Phoenix Society, 12, 13, 76–78, 79
Pick Up Girl, 213
Picnic, 214
Pilgrim Players, The, 165, 229
Pilgrim's Progress, 91
Pink String and Sealing Wax, 200
Pins and Needles, 101
Pioneer Players, The, 12
Pioneers, The, 81
Plant in the Sun, 100
Play Actors, The, 28, 81
Player Queen, The, 73
Players Theatre, 216–217
Playmates, The, 12
Pleasure Garden, The, 75
Plough and the Stars, The, 12
Point Valaine, 202
Polish Jew, The, 45
Precious Bane, 221
Pretenders, The, 58
Princess and Mr. Parker, The, 198
Princess's Theatre, Glasgow, 195
Prisoners of War, The, 79
Private History, 119
Professional Lover, The, 48
Progress, 75
Provoked Wife, The, 73, 76
Pygmalion, 115, 202

Q

Queen Bee, The, 135
Queen Christina, 75

R

Race with the Shadow, The, 45, 47, 50
Rape of the Locks, The, 97
Red Roses for Me, 225, 227
Red Rover's Revenge, The, 48
Regent Theatre, 12, 13, 171
Remembrance of Things Past, 83
Renaissance Theatre Society, 12, 78, 79
Repertory Players, The, 12, 80, 81
Reprobate, The, 75
Rest In Silence, The, 200
Return of the Prodigal, The, 20
Reverie of a Policeman, 213
Richard III, 58, 66, 130
Richard of Bordeaux, 14
Riding to Lithend, The, 58
Right You Are If You Think You Are, 166
Rising Sun, The, 61
Rivals, The, 20, 36, 67, 215
Riverside Nights, 37–38
Road to Damascus, The, 75
Road to Rome, The, 199, 222
Robin of England, 100
Romeo and Juliet, 66, 93, 130, 132, 221, 227
Rosa Bernd, 45
Rosmersholm, 171, 214
Royal Divorce, A, 226
Rumour, The, 70, 75
Russians, The, 135

S

S.S. Tenacité, 74
Sabotage, 101
Sadler's Wells Ballet 70, 83, 143–161, 163, 207, 229, 230
Sadler's Wells Opera, 208–209, 227, 229, 230
Sadler's Wells Opera Ballet, 157
Sadler's Wells Theatre, 224
St. Joan, 132, 169, 207
St. Pancras People's Theatre, 98–99
Sally Lunn, 98
Salome, 48
Savitri, 35
Scandal at Barchester, 202
Scandal in Assyria, 83
Seagull, The, 12
Serena Blandish, 119
Seven Deadly Virtues, The, 110
Shadow Factory, The, 213
Shakespeare Memorial Theatre, Stratford on Avon, 35, 36, 175–189
She Stoops to Conquer, 23, 36, 40, 133, 135, 229
Sheffield Repertory Company, 56
Shepherd and the Hunter, The, 100
Shilling Theatre, The, 218, 223
Ship, The, 199
Shirley, 201
Shoemaker's Holiday, The, 70, 130, 229
Show, The, 58
Showing-Up of Blanco Posnet, The, 91
Simpleton of the Unexpected Isles, The, 169,170
Skin Game, The, 18
Skin of Your Teeth, The, 152
Smaragda's Lover, 79
Socrates, 79
Soiled, 226
Spanish Village, 100
Spirit of Parsifal Robinson, The, 73
Springtime of Others, The, 98, 121
Spook Sonata, The, 26, 58
Squaring the Circle, 213
Stage Society, The, 12, 13, 14, 23, 72, 73–76, 79, 81, 83, 232
Strange Combat, 108, 111
Strange Orchestra, 14, 221
Strife, 18
Stronger, The, 23
Subway, The, 58
Sulky Fire, The, 107, 108, 202
Susannah and the Elders, 83
Sweetest and Lowest, 224
Switchback, The, 169

T

Taming of the Shrew, The, 168
Tantivy Towers, 40
Tavistock Little Theatre, 99
Tempest, The, 91, 98, 128, 133
1066 and All That, 163, 171, 172
Ten Minute Alibi, 222
Ten Nights in a Bar Room, 48, 163
Tennent Plays, Ltd., 222, 230
Theatre Royal, Barnwell, 55
Theatre Royal, Bristol, 135, 194, 229
Theatre of the Soul, The, 45
Theodore and Co., 17
Therese Raquin, 163
They Came to a City, 229, 230
This Way to the Tomb, 213
This World of Ours, 68
This Year, Next Year, 108

Three Hundred Club, 12, 78
Three Men on a Horse, 29
Three Sisters, The, 219
Threshold Theatre, 214
Through the Crack, 220
Thunder Rock, 214
Time and the Conways, 198
Time of Your Life, The, 134
Toad of Toad Hall, 199
Tobacco Road, 115
Tobias and the Angel, 211
Too Good to Be True, 119, 173
Toussaint L'Ouverture, 76
Tragedy of Good Intentions, 202
Travelling Repertory Theatre, The, 167, 227
Trial of a Judge, The, 212
Trial of Oscar Wilde, The, 110
Troilus and Cressida, 211
Tudor Wench, The, 222
Tuppence Coloured, 82
Twelfth Night, 23, 96, 120, 121, 158
Twenty Below, 47
Twenty Houses in a Row, 82
Two Children, The, 215

U

Uncle Tom's Cabin, 48, 50
Uncle Vanya, 74, 75, 201, 219
Unity Theatre, 99–103
Unknown Warrior, The, 91
Unnamed Society, The, 97
Unquiet Spirit, The, 74, 76, 117

V

Various Heavens, 112
Venice Preserved, 76
Venturers, The, 12, 81–82
Versailles, 97
Viceroy Sarah, 132
Victoria Regina, 14, 110, 111, 112, 115, 116, 123
Victoria Theatre, Burnley, 133
Vic-Wells Ballet*: see* Sadler's Wells Ballet
Village Wooing, A, 229
Vortex The, 13, 82

W

Waiting for Lefty, 100, 102
Waste, 211
Watched Pot, The, 215
Way of the World, The, 36, 37, 40, 97
West Riding Theatre, The, 194
Westminster Theatre, 70, 210–212, 234
Wet Paint, 81
What Happened to George, 199
When Crummles Played, 39
When We Dead Awaken, 214
Where's That Bomb?, 100
White Devil, The, 78
Widowing of Mrs. Holroyd, The, 79
Wild Duck, The, 221
Winter's Tale, The, 168
Winterset, 118, 167
Wise Have Not Spoken, The, 227
Women Beware Women, 78
Workhouse Ward, The, 23
World is Yours, The, 133
Would-Be Gentleman, The, 39

Y

Yahoo, 211
Yellow Jack, 98, 212
Yellow Star, 101
You Can't Take It With You, 199
You Never Can Tell, 229
Young Vic, The, 218
Young Woodley, 14, 74
Younger Generation, The, 34
Your Number's Up, 115